LAWRENCE M. FRIEDMAN is Professor of Law at the University of Wisconsin School of Law. He received his A.B., J.D., and LL.M. from the University of Chicago and has previously taught at the St. Louis University Law School and the Stanford University Law School. He is also the author of *Contract Law in America*.

GOVERNMENT AND SLUM HOUSING

". . . the housing problem . . . almost as immovable as the Sphinx . . ."

Edith Abbott (1936)

GOVERNMENT
AND
SLUM HOUSING
A CENTURY OF FRUSTRATION

Lawrence M. Friedman
University of Wisconsin

Rand McNally & Company • Chicago

RAND McNALLY POLITICAL SCIENCE SERIES
MORTON GRODZINS, Advisory Editor

BECKER, *Political Behavioralism and Modern Jurisprudence*
DAHL, *Pluralist Democracy in the United States*
DIAMOND, FISK, and GARFINKEL, *The Democratic Republic*
ELDERSVELD, *Political Parties: A Behavioral Analysis*
FRIEDMAN, *Government and Slum Housing*
FROMAN, *Congressmen and Their Constituencies*
GOLEMBIEWSKI, GIBSON, and CORNOG, eds., *Public Administration*
GOLEMBIEWSKI, WELSH, and CROTTY, *A Methodological Primer for Political Scientists*
GRODZINS, *The American System*
HAIGHT and JOHNSTON, eds., *The President: Roles and Powers*
MILBRATH, *Political Participation*
PARSONS, ed., *Perspectives in the Study of Politics*
PEABODY and POLSBY, eds., *New Perspectives on the House of Representatives*
PRESS and WILLIAMS, eds., *Democracy in the Fifty States*
SCHUBERT, ed., *Judicial Behavior: A Reader in Theory and Research*
STRAUSS, *The City and Man*
WILDAVSKY and POLSBY, eds., *American Governmental Institutions*
WILLIAMS and PRESS, eds., *Democracy in Urban America*

AMERICAN POLITICS RESEARCH SERIES, edited by *Aaron Wildavsky*
RAND McNALLY PUBLIC AFFAIRS SERIES, edited by *Robert A. Goldwin*
RAND McNALLY SERIES IN THE ORGANIZATION SCIENCES, edited by *Robert T. Golembiewski*

To my wife
and my daughters

Preface

THE STUDY which follows is essentially an essay in the history of American law. It attempts to explore and explain how a specific corner of law came to be—law which deals with control and reform of slum housing. The story cannot, of course, be meaningfully told solely through legal sources. Law is an instrument of society. To understand the meaning of a course of legal development, particularly law so close to the surface of social conflict as housing law, data from various disciplines—history, sociology, political science, and others—must be used.

The story of law and slum housing has been told, for the most part, without undue editorializing. But the story, which begins a century ago and marches up so close to the present (June, 1966), is so rich in policy implications, that at times I have felt it desirable to put aside the cloak of invisibility that scholars affect to wear (in general quite rightly, I think) and have made comments on what is right and wrong with housing policy, code enforcement, urban renewal, and the like. The reader will be able, I hope, to judge for himself, on the basis of the facts and arguments presented, whether or not my suggestions are sound.

A fair portion of the book represents original research and rests on primary sources. But much of it does not. There is a great deal of interest today in welfare legislation, in poverty problems, in the slums and their attendant miseries. Research in the history, politics, and laws relating to problems of poverty has been skimpy in the past and will not catch up to the demand for a number of years, if ever. I have relied on what secondary sources I could find and use, but the story touches on so many aspects of American life and straddles so many scholarly disciplines that much has been necessarily left out. Moreover, the account given here is brief, perhaps too brief for the subject. My aim has been to build a framework for future research and future discussion and to illustrate some of the possibilities of legal-historical scholarship. Much, then, of what is said here should be taken as hypothesis rather than proven fact. Where this is so will be, for the most part, quite obvious.

Since the text was completed (June, 1966), neither events nor scholarship stood still. A good deal of what was suggested about the nature of tenement landlordship, for example, has now been put on a firm footing by George Sternlieb of Rutgers University, whose excellent study of Newark, New Jersey, *The Tenement Landlord,* was published since the manuscript was completed. Other useful work bearing on the subject matter of this book has appeared or is in progress. New York City's experience with the receivership program has borne out the fears and reservations expressed in the text. Dissatisfaction with a punitive approach to housing law, always present, seems to be greater than ever. Militancy among the poor has led to far greater questioning of authority than in the past, and a number of pending lawsuits against housing authorities may prove to be catalytic agents of administrative change. On the other hand, preoccupation of government with problems of poverty seems to have lessened distinctly in the last year or so, occasioned no doubt by the budgetary and emotional demands of the war in Vietnam. Whether this is a passing phase of policy remains to be seen.

Many people have given me help and advice in writing this book. I will mention only the most salient. The last chapter owes much to the suggestions of Professor J. Willard Hurst of the University of Wisconsin Law School. The manuscript was carefully reviewed and criticized by Professor Henry Fagin of the Department of Urban Planning at the University of Wisconsin. I owe a debt of thanks also to Professors Joel Handler, Stewart Macaulay, and William A. Klein, Jr. of the University of Wisconsin Law School, to Professor Charles Meyers of Stanford University Law School, to Professor Warren Lehman of the Washington University School of Law, and to Professor Gilbert Steiner of the Brookings Institution. I particularly wish to thank the faculty, staff, and students of the University of Wisconsin Law School for support, encouragement, and the environment of scholarship at that institution. The Russell Sage Foundation has generously supported research and training in law and sociology at the University of Wisconsin. The Foundation has directly supported my research and, equally important, has produced the interdisciplinary climate without which this book would perhaps never have been written. I would also like to acknowledge my debts to and admiration for the scholars and reformers, from Lawrence Veiller to Charles Abrams, who have labored so hard to improve the lot of the urban poor, against such odds, and with such skill and patience. Finally, I thank my wife, Leah, for the many subtle ways in which she lent a hand.

March, 1967   Lawrence M. Friedman
Palo Alto, California

Table of Contents

Prologue

CONCERN OVER the poor and over poverty mixes old and new forms and techniques in each historical period. The American system of poor relief can be traced in some aspects all the way back to Elizabethan poor laws, whose "principal features linger in the welfare programs of all of our states."[1] The "war against poverty" is new; but some of its aims are the accretion of generations. The attack on slum housing embodies one such aim. Housing, in the broad sense, is often considered the key to the problem of poverty; the slum is the poor man's environment as well as his home. "No nation," wrote Edith Wood, "can rise higher than the level of its homes. Whether we approach the subject from the point of view of health, morals, child conservation, industrial efficiency, Americanization, or good citizenship, the housing problem is fundamental."[2] Many have shared this opinion; in successive generations, reformers have struggled against the slum, using one or another method of social control. All the major institutions of our legal system—legislative, judicial, and administrative—have been used by those who have made war on the slums; and they have been used, too, by the powerful economic and social forces which benefit from keeping things as they are. The story of the law and the slums thus makes a most instructive illustration of the way in which legal institutions can and cannot be brought to bear on social problems in the specific context of American life. It is not always a pretty or a hopeful story. A dark stain of failure runs through it. But there is, perhaps, a glimmer of hope at the end.

This study does not purport to tell the whole story of the origin of the various programs which constitute the legal attack on the slums. That story would take many volumes to tell. What is attempted here is rather a modest beginning. We will try, first of all,

---

[1] Jacobus ten Broek, "California's Dual System of Family Law: Its Origins, Development, and Present Status: I," *Stanford Law Review*, 16 (1964), 257, 258.
[2] Edith Elmer Wood, *The Housing of the Unskilled Wage Earner* (New York: Macmillan, 1919), p. 1.

1

to develop some general concepts and considerations. We will classify the various legal programs to alleviate housing conditions in the slums. Then we will discuss these programs, type by type, in their historical and social context.

First, we must make clear what this study is *not* about. Law and government touch on slum housing in innumerable ways. For example, general fire and health laws apply to slum housing as well as to standard housing and commercial buildings; the fire department and the board of health operate in the slums, at least in theory and increasingly in practice. Fire, health, and safety laws deeply affect the character of slum life. Over the past century, these general laws have greatly reduced the horrors of fire, plague, and calamity among the poor of the slums. This may well be the most solid accomplishment of our welfare laws among the poor. Very likely, specific slum programs have done less for the people of the slums than has been accomplished by the extension of general social services to the poor. But we will deal here only with housing programs strictly speaking—with programs which have directly attacked the problem of that noxious housing in which the poor of American cities live and have lived.

CHAPTER I

Some General Concepts

THE URBAN poor live, by and large, in special districts. They are not scattered randomly throughout the city. There are, to be sure, many poor people in districts where one would not expect to find them—particularly the aged poor. But many more of the poor live in dense, crowded masses, forming a "poverty-stricken urban proletariat."[1] The homes of these people constitute the slums.[2] Their homes are "substandard," though the standard to which they fail to conform has no fixed meaning. No scientific definition of a "slum" is possible. A house without plumbing is substandard by United States Census Bureau measures.[3] However, an American slum might pass for decent housing in Calcutta or Bombay where hundreds of thousands have no home at all and sleep on the streets.[4] The slum and its conceptual cousins, such as the "blighted area," can only be defined operationally and culturally. Much depends upon the purpose we have in mind when we define an area as a slum.

Definitions of slums and bad housing can be divided, however, into two broad classes. Housing can be described as meeting or not meeting certain physical standards: Does it have plumbing? How many people to the room? A slum would then simply be a neighborhood of substandard houses. A slum can also be defined in social terms as an area where people of a certain class live. One authority has succinctly described the slum as "the home of the

---

[1] Council for Research on Housing Conditions, *Slum Clearing and Rehousing* (London: P. S. King & Co. Ltd., 1934), p. 27.

[2] The phrase "rural slum" is sometimes heard, but basically a slum is a city section in which masses of poor people live. For other attempts at defining the slum, see James Ford, *et al., Slums and Housing,* I (Cambridge, Mass.: Harvard Univ. Press, 1936), pp. 1–14; and David R. Hunter, *The Slums: Challenge and Response* (New York: Free Press, 1964), pp. 12–19.

[3] See Hunter, pp. 31–33.

[4] Charles Abrams, *Man's Struggle for Shelter in an Urbanizing World* (Cambridge, Mass.: M.I.T., 1964), p. 3.

poor and the stranger."[5] Common sense tells us that the slum is
both a social and a physical fact. It is the home of the poor, and
the poor live badly. The two elements—physical and social—of a
definition of the slum are related to two key ways of analyzing the
problem of the slum. These are: (a) in terms of the costs imposed
by the slums on society at large, and (b) in terms of the costs imposed by the slums on the people who live in them. We can call
these, respectively, the *social-cost* approach and the *welfare* approach. They are not unique to the housing problem. Social legislation in general is proposed and defended on one or both of these
bases, either that it helps the poor or some worthy class or that by
helping the poor it helps us all. Most frequently, perhaps, both
justifications are used.

Since the dawn of American consciousness of the problem of slum
housing, the social-cost approach has been heavily emphasized by
those eager for reform. The whole community, we are told, bears
the scars of the slums. Jacob Riis, in 1890, labeled the tenements
as sources of crime, disease, fire, and corruption. They were "the
hot-beds of the epidemics that carry death to rich and poor alike;
the nurseries of pauperism and crime," they bred "a scum of forty
thousand human wrecks to the island asylums and workhouses year
by year." The tenements "turned out in the last eight years around
a half million beggars to prey upon our charities"; they maintained
"a standing army of ten thousand tramps"; and above all, they
touched family life "with deadly moral contagion."[6] In slum districts, masses of ignorant foreigners voted as they were told by their
bosses—at least so it appeared to reformers. A Boston settlement
study of 1898 warned that the slums had no "neighborhood life . . .
no watchfulness over common interests"; as a result, "political corruption" flourished and money was "laid out at election time."[7]
Jacob Riis darkly reminded his readers that Boss Tweed "was born
and bred in a Fourth Ward tenement."

---

[5] Charles J. Stokes, "A Theory of Slums," *Land Economics,* 38 (1962), 187, 188.
Stokes' full definition combines both physical and social elements. "The distinctive
feature of slums is not appearance as such, then, but the relation between the
slum and its inhabitants and that neighborhood and its inhabitants which the
city regards as having met minimum livability standards. . . . The function of the
slum . . . is to house those classes which do not participate directly in the economic
and social life of the city." See Charles Abrams, *The Future of Housing* (New
York: Harper, 1946), pp. 22–28, for a typology of slums.

[6] Jacob A. Riis, *How the Other Half Lives* (New York: Hill & Wang, 1957), p. 3.

[7] Robert A. Woods (ed.), *The City Wilderness* (Boston: Houghton, Mifflin &
Co., 1898), p. 3.

Human nature being what it is, it could hardly have been possible to rouse any substantial group of the comfortable to action
without awakening in them fears for their own health and satisfaction. This is an oft-told tale. In similar fashion, the rise of a public
health system was intimately bound up with the notion that un-
sanitary conditions anywhere endangered the health of the community. Thus, during the cholera epidemics of 1832 and 1849, the
idea was widely held that only drunks and paupers contracted
the disease; this belief made it easy for the gentler classes to ignore the problem of epidemic. By 1866 it was clear that

> Not the poor and the vicious classes alone will fall victims to
> the coming pestilence, for if the great Cholera-fields that now
> invite the epidemic in our city be not cleansed . . . the poisons
> which they will breed will infect and kill many persons among
> the more favored classes.[8]

This notion, as much as or more than a sense of compassion with
the suffering poor, sparked the creation of institutions of public
health in New York. In Boston in the 1890's, an Anti-Tenement
House League was formed to arouse public opinion against the
manufacture of clothing in sweatshops. When the legislature became convinced that clothes made in the slums spread germs to respectable people who bought them, it passed an "Act to Prevent the
Manufacture and Sale of Clothing Made in Unhealthy Places."[9]

---

[8] Quoted in Charles E. Rosenberg, *The Cholera Years* (Chicago: Univ. of Chicago Press, 1962), p. 189, an excellent study of the social, legal, and medical consequences of three epidemics, 1832, 1849, and 1866.

[9] Laws Mass. 1891, ch. 357.

Jane Addams, in *Twenty Years at Hull-House* (New York: New American Library, 1961), pp. 210–11, tells the story of a middle class widow who continued to
live in the Hull-House ward, but who remained "quite aloof from her Italian
neighbors" and was not interested in sanitary reform. Her two daughters went
to an Eastern college. One summer the girls came home for a summer holiday;
they contracted typhoid fever and "one daughter died because the mother's utmost
efforts could not keep the infection out of her own house. The entire disaster
affords, perhaps, a fair illustration of the futility of the individual conscience
which would isolate a family from the rest of the community and its interests."

A bill was introduced in 1908 in Massachusetts to consider establishing a state
agency "to represent and protect the interests of the home," to reduce taxation,
"to help the people . . . to develop naturally, and to prevent and ultimately
overcome all feebleness and deficiency which is now costing the people, through
the government, such great strain and expense." Quoted in Dorothy Schaffter,
State Housing Agencies (New York: Columbia Univ. Press, 1942), pp. 9–10. The
passage quoted points up one supposed social cost of bad housing and home environment very much in the minds of a generation concerned with eugenics.

Housing reform legislation was itself particularly early and noncontroversial where it sought to eliminate fire hazards. Fires obviously drew no class line; if they started in the slums, they could easily spread to the homes of the rich. The first tenement house laws, typically, were fire laws.[10]

Arguments of social cost, therefore, have often served to persuade and mobilize the indifferent; they generate the belief that slum clearance and slum relief serve the interests of the middle and upper classes as well as of the poor. Types of social-cost argument vary with the social context. The precise mode of concern with bad housing at any given time reflects social attitudes toward the poor, toward city life, and toward the interdependence of social classes. The social costs of the slums to the comfortable, if they did not increase absolutely, became more glaring as cities grew and filled with landless, largely foreign-born, poor people. They also grew in visibility with the growth of knowledge of the interconnections between man and man; the germ theory, for example, was a powerful engine of social reform. Technological and industrial advance and the urbanization of the country brought social classes face to face. In large cities today, the tremendous agitation over the crime rate—the cries of anguish that streets, subways, beaches, museums, parks, and sidewalks are no longer safe for decent people —provide ammunition for those who use the social-cost approach. This urban terror, if grounded in fact at all, reflects not so much an increasing crime rate as the accessibility to each other of different social strata in those parts of the city which are, so to speak, held in common. There are, of course, still ghettos in the cities; but the people of the ghettos roam the streets at will. They need return home only to sleep; they do not have to stay put as perhaps they once did. Michael Harrington has argued that the "millions who are poor in the United States tend to become increasingly invisible."[11] In one sense, at least, he may be wrong. Teenage gangs do ride the subways; skid row bums do stagger in the shadow of skyscrapers; unemployed Negroes do riot in the streets. Some of

---

[10] E.g., Laws Wis. 1895, ch. 355; see Lawrence M. Friedman and Michael J. Spector, "Tenement House Legislation in Wisconsin: Reform and Reaction," *American Journal of Legal History*, 9 (1965), 41, 42.

[11] Michael Harrington, *The Other America: Poverty in the United States* (New York: Penguin Books, 1963), p. 10.

the problem poor are all too visible to the middle-class masses.[12]
This visibility engenders, if not pity or love, an urge toward action
of some kind.

Social-cost arguments have legal usefulness as well as political usefulness. American social legislation operates necessarily in a constitutional context. Under the American system of government, the
courts have the power to review legislation to determine if it meets
constitutional standards. In the late nineteenth century, the federal
and state courts developed the concept of substantive due process
which they then used to limit the right of legislative bodies to enact
social and economic legislation. Both the limits of the courts' powers
of judicial review and the corresponding limits of the states' rights
to enact new forms of law were vague and controversial.[13] Though
the federal courts have virtually abandoned use of the doctrine of
substantive due process, the concept retains some measure of vitality
in the states.[14] A major piece of economic or social legislation must
prove its validity by fitting itself within some historically recognized branch of governmental power (the "police power" of government) or find some other conceptual means to defend itself
against legal attack. The limits of the police power roughly correspond—in verbal formula at least—to the limits of the concept of
social cost. Indeed, roughly speaking, the concept of police power
is a concept of social cost; it validates legislation designed to limit
or alleviate the burden of social costs. On the basis of the police-
power concept, it becomes possible to reconcile strict free-enterprise
economics with regulation by the state in the name of public health,
safety, or welfare. Even so rigorous an opponent of state intervention in the economy as Milton Friedman has room in his scheme of

---

[12] Is the converse also true? Lillian Wald, in her book *Windows on Henry
Street* (Boston: Little, Brown, 1934), p. 34, reported that at one time "the appear-
ance of a carriage in our block was exciting. . . . To-day taxis are easily accessible
. . . [S]trangers . . . find their way from other parts of the city to our quarter.
Indeed, with the broad, well-paved, new streets that have followed the use of the
automobile . . . the lower East Side is no longer an unknown and foreign land."
And yet, how many whites visit Harlem?

[13] The "public-use" doctrine was another classic doctrine of limitation developed in the nineteenth century. Government could not legitimately exercise its
power to take private property, unless it could show that the taking was for a
"public use." This doctrine, too, has lost considerable vitality.

[14] See John A. C. Hetherington, "State Economic Regulation and Substantive
Due Process of Law: State Courts," *Northwestern University Law Review*, 53
(1958), 226.

things for government action to reduce social costs, which he calls "neighborhood effects."[15]

During the high days of judicial review, legislation had to be prepared to justify itself by working out some sort of social-cost analysis. Today, of course, the police-power concept has been vastly expanded by the courts. Cooley and Tiedeman—the major theorists of constitutional limitations on government—would hardly recognize it. In 1926 the United States Supreme Court, by a narrow five to four margin, upheld the validity of zoning ordinances; in 1954 a unanimous Court upheld the District of Columbia Redevelopment Act of 1945.[16] Justice Douglas, who wrote the majority opinion in the latter case, remarked that "public safety, public health, morality, peace and quiet, law and order . . . merely illustrate the scope of the [police] power and do not delimit it." Nevertheless, courts still formally examine legislation to see if a legislature could rationally believe that the measure in question affected the public health, safety, or welfare. Showing that a proposed law eliminates "neighborhood effects" is, therefore, still valuable even today as a kind of formal prerequisite to the passage or legitimation of social legislation. For example, a California act of 1933, authorizing the formation of limited-dividend companies to build housing for the poor, declared that

> . . . congested, unsafe and unsanitary housing conditions which exist in certain slum areas of the State are a menace to the health, safety, morals and reasonable comfort of the residents of this State.[17]

---

[15] "An obvious example is the pollution of a stream. The man who pollutes a stream is in effect forcing others to exchange good water for bad. These others might be willing to make the exchange at a price. But it is not feasible for them, acting individually, to avoid the exchange or to enforce appropriate compensation." Milton Friedman, *Capitalism and Freedom* (Chicago: Phoenix Edition, Univ. of Chicago Press, 1962), p. 30.

[16] The cases are, respectively, *Euclid* v. *Ambler Realty Co.*, 272 U.S. 365, 71 L. Ed. 303 (1926); *Berman* v. *Parker*, 348 U.S. 26, 99 L. Ed. 27 (1954).

[17] Cal. Stats. 1933, ch. 538. The Act went on to recite that "the correction of these conditions is a public necessity and the acquisition of property necessary to permit the clearance and reconstruction of slum areas is hereby declared . . . a public use within the meaning of the laws . . . relating to . . . eminent domain." The preamble to the Wisconsin "blighted areas law," Wis. Stats. §66.43(2) even more emphatically carries the reasoning past police power to eminent domain:

It is hereby found and declared that there have existed and continue to exist in cities within the state, substandard, insanitary, deteriorated, slum and blighted areas which constitute a serious and growing menace, injurious **and**

Such preambles are invitations to the judiciary to accept, as a rational basis for upholding the law, the "facts" as "found" by the legislature. Increasingly the courts are willing to accept these verbal formulae. Justice Douglas declared, in *Berman* v. *Parker,* that any attempt to define the reach of the police power was "fruitless"; definition was "essentially the product of legislative determinations." When the legislature speaks, "the public interest has been declared in terms well-nigh conclusive. . . . [T]he legislature, not the judiciary, is the main guardian of the public needs to be served by social legislation."[18] It would be wrong to conclude that without their preambles housing acts and other social legislation would fail. But preambles with their "findings" are part of the etiquette of constitutional dialogue and may play at least a marginal role in enhancing the legitimacy of welfare statutes.

Of course, computing the social costs of the slums raises empirical questions of ferocious difficulty. Few of these questions have been resolved. Do slums really breed crime, so that the elimination of slums would eliminate organized crime, criminal gangs, and juvenile delinquency? It is difficult to investigate this question. Classically, the answer was believed to be "Yes"; but some modern sociologists (perhaps wrongly) are dubious and indeed speak of the "demoralizing effect of the massive slum-clearance programs which

inimical to the public health, safety, morals and welfare of the residents of the state; that the existence of such areas contributes substantially and increasingly to the spread of disease and crime (necessitating excessive and disproportionate expenditures of public funds for the preservation of the public health and safety, for crime prevention, correction, prosecution, punishment, and the treatment of juvenile delinquency and for the maintenance of adequate police, fire and accident protection, and other public services and facilities), constitutes an economic and social liability, substantially impairs or arrests the sound growth of cities, and retards the provision of housing accommodations; that this menace is beyond remedy and control solely by regulatory process in the exercise of the police power and cannot be dealt with effectively by the ordinary operations of private enterprise without the aids herein provided; that the acquisition of property for the purpose of eliminating substandard, insanitary, deteriorated, slum or blighted conditions thereon or preventing recurrence of such conditions in the area, the removal of structures and improvement of sites, the disposition of the property for redevelopment incidental to the foregoing, and any assistance which may be given by cities or any other public bodies in connection therewith, are public uses and purposes for which public money may be expended and the power of eminent domain exercised; and that the necessity in the public interest for the provisions herein enacted is hereby declared as a matter of legislative determination.
[18] *Berman* v. *Parker,* 348 U.S. 26, 32, 99 L. Ed. 27 (1954).

have recently been undertaken" and of the "divisive influence of public-housing programs."[19] It is even more difficult to approach some of the more value-loaded counts in the indictment of the slums. Have the slums corrupted local government by breeding boss-rule? To this question no scientific answer is possible. There are even defenders of the bosses.[20] Yet the logic of the social-cost approach seems to demand an accounting. It seems to demand that we ask: Is reform worth the price?

Quite a different kind of cost-benefit analysis is required by a welfare approach to the slums. Under this approach, the problem of the slums is perceived as a problem of the suffering people who live there, whether or not the slums hurt society at large. Relieving their pain is worthwhile in itself, unless the mode of doing so is inordinately harmful to other social values. In the 1960's, legal-constitutional barriers do not seriously inhibit or imperil the major aspects of a war against poverty and slums. This means that direct slum action by government is not deemed to endanger social, economic, or political values insofar as they are constitutionally protected. Most people would probably agree that the government can and should increase economic and social opportunities for the poor, at least as an abstract proposition. Indeed, even in the palmiest days of the Fourteenth Amendment, when the concept of substantive due process terrorized social legislation, few people seriously questioned the right of government to help the poor and helpless. Public aid to the destitute poor was acceptable to Queen Elizabeth I and to Cotton Mather; it was also constitutionally acceptable to nineteenth century America. Constitutional and political problems were raised, however, by considerations of the level of government at which poor relief should be administered and financed. President Pierce vetoed a bill in 1854 which provided federal land-grant support for insane asylums and homes for the deaf. The bill, in his estimation, was the opening wedge for federal intervention into poor relief; and there was no authority in the Constitution "for making the Federal Gov-

---

[19] Richard A. Cloward and Lloyd E. Ohlin, *Delinquency and Opportunity: A Theory of Delinquent Gangs* (New York: Free Press, 1963), pp. 209–10. A thorough review of the evidence on the impact of slums on their inhabitants is Alvin L. Schorr, *Slums and Social Insecurity* (London: Thomas Nelson, 1964).

[20] E.g., Robert K. Merton, *Social Theory and Social Structure* (Glencoe, Ill.: Free Press, 1957), pp. 73–78, 193–94, to some degree.

ernment the great almoner of public charity throughout the United States."[21]

Private charity work in the slums went on throughout the century. Much of it was religiously motivated. Workers among the poor were eager to rescue bodies and souls in the slums from drink, degradation, evil company, and irreligion. It was easy to be discouraged at the magnitude of the task. As time went on, slum workers became more and more convinced that moral preachment and good example were not enough to help the masses of the poor in the dark alleys, back yards, and grim barracks of the city. But the corps of workers kept on; they never abandoned the welfare ideal, the notion that their aim was the salvation of the poor, not the safeguarding of society. The ideal remained strong during all the years of agitation over the slums. Reformers kept their eye on one goal: the erection of "standards of health, intelligence, and morality, below which the general level of the population cannot fall." They demanded that government refuse "to allow the sick or the hungry to go uncared for," that it insist "that children shall not grow up in illiteracy," and that it "especially" guard against "chief avenues" to "degradation." Government should

> proceed first to see that no family shall be without assistance toward recovering honorably from material disaster, and secondly to supply in general some of the means of a happier and nobler existence. By this voluntary effort additional checks are put on the *encroachment of social tendencies upon personal and domestic welfare.*[22]

This statement appeared in a settlement-house survey of conditions in Boston's South End at the turn of the century; it expressed some of the noblest sentiments of those for whom welfare was the goal. The emphasis was the reverse of the social-cost approach: "checks" sought against the "encroachment" of society on the poor man, rather than the reverse. Moreover, many people by 1900 had abandoned the idea, once strongly held, that poverty was either a virtue (it provided an incentive to work) or, somewhat inconsistently, a

[21] Quoted and discussed in Robert H. Bremner, *American Philanthropy* (Chicago: Univ. of Chicago Press, 1960), p. 70. In addition, the President doubted whether massive government intervention would not be "prejudicial" to the "noble offices of charity."

[22] Woods, p. 290 (emphasis added).

curse which descended on those who failed morally in society—those
who "brought it on themselves." This attitude had been replaced
by a greater sympathy for the poor, a greater tendency to blame society for the social ills of the slums.[23]

Neither the welfare nor the social-cost approach is usually found
in rhetorical isolation; both are powerful arguments against the
slum, and those whose emotions are engaged by the one are apt to
enlist the other for aid and persuasion of the doubtful. The social-
cost argument has, perhaps, packed more power to move legislation;
but the literature, from Jane Addams and Jacob Riis down to
Michael Harrington, has been strongly infused with a passion for
welfare.

Both approaches imply at least logical differences in modes of
housing and slum reform. A man who emphasizes the price society
pays for the results of slum housing is apt to look for measures
which, for the fewest dollars, eliminate the evil as it touches him.
He might be content merely to neutralize the effects of the slums—
to quarantine the poor in their districts, if possible. Mature
deliberation usually leads to the conclusion that quarantine is impractical and short-sighted; but not everyone is capable of mature
deliberation. Throughout American history, then, men have frequently advanced solutions to urban housing problems which meet
external difficulties only. The law has emphasized fire prevention,
sanitation, minimum standards of building and maintenance, and
outright demolition of the slums. These are ways of protecting society from contamination rising out of the slums. The pathology of
this branch of the social-cost approach is its tendency to disregard
the problems of the people who live in the slums. If they are criminals and endanger others, they must be put in jail.[24] If they are
infectious, they must be isolated. Containment is viewed as an
adequate, if not an ideal, solution.[25]

---

[23] See, in general, Robert H. Bremner, *From the Depths: The Discovery of
Poverty in the United States* (New York: New York Univ. Press, 1964), especially
pp. 123–39.

[24] There is a tendency to differentiate between crimes which cross the class-lines
and those which do not. The police may break up a brawl in a poor neighborhood
without arresting anybody; an attack by a poor person on a member of the middle
class may be more likely to bring an arrest. What "they" do to each other in their
own ghettos is not of much concern to "us."

[25] Many Americans who are outraged by domestic containment are quite quaran-
tine-minded when it comes to the international poor; we close our borders to
sick, indigent foreigners.

Another kind of social-cost approach is to look for programs which turn a profit for the larger society. Some people are fond of pointing out that the slums cost more than they bring in. Slums require

> more in direct . . . expenditures for police protection, fire fighting, garbage removal, welfare, and health . . . [S]lums, representing 20 per cent of the average American city's residential area, cost taxpayers 45 per cent of all city service expenditures and still produced excessive health, welfare, housing, crime, and fire problems.[26]

Programs are good if they turn this red ink to black. Slum clearance followed by urban redevelopment is good, we are told, because it raises a city's tax base. Some programs are called good because of their benefits to other groups or society at large outside of the slums. So public housing construction can be advocated because it stimulates the economy and puts masons and bricklayers to work.

The welfare approach has problems of its own. It is possible to ignore social costs and concentrate unduly on the burdens of discrete individuals. Too great solicitude for the welfare of the current poor could conceivably lead to neglect of ultimate causes and solutions. A program of temporary ruthlessness might be necessary for long-term solution to serious social disorders. Someone may have to be hurt. If we respect the right of people to choose to stay where they are, nothing would ever get built. One tearful widow or one sentimental old-world family could ruin a mighty plan. Similarly, a demand for complete and perfect relocation would kill or cripple slum clearance of any kind. It would be almost impossible, under present technology, to move every family into a new and better house before uprooting the old house.[27]

Pathologies follow neither logically nor inevitably from the essence of the two approaches. Most able social reformers have held both views in balance. If slums are evil, they are so both because they destroy the lives of those who live in them and because they harm society as a whole. Slum housing reform must meet both needs and

---

[26] Hunter, p. 82.

[27] At any rate, it would take more money than any community has currently been willing to spend. Alternatively, of course, new housing could be constructed on vacant land. Relocation could be immediate and relatively painless. Politically, this solution is difficult.

use both approaches, or it is likely never to become law—or if made law, to lack full force.

Historically, the welfare approach has provided housing movements with their passion and to some extent also their concrete programs. But to enact a law takes more than passion. Social legislation usually demands some sort of coalition of political forces, cemented together by an appeal to material or other vital interests of some numerous or powerful group. These interests may be general social interests—everyone's stake in the reduction of the external effects of the slums; or they may be something more vulgar and direct. Proposals to build public housing were particularly appealing during the great depression of the 1930's because the program was certain to create construction jobs. Naturally, building-trades unions looked with favor on the program; in 1935 the American Federation of Labor went on record to express its "sympathy with the Slum Clearance and Low Rent Housing Program which has for its purpose provisions that will furnish employment to those engaged in the building and construction industry."[28] Social cost considerations have weighed heavily in the passage and continued success of urban renewal programs. Decay, tax attrition, and a bad image were assumed to be social costs imposed upon cities by their large tenement districts and by the dingy areas which strangled the downtown heart. Downtown merchants saw urban renewal as a chance to stop downtown decay and to upgrade the value of their property. Mayors and local politicians saw a chance to make a name as dynamic leaders. Professional planners within local government saw a chance to increase their sphere of influence and authority. Some influential men (Senator Taft, for example) wanted to stress housing and slum clearance partly for social-cost reasons and partly for reasons of welfare. The Senator and those who agreed with him made a strong mark on the character of the 1949 urban renewal law; but the basic design of that act and the subsequent legislation followed the interests of city politicians, merchants, and planners.[29]

In short, the welfare approach has been a useful catalyst, a goad to the national conscience. By itself, it has rarely succeeded in pass-

---

[28] Quoted in Timothy L. McDonnell, *The Wagner Housing Act: A Case Study of the Legislative Process* (Chicago: Loyola Univ. Press, 1957), p. 118.

[29] On the legislative history of the 1949 Act, see Ashley L. Foard and Hilbert Fefferman, "Federal Urban Renewal Legislation," *Law and Contemporary Problems,* 25 (1960), especially pp. 662–63.

ing a law; it needs allies. Nor does zeal alone ensure that a program will remain vital, actively enforced, and responsive to new needs. Passion is transient; interest remains. By and large, in the history of government and housing, welfare-oriented legislation has not had staying power, unless it could enlist in its aid some coalition of groups with a strong nonwelfare stake or a bureaucracy with a vested stake in keeping the program alive.

The urban poor, by and large, are not such a powerful interest group. They are a numerous tribe, and they vote; they have, therefore, some political power. But the history of housing legislation strongly suggests that little action so far can be traced directly to the political strength of the urban masses. The poor may be underrepresented in legislatures; their political representatives may be corrupt or corruptible. Even aside from these considerations, the urban poor (those who would benefit from programs to remedy slum housing conditions) have been too few and too weak to have their way against the opposition of the middle class.[30] Significantly, the first, major, federal housing program was enacted during the New Deal period (1933–1937) when, alas, tremendous numbers of new and unwilling recruits joined the ranks of the unemployed, the underemployed, and the marginally employed. Millions of the new poor were culturally members of the middle class who had fallen from economic grace after 1929. Many of these were articulate, educated people; they were used to a better way of life. As a whole, these people were better equipped to demand measures of alleviation than the lowest group of the urban poor before or since. The later career of public housing also attests, in a negative way, the power of influence and numbers. The war, of course, interrupted housing construction. Afterwards, the housing energies of government were diverted to the quite distinct task of providing "veterans' housing"—housing for the benefit of a large, powerful, articulate, and by no means poverty-stricken group. In the period of postwar prosperity, public housing lost most of its middle-class clientele. With the decline of veterans' housing, the program suffered from failure of momentum; it survived in an arrested form, while the urban renewal program—middle-class and social-cost oriented—took the center of the stage. Public housing has

---

[30] Majority rule, of course, is much more than a matter of a headcount. Other factors, such as the intensity of positions taken by those with a voice in the question, are equally important. For the purposes of this general discussion, however, these other factors will be ignored.

begun to show signs of life again under the auspices of the war against poverty or at least as a by-product of the recent, fresh infusion of welfare passion. We shall have occasion to tell this tale again in more detail. For now, we are content to notice one lesson: How greatly the interests of a politically potent or impotent clientele influence the passage and form of welfare legislation.

SOME GENERAL CONCEPTS: ON THE NEGATIVE SIDE

We have so far accentuated the positive, discussing concepts and reasons for the war on the slums. But there must be concepts and reasons on the other side. Indeed, each positive concept or force has its negative; and the negative has been powerful, since housing legislation has not, in general, had a particularly easy road to enactment. There have been those with material interests (real or imagined) opposed to housing legislation, e.g., landlords and the housing industry. The negative counterparts of the reformers have been those, from early times to the days of the Newburgh plan, who distrust the poor and believe they deserve their fate or who, in crushing numbers, are indifferent to reform and allow it to be stifled and side-tracked. Both the social-cost approach and the welfare approach have a logical negative—the notions either (1) that the slums are beneficial to society, or (2) that slum life is beneficial to the people who live in slums.

These are, on the surface, rather unpalatable propositions, and we are unlikely to find them baldly expressed in real life. But corollaries of the first proposition are commonly, widely and deeply held. Many people, for example, believe that it is good for society to segregate the poor. In its extreme racial form, this is an argument for *apartheid* or strict residential segregation. Much of the white middle class believes firmly and persistently in segregation by income and race.[31] The main argument that the poor should live by themselves stems from the conviction of the middle class that their own lives are richer, safer, and more pleasant without poor people about. The popularity of race segregation, obviously, and income segregation, less obviously, has played a powerful role in preventing the passage of certain kinds of housing legislation and in distorting or delaying existing pro-

---

[31] See Lawrence M. Friedman, "Suburbs and Slums in Perspective," *Wisconsin Law Review* (1964), pp. 523, 526–27.

grams. A notorious example is the location politics of public housing in the cities. In Chicago, for example, in the late 1940's and early 1950's, substantial majorities of the city board of aldermen were in favor of the *principle* of public housing—after all, the federal government was paying most of the bill; but the same aldermen definitely did *not* want public housing built in their own wards. They did not want low-income neighbors, and they wanted no Negroes of any kind. The battle over location nearly crippled public housing in Chicago. A construction program of new public housing did survive; but the victorious sites were not located in what the Chicago Housing Authority would have considered the right and proper places. They were placed where they would not interfere with racial lines and lines of economic class.

Segregation, at least in theory, does not *necessarily* mean that the slums must remain undesirable, only separate. In practice, of course, there cannot be separate but equal areas for the poor. Yet among those who have been most vehement in demanding income segregation are many who, in all honesty, want the poor to be decently though separately housed.

There are also those who warn us that what we call slums are not an unmixed curse. Particularly since the advent of urban renewal, some scholars and reformers have pointed out that some "slums" and "blighted areas" are really stable low-income communities; they provide those who live in them with many advantages. Society is not ready to help the slum-dwellers on their own terms, nor is it providing substitutes for the advantages of the slums, such as cheap rents. For these and other reasons, it is a disservice to the poor to destroy their neighborhoods.

Serious scholars who have argued this way have not generally suggested that *all* slums have positive qualities. They have pointed out and defended particular low-income areas. Herbert Gans carefully studied an Italian working-class neighborhood in Boston, which was condemned and cleared for urban redevelopment. Gans argued that it was wrong to clear this neighborhood; what appeared to the outside world as a slum was in fact no slum at all; it was a decent, tightly-knit, low-rent home for working-class people. It was a good place to live for those who wanted to live there. Gans would reserve the term "slum" only for areas which are "proven to be physically, socially or emotionally *harmful* to their residents or to the larger community."[32] Meyerson and Banfield make much the same point when they lament the passage of the old ethnic enclaves: the banishment of the "old Italian who made his living by selling sausages from a sidewalk cart"; the priest who is "left without a parish"; the "dispersal of the Greek slum," which "meant an end to the shadow plays which, to the deep satisfaction of the older men, portrayed Greek history, scenes of peasant life, and the glories of strife with the Turks."[33] Other writers have found positive benefits even in areas they are willing to label as slums. One such writer has coined the term "slums of hope" to describe areas which serve a useful purpose as a way-station for acculturation of immigrants.[34] A somewhat similar slum is the boarding-house belt which surrounds many American universities.[35] Here students find cheap, convenient, if sometimes unpleasant, housing. These areas are different from other slums in that most of the residents have a middle-class background. They are deliberately foregoing better housing which they could afford if they went on the job market rather than to college. By deferring some satisfactions and living cheaply, they are acquiring the priceless asset of a good education and, more tough-mindedly, a ticket to increased lifetime earnings.

Romantic or hard-headed praise for the slums probably plays little part in legislative debate on the propriety of fresh housing legislation. More frequent are arguments that the costs of slum reform are too great, that the cure is worse than the disease. If so, then social-cost accounting demands that matters be left as they are. Similarly, it can be argued that the welfare of the poor is impaired by reform legislation because these programs necessarily backfire. Therefore, welfare considerations demand that things be left as they are.

The first of these is the free-enterprise argument, strictly speaking. But the second point, too, has been urged by economic conservatives (or liberals, as they choose to style themselves). Milton Friedman argues that

> Public housing cannot . . . be justified on the grounds either of neighborhood effects or of helping poor families. It can be justi-

---

[32] Herbert J. Gans, *The Urban Villagers: Group and Class in the Life of Italian-Americans* (Glencoe, Ill.: Free Press, 1962), p. 309.

[33] Martin Meyerson and Edward C. Banfield, *Politics, Planning, and the Public Interest* (Glencoe, Ill.: Free Press, 1955), p. 99.

[34] Stokes, p. 187.

[35] See "The Gamut of Campus Housing," *Daily Cardinal Magazine*, 2, No. 2 (Dec. 9, 1964).

fied, if at all, only on grounds of paternalism; that the families being helped "need" housing more than they "need" other things but would themselves either not agree or would spend the money unwisely. The liberal will be inclined to reject this argument for responsible adults.[36]

A kind of sociological *laissez faire* is possible, too: the notion that slums or slum communities perform vital functions, manifest or latent. If so, government intervention in the form of wholesale slum clearance may well do more harm than good. Probably no sociologist stands for so extreme a position. But Herbert Gans and others have argued with great force that not all so-called slums are antisocial; indeed, they have stated that the measures taken against the slums are themselves frequently antisocial and that, at the very least, a cautious accounting of benefits and burdens ought to be undertaken by government before a neighborhood is destroyed.

Modern conservatives, such as Milton Friedman, usually insist that they are not enemies of the welfare principle. They believe that government should put some kind of floor under human misery. Their quarrel is with means and not with ends. Older conservatives, by way of contrast, were often leery of *any* government social program, particularly a federal program. Some believed that it was futile and wicked for government to meddle with the social system. It was a common, though by no means universal, belief in the early nineteenth century that charity itself—private or public—was degrading and evil in its effects. The New York Society for the Prevention of Pauperism, in an 1818 report, listed the "numerous charitable institutions of the city" as one of the causes of pauperism:

> Is not the partial and temporary good which they accomplish . . . more than counterbalanced, by the evils that flow from the expectations they necessarily excite; by the relaxation of industry; . . . by that reliance upon charitable aid, in case of unfavorable times, which must unavoidably tend to diminish, in the minds of the labouring classes, that wholesome anxiety to provide for the wants of a distant day, which alone can save them from a state of absolute dependence . . . ?[37]

---

[36] Milton Friedman, pp. 178–79. Friedman also argues that public housing has hurt the lot of the poor by destroying more houses than it builds.

[37] Quoted in David Schneider, *The History of Public Welfare in New York State 1609–1866* (Chicago: Univ. of Chicago Press, 1938), p. 213.

Some also believed that charity was wicked and futile in that the poor deserved their lot.[38] To many people, the slums were the natural habitat of drunks, moral cripples, and emotional and physical weaklings. This view has been banished from all respectable forums. But it has enormous power in a subterranean way, just as the notion of income segregation or race segregation has, at least in the North, few defenders but many adherents. The middle-class citizen does not understand the poor of the slums, and he judges them harshly. He tends to feel that public money is wasted on them. The smell of urine in public housing projects is taken as evidence that public money is squandered by and on the poor.[39] One result of this point of view is a search for housing measures which will distinguish between the good poor and the wicked poor. The strength of this distinction can be seen at many points in the history of housing legislation. Public-housing projects are reserved to those low-income families who meet middle-class standards; problem families are eliminated. A reporter writes that, at Chicago's Taylor homes,

> All tenants are subject to an annual house-keeping inspection. Those who don't make the grade may lose their lease, and this does happen to at least some of the tenants who can't give up their slum ways.[40]

Public housing tenants have been evicted because they have given birth to bastards, because their children misbehaved, because a member of the household was a dope addict, and even because the head of the family was in jail.[41] Eviction policy can be justified on a number of grounds, including administrative efficiency, but undoubtedly more is involved. Housing projects are conceived of as places where the *potential middle class* can profit from a change in environment or where members of the *submerged middle class* can be helped back on their feet. Indeed, the concepts of the potential and the submerged middle class are central to an understanding of housing history in this country. The key notion is that there are unfortunate

---

[38] Bremner, *From the Depths*, pp. 16–20.

[39] The equivalent of this urine in another generation was "the old story of the bathtubs in model tenements which had been turned into coal bins." Addams, p. 221.

[40] M. W. Newman, "Trouble Boils Over in Ghetto Oven," *Chicago Daily News*, April 13, 1965, p. 10, col. 8.

[41] See the discussion below, pp. 136–38.

individuals who are culturally members of the middle class but who have been prevented by unfortunate circumstances from taking their proper place in the social order or who have, through no fault of their own, dropped down a notch in society. American housing programs, by and large, have been designed for these people and not for the "true" poor. The real poor, the problem families, the deviant poor—these fill the slums to an ever greater degree, and they find their way into public housing projects, too; but the standard reaction to these members of the poor is exile and rage. A parallel kind of development is found in other government welfare programs. Even Aid for the Families of Dependent Children, which does not seem to draw this cultural line, can be traced back to a program for worthy widows of the submerged middle class.[42] When the worthy widows "graduated" to social insurance[43] and the Negro and problem poor inherited the program, it became, like public housing, desperately unloved. The American belief in the innocence and perfectibility of children may be all that protects AFDC from the full impact of public rage.

SLUM HOUSING: STANDARDS AND REMEDIES

Slum housing can be defined, as we have seen, in terms of its physical standards or in terms of the social conditions of slum neighborhoods. Both physical and social definitions can be used by those who adopt a social-cost approach. Slums can be defined, for example, as aggregations of rat-infested firetraps or as neighborhoods with high rates of crime or alienation. Similarly, the welfare approach can emphasize physical conditions (equating welfare with material comfort) or social conditions (equating welfare with proper integration into the larger society).

Housing reformers of the late nineteenth century stressed legislation designed to prevent fires, reduce overcrowding, introduce proper sanitary conditions, and provide more light and air in the slums. The first period of housing reform was climaxed by the passage of tenement house laws, the forerunners of modern housing codes.

Regulatory, restrictive housing legislation by its nature tends to emphasize the physical condition of buildings, though usually there

---

[42] See Winifred Bell, *Aid to Dependent Children* (New York: Columbia Univ. Press, 1965), pp. 3–19.

[43] *Ibid.*, p. 60.

is an implicit assumption that physical change will lead to social change. The twentieth century discovered slum clearance and rebuilding as a way of recasting the total environment of the poor. The difference between public housing and housing-code enforcement might therefore seem to be the difference between social and physical solutions to the slum problem. But there is no clear mark of separation between the two; programs tend to be ambivalent. Public housing certainly aims at improving the physical conditions in which poor people live, as well as providing a new environment. A city may try vigorous enforcement of its housing and building codes as a technique to upgrade the slums and change the environment of the poor without bulldozing houses. Positive and negative measures can be manipulated, then, either for physical or social ends.

The same mixture is visible in the history of urban renewal. Initially, urban renewal emphasized the objective manifestations of "blight" and therefore seemed to favor a rigorous physical definition of deteriorated neighborhoods. Blight can be measured by the degree of dilapidation. "We have urban blight, and then slums," said the Commissioner of the Urban Renewal Administration in 1955, "primarily because all physical facilities, both buildings and their surrounding neighborhoods, wear out."[44] In the opinion of Herbert Gans and others, this purely physical approach leads to mistakes in classification and to the bulldozing of perfectly good neighborhoods.[45] On the other hand, blight has increasingly been defined in sociological terms. And the original remedy of redevelopment was clearance and rebuilding: a radical solution that lent itself both to physical and to social reform. Since 1949, when the federal urban redevelopment program first became law, national policy toward slum clearance has gradually moved away from a one-sided approach. Hopefully, future attacks on the slums will balance the physical and the social in definition, solution, and operation.

A NOTE ON CLASSIFICATION

Basically, there are two ways in which government can attack the problem of the slums. First, there is a restrictive or negative approach. Society can attempt to get rid of bad housing by forbidding

[44] "Slums and Blight . . . a disease of urban life," *Urban Renewal Bulletin*, No. 2, URA, HHFA (1955), p. 1.
[45] Gans, pp. 308–17.

it. It may regulate the building and maintenance of places where human beings live. Government may also use a positive approach; not content to forbid bad housing, it may concern itself actively with providing good housing.[46] Under the one approach, the government expects private owners to be goaded or cajoled into maintaining a stock of decent housing; under the other, government provides alternatives to existing, substandard housing through its own activities. Many programs, of course, use both approaches; they set up measures of control and provide, in addition, for positive public alternatives. Still other programs are half-breeds of the two.

Positiveness and negativeness, as described above, are aspects of the degree of *public* participation. Many people outside of government have been actively engaged in doing something about the problem of slum housing. Sometimes private agencies have asked for (or had to be satisfied with) a limited amount of public help. Some private programs use more of the resources of government than others— taxes, subsidies, law enforcement techniques. Others content themselves with purely private resources, by choice or by compulsion. The purely private programs are beyond the scope of this study; but they will be mentioned and at times discussed for the sake of completeness and enlightenment. The public programs are our true subject. The degree of public participation in slum housing programs has varied tremendously. Government has built and operated its own low-income houses; it has subsidized others. Other programs of government "aid" go no further than to legitimate private activity, e.g., through passing laws to authorize essentially private efforts. Public and private efforts, of course, are in constant interaction; the failure of a private effort to replace slum housing may lead to increased pressure for public efforts, and vice versa. The adequacy of dwellings, the rate at which houses are built, the kind of houses that are built, and private market conditions of every sort—all of these influence governmental decisions to build or not to build, to control or not to control. This complex interaction will be frequently noted in

---

[46] See Edith Elmer Wood, *The Housing of the Unskilled Wage Earner* (New York: Macmillan, 1919), pp. 19–20. A third solution, of course, is to do nothing, either because the problem is insoluble or because it will solve itself. Martin Anderson, for example, argues that the free market is rapidly "solving" the problem of inadequate housing. By now "there is not a physical shortage of decent housing units. The real problem is that there is a certain group of people who either cannot or will not spend enough money to rent or to buy this housing." Martin Anderson, *The Federal Bulldozer* (Cambridge, Mass.: M.I.T., 1964), p. 200.

this study. Nonetheless, analytically we can distinguish between public and private efforts, and within each sphere, between the positive and the negative approach.

In this study we are concerned with the process of formation of social policy as expressed in formal law. Though we omit the purely private efforts, we will organize our discussion to some extent in terms of whether public programs (either negative or positive) seek to stimulate the private sector or choose to do the job in a wholly public manner. We shall begin with a discussion of the *negative* approach—the path taken by tenement house laws, housing codes, and some lesser programs. The discussion of *positive* programs follows in which the major emphasis is on public housing. Next we will turn to a consideration of urban redevelopment and renewal, a recent movement of mighty proportions which unites in itself so many elements of the past. Still another chapter will consider proposals and programs which seem to constitute the opening wedge of the future and will attempt some words of assessment. A final chapter will use the lessons of housing history to make some remarks on the nature and growth of welfare legislation.

CHAPTER II

Housing Reform: Negative Style

(1) PUBLIC RESTRICTIONS ON SLUM HOUSING: TENEMENT HOUSE LAWS AND THEIR DESCENDANTS

The negative approach to slum reform, using restrictive housing laws, is the oldest and most persistent of the housing solutions. Constant criticism of its efficacy and adequacy has not succeeded in ending reliance upon it. Public housing and urban renewal have not ousted this ancient rival; rather they have assimilated restrictive measures into themselves and assigned them a major role in the design of their programs.

Building restrictions are of ancient lineage and appeared quite early in American history. In New York, for example, pre-Revolutionary laws tried to prevent people from keeping hay, straw, pitch, tar, and turpentine where the danger of fire was great; a law of 1766 created a fire zone where houses had to be made of stone or brick and roofed with tile or slate.[1] These and later restrictions were not confined to slum areas. The New York tenement house law of 1867 was a different kind of law. It applied only to dwellings. It set up minimum standards that had to be observed by "tenements," which it defined as

> every house, building, or portion thereof which is rented, leased, let or hired out to be occupied, or is occupied as the home or residence of more than three families living independently of another, and doing their cooking upon the premises, or by more than two families upon a floor, so living and cook-

---

[1] Joseph D. McGoldrick, Seymour Graubard, and Raymond J. Horowitz, *Building Regulation in New York City* (New York: Commonwealth Fund, 1944), pp. 34–35.

ing, but having a common right in the halls, stairways, yards, waterclosets or privies.[2]

This definition covered virtually all the houses in the slum areas and virtually none of the houses of the well-to-do. The age of the apartment house and the apartment hotel had not yet arrived; the vast majority of the rich lived not in apartments, but in private houses which were excluded from the act.[3]

The New York law of 1867 is, if not the ancestor of all succeeding tenement and housing codes, quite close to the evolutionary root.[4] It exerted a powerful, direct impact on much later legislation, e.g., the Massachusetts tenement house law of 1868[5] and the Milwaukee housing ordinance of 1905.[6] Whether or not later legislatures helped themselves to the language of the 1867 act or of some other model is

---

[2] Law N.Y. 1867, ch. 908, §17. The act also applied to lodging-houses, defined as "any house or building, or portion thereof, in which persons are harbored or received, or lodged for hire for a single night, or for less than a week at one time, or any part of which is let for any person to sleep in for any term less than a week."

[3] See James Ford, *et al.*, *Slums and Housing*, I (Cambridge, Mass.: Harvard Univ. Press, 1936), pp. 867, 869. On the rise of the apartment hotel, see *Grimmer* v. *Tenement House Department*, 204 N.Y. 370, 97 N.E. 884 (1912). The account in McGoldrick, Graubard, and Horowitz, p. 7, claims that the apartment hotel was invented in 1919 as an evasion of the Tenement House Law. But the Grimmer case proves that the device was older. On the rise of the apartment house, see Christopher Tunnard and Henry Reed, *American Skyline* (Boston: Houghton Mifflin, 1956), pp. 122–24.

[4] Modern housing codes are mostly municipal ordinances. Some states have or have had statutory codes. The housing codes may exist by themselves, or they may be mixed in with building codes, plumbing codes, or the like. The word "tenement" has unfortunate connotations; New York's present state law uses the phrase "multiple dwelling," which is more neutral in tone. The New York Multiple Dwelling Law was passed in 1929. It applied to cities of more than 800,000 population, though smaller municipalities could elect its provisions (N. Y. Mult. Dwelling Law, §3(2)). A tenement house law remained on the books in New York state, but it applied only to the city of Buffalo. That city elected to come under the Multiple Dwelling Law in 1949. The Tenement House Law then became a dead letter. It was repealed in 1952 (Laws N. Y. 1952, ch. 798). In 1950 the Multiple Dwelling Law was amended to make its provisions mandatory for cities with more than 500,000 population, i.e., Buffalo and New York City (N. Y. Mult. Dwelling Law, §3(1)). Useful information on the background of the Multiple Dwelling Law is given by MacNeil Mitchell, "Historical Development of the Multiple Dwelling Law," *Consolidated Laws of New York Annotated*, Vol. 35-A (1946), pp. ix–xxi.

[5] Laws Mass. 1868, ch. 281.

[6] Lawrence M. Friedman and Michael J. Spector, "Tenement House Legislation in Wisconsin: Reform and Reaction," *American Journal of Legal History*, 9 (1965), 41, 52–53.

irrelevant. The tenement law idea spread not by textual persuasion but through the spread of circumstances similar to those which led to the passage of the original act or acts. (Reform movements, of course, are as much a circumstance as the condition of plumbing is.) There has been, in fact, a great deal of borrowing in housing legislation. Detail varies greatly over time, if only because codes more or less must keep up with technological and social change in housing standards. But the basic idea of restrictive housing legislation is much the same now as it was in 1867.

The 1867 law was divided into 19 sections. It ordered tenement and lodging houses to be equipped with ventilators, fire escapes, "good and sufficient water-closets or privies" (§5), "proper and suitable conveniences or receptacles for receiving garbage and other refuse matters" (§8), and adequate chimneys. Another provision declared that "the roof of every such house" had to be "kept in good repair . . . so as not to leak" (§4); another restricted the habitation of cellars. Some provisions applied only to buildings erected after the effective date of the act, e.g., provisions relating to ceiling height and window area (§14). The law concerned itself primarily with gross physical characteristics of tenement buildings. But some attempt was made to cut down overcrowding on lots with one building already on them (§14). Thus, in embryo at least, the law of 1867 had some slight regard for slums as social settings, as well as aggregations of brick and stone.

Primarily, however, the law of 1867, like later laws, assumed that a slum was a physical entity, whatever else it was; control of physical abuses was *per se* a contribution to solving the evils of the slums. No one has expressed this view better than Jacob Riis. Describing the destruction of the so-called "Mulberry Bend," a notorious block in New York, Riis asked the rhetorical question: "Are we better off for scattering the poison and the poverty of the Bend?" His answer was a resounding, "Yes."

It is not scattered. The greater and by far the worst part of it is destroyed with the slum. Such a slum as this is itself the poison. It taints whatever it touches. Wickedness and vice gravitate toward it and are tenfold aggravated, until crime is born spontaneously of its corruption. Its poverty is hopeless, its vice bestiality, its crime desperation. Recovery is impossible under its blight. Rescue and repression are alike powerless to reach it. There *is* a connection between the rottenness of the house and that of the tenant that is patent and positive. Weakness characterizes the slum criminal, rather than wickedness. Chameleon-like, he takes the color of his surroundings. It is not where they shall go, but that they shall not go there at any rate, that is the important thing. In this much are we, are they, better off, that there will never be another Mulberry Bend for them to go to. In its place will come trees and grass and flowers; for its dark hovels light and sunshine and air.[7]

The prediction, of course, has not been borne out—a fact that casts doubt on the assumptions that underlay it.

New York was the pioneer in tenement house legislation. This fact should not surprise us. Tenement house legislation concerned the urban poor; the largest city in the country was in New York State—New York City had more foreign-born, more poor people, and more crowded slums than any other city.[8] Slum conditions at the time of the law of 1867 were appalling. New York City had grown like a weed since the turn of the century. Many of the immigrant poor and the poorer workmen lived in converted houses from which the rich had run; thousands of others lived in cellars, in rear tenements thrown up on the back of small lots, and in specially built "tenant-houses." In the slums, conditions of overcrowding, filth, misery, and degradation were indescribable. A legislative report of 1857 spoke of the

> hideous squalor and deadly effluvia; the dim, undrained courts oozing with pollution; the dark, narrow stairways, decayed with age, reeking with filth, overrun with vermin; the rotted floors, ceilings begrimed, and often too low to permit you to stand upright; the windows stuffed with rags . . . the gaunt, shivering forms and wild ghastly faces, in these black and beetling abodes.[9]

The characteristic Manhattan tenement was taller than the characteristic home of the poor in other cities, if only because New York

---

[7] Jacob A. Riis, "The Clearing of Mulberry Bend," *Review of Reviews,* 12 (1895), 172, 177; see Ernest Flagg, "The New York Tenement-House Evil and Its Cure," *Scribner's Magazine,* 16 (1894), 108, blaming much of the vice of New York's tenements on the standard 25' x 100' lot.

[8] Perhaps the character of the city's elite is an alternative or better explanation for the timing of tenement house reform. Both New York City and Boston were pioneers in tenement house reform; both cities had well-established leisure classes with strong senses of social obligation. Frontier Chicago had a quite different kind of "society." I am indebted to Martha Derthick for this suggestion.

[9] Quoted in Ford, *et al.,* I, p. 134.

is a long, narrow island, where space is at a premium. Chicago, by way of contrast, spread out in all directions, developing slums of small frame houses, "shambling, dilapidated," but in "striking contrast to the closely built, tall brick buildings that extend in deadly uniformity . . . in New York's poverty areas."[10] Yet the law of 1867 was not a *welfare* response to New York's especially blatant and obnoxious conditions. It was in an important sense a law to reduce social costs. The 1867 legislation was a by-product of one of New York's recurrent cholera epidemics which ravaged the city just after the end of the Civil War. In 1866, the Metropolitan Board of Health was created for the city, and this agency was the prime "beneficiary" of the law of 1867; it was granted major administrative powers under the act.[11]

The act of 1867 was a failure in several senses. Few states or municipalities followed its example, at least before 1900. Moreover, the law was not well-enforced. Certainly, it failed to check the growth of the slums. Conditions became or seemed to become worse than ever. By 1900, the city was more crowded, the poor suffered more, and the moral and physical stench from the slums was more offensive than ever to the respectable members of the community. Articulate men of the age were obsessed with fear—fear that the American dream was being destroyed, that the American social system was decaying, that the country was undergoing radical changes for the worse. Prominent New Yorkers could easily hold to these opinions. Political corruption, crime, drunkenness, and juvenile delinquency were, if not more prevalent, more socially visible than before. The gentler classes trembled at the crowds of immigrants pouring into the cities and worried about the lawlessness of strikers, about the concentration of wealth, and about the spread of radicalism—worried, in general, whether America could survive the passing of the symbolic frontier. Whether the problems of the times were as new or as serious as people thought is irrelevant. The sense of crisis was crucial.[12]

---

[10] Edith Abbott, *et al.*, *The Tenements of Chicago 1908–1935* (Chicago: Univ. of Chicago Press, 1936), p. 170.

[11] Charles E. Rosenberg, *The Cholera Years* (Chicago: Univ. of Chicago Press, 1962), pp. 192–234; Roy Lubove, *The Progressives and the Slums: Tenement House Reform in New York City 1890–1917* (Pittsburgh: Univ. of Pittsburgh Press, 1963), pp. 1–28.

[12] See, in general, Richard Hofstadter, *The Age of Reform* (New York: Alfred Knopf, 1955).

In this age of upheaval, the disease of the slums was perceived as
a disease of the whole body politic. The sense of the social costs of
the slums was dramatically heightened; it affected even stalwart
conservatives. Justice Peckham of New York, whose chief claim to
fame is his bitter hostility to social legislation as a New York and
federal judge, conceded the need for a war on the slums. In his view,
the evils of the slums endangered society and called for legal action:
fires, disease, "tendencies to immorality and crime where there is a
very close packing of human beings of the lower order in intelligence and morals . . . must arouse the attention of the legislator."[13]
The sense of social cost set the reform conscience free from the
crippling effects of a moralizing attitude toward the poor. The careers
of a band of vigorous, reform-minded men and women coincided hap-
pily with a point of history in which a heightened sense of the social
costs of the slums made tenement house legislation finally possible on
a grander scale than before. This took place from 1900 to the present.

The conditions laid bare by men such as Jacob Riis, by the writers
in the popular press, and by various state and local investigating
bodies were in fact not new; but they were still appalling. The New
York Tenement House Committee of 1894 found that "only 306
persons out of a total of 255,033, whose living conditions were carefully examined by its investigating staff, had access to bathtubs in
their homes." In 3,984 tenements, with a population of 121,323,
there were only 51 private toilets; others had to content themselves
with access to toilets in yards, basements, or halls.[14] Most of these
were unspeakably filthy: "Foul, malodorous privy vaults, filled to
the yard level and, in many cases, overflowing into the yards and
draining into adjacent cellars, the floors and even the walls covered
with an accumulation of fecal matter." This was the story in New
Jersey.[15] Every other sanitary sin was found in the tenements: broken
pipes with sewer gas escaping, heaps of trash and broken bottles,
garbage strewn everywhere. But there were worse things about the
tenements. In the tall, densely-massed tenements, suffering men and
women were crowded into tiny rooms; no sunlight penetrated into
the blackness. Life on the teeming streets showed the horrified eye

---

[13] J. Peckham, in *Health Department* v. *Rector, etc., of Trinity Church*, 145
N.Y. 32, 50 (1895).

[14] Quoted in Lubove, pp. 91, 92. In 1892, in the one-third square mile adjacent
to Chicago's Hull-House, there were only three bathtubs. Jane Addams, *Twenty
Years at Hull-House* (New York: New American Library, 1961), p. 221.

[15] Board of Tenement House Supervisors of New Jersey, *First Report* (Executive Document No. 26, 1904), p. 35.

of a beholder every kind of crime, immorality, and corruption. Hunger and disease prowled the dirty corridors. This, as Jacob Riis described it, was "how the other half lives."[16]

Riis was a journalist; other reformers worked within government for passage of tenement house laws. One critical aim of the reformers was to arouse the sleeping public—to show the world how bad conditions were, how much society itself was a victim of the slums. They wrote government reports and studies as well as articles in the press and magazines. A federal study of the slums was published as early as 1894.[17]

No housing reformer used publicity more astutely than Lawrence Veiller of New York. He, more than anyone else, was responsible for the New York Tenement House Law of 1901. He had been active in the Tenement House Committee of New York's Charity Organization Society; and in 1899 he set out before the public at the Sherry Building on Fifth Avenue a "tenement house exhibition" with maps and photographs of the horrors of the slums.[18] He induced the legislature to create a Tenement House Commission in 1900, which he dominated. The Commission produced a monumental study, a vivid yet dispassionate document of life in the lower depths. Photographs of conditions in the tenements were included in the study for those who would not read or for whom the written word was too pale. The technique was a fruitful one. Wisconsin, too, had a tenement house study preceding its law of 1907; its Commission also produced a report, complete with photographs, to shock the conscience and stir the Assembly.[19]

---

[16] Many articles in popular magazines and the press between 1885 and 1910 graphically described these conditions. See, for example, Edward T. Devine, "Housing Conditions in the Principal Cities of New York," *Charities,* 7 (1901), 491; Edessa Kunz, "The Housing Problem in Wisconsin," *Charities and the Commons,* 18 (1907), 251; Alice Rollins, "The Tenement-House Problem," *Forum,* 5 (1888), 207. Not all painted a totally black picture of the tenements. See, for example, William T. Elsing, "Life in New York Tenement-Houses as Seen by a City Missionary," *Scribner's Magazine,* 11 (1892), 697.

[17] Carroll D. Wright, *The Slums of Baltimore, Chicago, New York, and Philadelphia* (Washington, D.C.: House of Representatives, Executive Document No. 527, 7th Special Report, U.S. Commissioner of Labor, 1894).

[18] Lawrence Veiller, "The Tenement-House Exhibition of 1899," *Charities Review,* 10 (1900), 19.

[19] Robert W. DeForest and Lawrence Veiller (eds.), *The Tenement House Problem,* 2 vols. (New York: Macmillan, 1903); Bureau of Labor and Industrial Statistics of Wisconsin, "The Housing Problem in Wisconsin," *Twelfth Biennial Report,* Part IV (1905–1906). This study was authorized by Laws Wis. 1903, ch. 203. For other reports, see Edith Elmer Wood, *The Housing of the Unskilled Wage Earner* (New York: Macmillan, 1919), pp. 46–59.

The public opinion that was mobilized was a narrow and select one; its extent must not be exaggerated. Newspapers made comments, a few key citizens were aroused, and a few key legislators were persuaded or embarrassed.[20] What may be more critical in explaining the "success" of the tenement house movement in the age of Veiller was the nature of the economic opposition. Tenement house reform did not evoke opposition from any major, powerful economic group. To be sure, builders and owners of tenements opposed the passage of the law of 1901; but most of these were small men, not great landlords.[21]

We might know more about the dynamics of housing legislation if we knew more about the tenement house business. What is known, though spotty and speculative, suggests that the lords of the land were not big business. Many small tenements were owned by men and women of the same ethnic background and originally of the same social class as their tenants. Perhaps this was less true of New York City than elsewhere. The tall tenements of New York took considerable capital to build. But the physical nature of tenement houses in other cities suggests a good deal about the nature of their ownership. In cities outside New York, most tenements were small frame houses, rear shanties, or the discarded mansions of the rich, broken up into tiny segments. In Chicago at the turn of the century, the slums consisted of "dilapidated frame structures" and small brick or wooden houses:

> Sometimes an entire block will be covered by cottages and two-storied houses. Many of these are little, unpainted tenements, rickety and awry from age and poor building. In the rear one

---

[20] See Friedman and Spector, p. 41, for the state of public opinion in Wisconsin.

[21] Some landlords—New York's Trinity Church, for example—were particularly vulnerable to public opinion. The first attacks on Trinity as a landlord came in the decade of the 1890's. The church's image was not helped by its losing struggle against the Board of Health, which insisted that water be furnished to tenants in upper stories of tenements. See *Health Department* v. *Rector, etc., of Trinity Church*, 145 N.Y. 32 (1895). Major reforms were undertaken in 1909 and 1910. See *Report as to the Sanitary Conditions of the Tenements of Trinity Church* (New York: Trinity Church, 1895); Charles T. Bridgeman, *The Parish of Trinity Church in the City of New York*, VI (New York: Trinity Church, 1962), pp. 116–28; *Yearbook and Register of the Parish of Trinity Church* (New York: 1909), pp. 386–402; Robert H. Bremner, *From the Depths: The Discovery of Poverty in the United States* (New York: New York Univ. Press, 1964), pp. 116, 208.

often sees an irregular line of closely packed shanties, chicken-coops to all appearances, dilapidated sheds of almost piano-box size, with stove pipes extending a foot above the top.[22]

In Washington, D.C., the characteristic slum house was the alley house, put up for Negroes in the period starting with the Civil War. The alley house had no sewers, no water mains, no indoor plumbing, "no pavement, no lights, no provision for the removal of garbage."[23] It was bare shelter, little else. Life in these shanty-towns was grim and unyielding; but it was not a life dominated by baronial overlords. No class of big tenement house owners corresponded to the big businessmen, manufacturers, and bankers of the day. To a striking degree, the slum landlord was himself a product of the slums. He was often an uneducated, half-impoverished man of immigrant stock. As we shall see, some of his sins can be ascribed to his environment—legal, social, and moral—as much as the sins of his tenants can.

The New York law of 1901 was the most elaborate tenement house act yet passed. It was a considerable advance on its predecessor, the much-amended law of 1867.[24] Superior sophistication in draftsmanship and experience with the failings of the older act account for much of this technical advance. Credit must also be given to the political skill of Lawrence Veiller who fought for the bill and prevented its dilution in Albany. The new law ran to more than one hundred sections. Once again, a sharp distinction was made between existing tenements and tenements to be constructed or converted in the future. Out of this distinction grew the expressions "old-law" and "new-law" tenements which passed into the language of New Yorkers. The main emphasis of the New York law was on the physical condition of the tenements. But the social needs of life were not totally neglected; light, air, and space were as important to the draftsmen as plumbing and fire protection and not merely for

---

[22] "Chicago's Housing Conditions," *Charities Review*, 10 (1901), 292.
[23] Wood, p. 47.
[24] Amended in Laws N.Y. 1879, ch. 504; Laws N.Y. 1880, ch. 399; Laws N.Y. 1884, ch. 272; Laws N.Y. 1884, ch. 448; Laws N.Y. 1887, ch. 84; Laws N.Y. 1887, ch. 288; Laws N.Y. 1888, ch. 422; Laws N.Y. 1889, ch. 211; Laws N.Y. 1890, ch. 486; Laws N.Y. 1891, ch. 39; Laws N.Y. 1891, ch. 204; Laws N.Y. 1892, ch. 329, ch. 655, ch. 673; Laws N.Y. 1893, ch. 173; Laws N.Y. 1894, ch. 247; Laws N.Y. 1896; ch. 991; Laws N.Y. 1900, ch. 279.

reasons of health. The morality of slum life was also carefully considered by the draftsmen. The act provided, for example, that

> In every apartment of three or more rooms in a tenement house hereafter erected, access to every room, including bath rooms and water closet compartments, shall be had without passing through any bedroom.
>
> *   *   *
>
> No room in any tenement house shall be so overcrowded that there shall be afforded less than four hundred cubic feet of air to each adult, and two hundred cubic feet of air to each child under twelve years of age. . . .[25]

The privacy provision is a good example of middle-class morality imposed upon the slums. Lack of privacy was and is a characteristic of slum life; but the clause in question had a special kind of privacy in mind.[26] It reflects a climate of opinion which saw moral degradation as one of the chief evils of the slums—the temptations to which small children were exposed, the absence of sexual restraint, and the fact that innocents were forced to live in close proximity to prostitutes. The New York Tenement House Department solemnly reported that when "dissolute women enter a tenement house their first effort is to make friends with the children. Children have been lured into their rooms, where they beheld sights from which they should be protected." The Tenement House Law of 1901 provided "severe and drastic measures so as to drive these women out of the tenement houses where respectable working men and their families lived." The law did not "seek to regulate the evil of prostitution generally, but solely to remove such contaminating influences from the tenement house dwelling, believing that such conditions should not exist in the homes of the poor."[27] The aim of the privacy provision was to reshape the moral environment of the areas where poor people lived. Characteristically, for its period, it attempted to mold social reality through manipulating housing design. The provision

---

[25] Laws N.Y. 1901, ch. 334, §75, §112.

[26] Veiller inserted a similar provision in his model housing law and remarked that, "This provision is made especially necessary in the case of tenement houses, because of the practice of tenants taking lodgers and boarders into their apartments." Lawrence Veiller, *A Model Housing Law* (2nd ed.; New York: Russell Sage Foundation, 1920), p. 146. Edith Elmer Wood called the privacy provision "a safeguard of far-reaching sociological importance," Wood, p. 68.

[27] Quoted in Tenement House Department of the City of New York, *First Report*, I (1902-3), pp. 93, 94.

against overcrowding was a less obvious example of the same impulse and the same solution. Overcrowding is a social and moral evil as well as a sanitary sin.

Nonetheless, the physical emphasis was primary. The provision on overcrowding, for example, reflected strong views on the noxiousness of dark and uncirculated air, as much as anything else. Moreover, nonphysical reforms were pursued through physical means. From a mid-twentieth-century viewpoint, the idea of improving moral conditions through changes in housing design and construction seems curiously archaic. Many housing experts, though not all, think that public housing and its problems teach us the futility of social reform through better plumbing and more space. We shall return to this problem again. In Veiller's day, we should remember, the path to reform lay precisely in the direction of stressing physical improvement. The argument that reformers had to make was that the poor were no different from the rich in innate morality and sense. "The rich and the poor," wrote Veiller, "are indeed alike in all essential particulars."[28] The point was to demonstrate that reform would not be wasted on the poor. Were poor people dirty? It was because they had no bathtubs. Public baths, when provided, were heavily used by the multitudes.

> Few people realize the efforts made by most of the tenement house population to keep clean under the most adverse conditions. When all the water that can be obtained must be carried up several flights of stairs, cleanliness is indeed a virtue.

As conditions changed, so did people's habits, Veiller argued. "We all live up to our environment, more or less, like the beggar in the bed of the king."[29] In 1900, to argue that the poor suffered from special disabilities of mind, family, personality, and social organization was to argue for doing nothing about the slums. Two generations later, the same arguments implied not less but more government intervention.

An important feature of the 1901 law was its meticulous attention to problems of administration and enforcement of the law. The law of 1867 had created a flexible, discretionary system with great

---

[28] Lawrence Veiller, *Housing Reform* (New York: Russell Sage Foundation, 1910), p. 16.
[29] *Ibid.*, pp. 17, 18.

power lodged in the Metropolitan Board of Health, which was created just prior to the law. The system of administration was a natural outcome of the background of the act. Fear of a cholera epidemic radiating out of the slums led to creation of the Board and passage of the act. The 1901 law sharply limited areas of formal discretion; it attempted to lay down rules which were objective, clear, and therefore easily enforcible. Administrative discretion was limited, so that city departments could concentrate on enforcement rather than interstitial decision-making, free from the temptations to laxity inherent in discretionary systems.[30] A "total window area in a water-closet [of] . . . not . . . less than three square feet"[31] cannot be mistaken, and anyone can tell by the use of a tape-measure whether a water-closet violates this law. The New York act also called for a system of building permits and a registry of all tenement houses. Veiller wanted as little as possible left either to politics, to chance, or to the human failings of administrators.

The New York law was followed by tenement house laws in a number of other states: New Jersey, Connecticut, Wisconsin, and Indiana.[32] Most of these laws adhered closely to the main outlines of New York's statute. Wisconsin was exceptional. Here, for complex reasons—perhaps a mere blunder—the tenement house law provided for no special administrative machinery. General law enforcement officers, local city officials, and state factory inspectors would presumably carry out the act. No permit or registry system was established. Yet the act had the broadest coverage of any state statute. New York's law was confined to "first class cities" (New York City and Buffalo were the only members of this class); and Connecti-

---

[30] The New Jersey Board found this a positive virtue despite "criticism" of the board's lack of "discretion": "the absence of general clauses in the law" prevents "the use of influence to obtain special favors and concessions, relieves the Board of much useless argument and protects . . . the public . . . from . . . loose administration." Board of Tenement House Supervisors of New Jersey, p. 64.

[31] Laws N.Y. 1901, ch. 334, §69.

[32] Laws N. J. 1904, p. 96; Laws Conn. 1905, ch. 178; Laws Wis. 1907, ch. 269; Laws Ind. 1909, ch. 47. None of these acts was a verbatim copy of the New York law. The New York law was used as a draft or model from which the draftsmen worked. Thus, the Connecticut law was much shorter than the New York model. It omitted the fire protection sections. It changed many of the specific dimensions required, e.g., minimum room heights were 8 feet 6 inches in Connecticut, and 9 feet in New York. There were also differences in definitions, in the scope of the law, and in administrative provisions.

Laws Pa. 1895, No. 110, p. 178, naturally owed nothing to the New York law. The Pennsylvania act seems to have had little or no influence outside of the state.

cut's law was restricted to cities of more than 20,000 population.[33] Wisconsin's law was unlimited. This was another blunder. Weak administration and excessively bold coverage was a fatal combination. The law, passed in 1907, lasted one year only. It was declared unconstitutional in 1908 in the case of *Bonnet* v. *Vallier*.[34] But the Wisconsin court went out of its way to express approval of the general aims of tenement house legislation. The court confined its critique of the act to particular aspects of this particular law; it did not cast doubt on the general legality of housing reform. The court's opinion was frank; tenement house legislation was a good thing, but only for major metropolitan areas. The 1907 law was "unreasonable" in its scope and detail. Indeed, the court suggested what the "reasonable" contents of a new law might be, almost inviting passage of a better act. This hint bore fruit in 1909.[35]

The Wisconsin decision stands alone. Courts have sustained state tenement house laws against constitutional attack whenever the problem has arisen.[36] This is a particularly significant fact in that the tenement house laws were passed at a time when social and economic legislation was unusually vulnerable to judicial review. Yet the number of cases was small, and the results (except perhaps in the Wisconsin case) no comfort to opponents of the laws. Perhaps the invisibility of the slum owner, the fact that he was typically a small businessman, often of immigrant stock, allowed the courts to see these statutes as entirely wholesome, not as interferences with the free market or as disturbances to the American system. No such difficult choices faced the courts as in labor cases, where bloodshed and violence stalked the streets outside the courtroom. In the tenement house cases, the social costs of slum housing could be reckoned without strong countervailing arguments or interests.

Even *Bonnet* v. *Vallier* was in a sense no anomaly. The court constantly stressed that the Wisconsin law was inappropriate except in

---

[33] Laws Conn. 1905, ch. 178. Smaller cities could choose to come under the act if they wished. The act originally applied to the cities of Hartford, New Haven, Waterbury, New Britain, and Meriden. After the 1910 census Danbury, Stamford, and Norwich were added. Bureau of Labor Statistics of Connecticut, *24th Report* (1910), p. 203.

[34] 136 Wis. 193, 116 N. W. 885 (1908).

[35] Laws Wis. 1909, ch. 394, ch. 592.

[36] In New York, see *Tenement House Department of the City of New York* v. *Moeschen*, 179 N.Y. 325, 72 N. E. 231 (1904), *aff'd per curiam*, 203 U. S. 583, 51 L. Ed. 328 (1906); *Adler* v. *Deegan*, 251 N.Y. 467, 167 N. E. 705 (1929) (Multiple Dwelling Law).

crowded urban centers. The notion that tenement house legislation could be applied to honest small-town Americans was offensive to the court. The tenement house laws met with approval only as measures imposed upon the lawless, filthy, un-American urban slums. In 1912, in *Grimmer* v. *Tenement House Department of New York*[37] the highest court of New York held that the New York tenement house law did not apply to an "apartment house with certain hotel features," in other words, to the kind of building usually called an apartment hotel. The New York statute defined a tenement house as one occupied by three or more families living independently and doing their cooking on the premises. It did not distinguish between apartments for the rich and for the poor. Grimmer's apartment hotel literally fit the statutory definition. The court's strictly legal arguments for exempting the apartment hotel have something of a specious ring. Most likely the court simply could not see why a building should be subjected to regulation as a tenement when it had "parquet floors of oak," entrance halls "covered with imported Vienna marble," floors of "white Italian marble," ceilings and cornices "decorated in metal," servants' quarters, and many baths, gas ranges and sinks. The spirit of the legislation did not apply to buildings whose tenants were of an "independent" class, "able to exact proper living conditions without the help of such drastic provisions as are found in the Tenement House Act."

In the early part of the twentieth century, what could be called a national housing-reform movement came into being.[38] In 1910, Lawrence Veiller helped found a National Housing Association, with the support of the Russell Sage Foundation. He extended his influence by publishing a number of books and pamphlets on housing; in 1910 he published a *Model Tenement House Law* and in 1914 a *Model Housing Law*. Both of these bore the imprint of the Russell Sage Foundation. These model laws were useful as sources of textual inspiration. It was necessary to avoid slavish imitation of New York's laws which Veiller thought unsuitable elsewhere.[39] Veiller traveled frequently to cities and states which were considering housing legislation to exert influence and pressure. His energies helped achieve a substantial spread of the housing-law idea. Ken-

---

[37] 204 N. Y. 370, 97 N. E. 884 (1912).

[38] Lubove, p. 143ff.

[39] Lawrence Veiller, *A Model Tenement House Law* (New York: Russell Sage Foundation, 1910), p. 2; Veiller, *A Model Housing Law*, 2nd ed., p. v.

tucky, Indiana, Massachusetts, Pennsylvania, and California enacted state housing laws by 1917; Michigan, Minnesota, and Iowa by 1919.

By 1920, about twenty cities had enacted new housing codes while twenty more had inserted housing provisions in their building and health ordinances. Virtually all of these cities—which included Syracuse, St. Paul, Grand Rapids, Duluth, Berkeley, Cleveland, Columbus, Lansing, Portland, Oregon, and Salem, Massachusetts—adapted their codes from the New York law or Veiller's model laws.[40]

Successful enactment of tenement house reform was due to a number of factors: (a) a heightened perception of the problem of urban slums; (b) a corps of dedicated and organized reform workers committed to housing reform; (c) the absence of strong ideological opposition; and (d) the absence of strong economic opposition. These four factors were interrelated. The judicial history of the laws indicates, for example, that judges were able to see, grasp, and advance the objectives of the movement; validity failed where judges saw no true need for reform *(Bonnet, Grimmer)*. Tenement house legislation was in a classical tradition of American reform; unlike public housing, it was not socialistic; it required no direct government intervention, only "regulation," and it was therefore "moderate" in scope (Veiller himself was bitterly opposed to public housing).[41] The laws were framed or construed to apply only to the urban poor who, arguably, were beyond the help of the market system. The absence of strong economic opposition probably played a key role in ensuring the passage of these laws. Many slum landlords themselves lived in the slums; others were one generation or less away from slum life; in neither case was the landlord a member of polite business society. It was relatively easy to override or ignore the opposition of unorganized small businessmen of this kind.

The Slumlord: Rise of a Scapegoat

The point about the slum landlord is worth dwelling on. The tenement house movement helped fix him in his permanent position as an American devil and scapegoat. Albion Fellows Bacon, who led

---

[40] Lubove, p. 146; see also Wood, pp. 60–90.
[41] Lubove, pp. 179–81.

a movement for housing reform in Indiana, cried out that "to col-
lect rent from our old death-traps of tenements is really to take
blood money."[42] Jacob Riis agreed; he blamed much of the problem
of the slums on "human greed"; a man "has no right to slowly kill
his neighbors, or his tenants, by making a death-trap of his house."[43]
Moreover, "reform by law must aim at making it unprofitable to
own a bad tenement."[44] This was an early sounding of the cry to
"take the profit out of the slums," a cry that has echoed down to the
present day. A belief that landlords were greedy villains was a necessity for the housing reformers. Since reform laws imposed costs on
landlords without reimbursing them in any way, and since no one
expected or wanted rents to rise, it was morally necessary to believe
that rents were exorbitant and that costs could be absorbed without
giving up a fair return. It was convenient, therefore, to assume that
landlords were a class of evil men, overcharging ignorant tenants
and callous to the point of criminality. The fact that tenement
house owners were not respectable old-American businessmen, by
and large, made it easier to adhere to this notion. Successful management of small slum houses may demand that the owner live in the
house; this was too high a price to pay for anyone with alternative
avenues of profitable investment. Simple economics then suggests
that only slumdwellers could "afford" to own at least some of the
slums. In fact, the evidence shows that many slum landlords did
live in the slums. A study of Jersey City housing, published in 1903,
found 111 resident owners of 539 tenements studied—more than one
out of five. "As a number of these landlords own two or more houses,
while a number of other houses are owned by landlords in neighbor-
ing streets, the actual number of houses managed by owners practically resident is considerably greater."[45] Of course, most landlords
were absentees. Some people grew rich on the slums and moved else-

---

[42] Albion Fellows Bacon, *What Bad Housing Means to the Community* (Boston:
American Unitarian Association, n.d.), p. 14.

[43] Jacob Riis, *How the Other Half Lives* (New York: Hill & Wang, 1957), p. 205.

[44] *Ibid.*, p. 217.

[45] Mary B. Sayles, *Housing Conditions in Jersey City* (Philadelphia: Supplement
to Annals of American Academy of Political and Social Science, 1903), p. 51. Approximately similar findings for Chicago are in Abbott, *et al.*, pp. 363–400. The
1894 federal report on Chicago, Baltimore, Philadelphia, and New York found considerable variation in tenure. In Baltimore 80.44 per cent of the families in tenements were renters, in Chicago 89.77 per cent, in New York 99.15 per cent, and in
Philadelphia 92.45 per cent. Wright, pp. 584–94.

where. Slums were owned by the Astors and by Trinity Church. But slum ownership, by and large, was and is more local, more decentralized, and more widely-spread than most other forms of enterprise. A study of some 300 properties in a Los Angeles slum found that one-third of the properties were owned by occupants; and another third were owned by people in the same postal zone.[46] A Milwaukee study showed a somewhat similar pattern.[47] New York City of course is more concentrated in ownership. Milwaukee and Los Angeles may deviate somewhat from the ownership pattern in older large cities. But it is clear that the business of low-income residential property is not highly concentrated; there is no equivalent of General Motors or the A & P among slumlords.

In any event, nothing impeded the progress of the notion that slum money was tainted money; and belief in the evils of slum ownership became a self-fullfilling prophecy. Bad reputation is a cost to a man, even if it cannot be measured exactly and valued in dollars. The business of selling illegal property or services, such as drugs or gambling, necessarily demands exorbitant profits; investors must be attracted by high returns into occupations of great risk and small prestige. Slum ownership has something of the same quality. As tenement house legislation became more stringent in its demands, slum ownership became virtually as legally perilous as running a brothel. If tenement house rules are too strict, in the economic sense, they cannot be obeyed without loss of profits. When the rules are overstrict, corruption sets in; landlords will "purchase . . . code revision through payments to building inspectors."[48] The codes will, moreover, be variably enforced. Laxity and corruption will alternate with periods of severe crackdown—perhaps following a disastrous fire or a scandal. But variable enforcement is merely another aspect of the high risk of slum ownership. Unpredictable enforcement makes one's livelihood a gamble; the pay-off cannot completely avoid the risk of exposure and punishment. These risks, like the bad reputation of the landlord, are real costs to an owner, and ownership of slum property will in time come to reside in those men

---

[46] Letter from Professor Fred E. Case, Graduate School of Business Administration, University of California, Los Angeles, March 15, 1966.

[47] Eugene Edward Molitor, *The Significance of Slum Ownership to the Urban Planning Function: A Case Study in Milwaukee* (Unpublished master's thesis, University of Wisconsin, Madison, 1961).

[48] Warren Lehman, "Building Codes, Housing Codes and the Conservation of Chicago's Housing Supply," *University of Chicago Law Review,* 31 (1963), 180, 189.

who can take the heat. At least this is a plausible hypothesis. More precise work on the economics and sociology of slum ownership might shed more light on the question of who owns the slums and how much they earn from this source.

Whatever the facts, the persistent model of the evil slumlord characterizes—and probably hampers—housing movements to this day. (The converse notion—that good houses, well-run by respectable businessmen, would return fair profits—lies at the base of the model tenement house movement, which will be discussed below.) Not that the notion of the evil slumlord is completely untrue. It can be assumed that over the years a kind of filtering-down process of landlords has occurred. The process is difficult to document, particularly for past generations; but it seems clear that it has taken place. The costs, risks, pains, and annoyances of slum ownership are too much for the "reputable" man. During the New York wave of rent strikes, a lawyer who represented a client with a building in the rent strike area claimed that eleven real estate firms refused to take over the management. The president of the New York Real Estate Board claims that owners "who once maintained well-kept tenements . . . have left the business," selling out to "quick-profit speculators."[49] Many of the worst landlords are those at the very end of the filtering-down process. This seems apparent from frequent articles in the newspapers on the difficulty of locating and pinning down slum landlords. One tenement house, which was in the news in New York in 1965 and which had been declared unfit for human habitation, was fined twelve times for code violations. The violations were charged to three different men, Gluck, Haver, and Samuel Braun. The tenants "believed the owner was Seymour Gelfand, but they sent their rent to Arthur J. Clyne." Gelfand said he had merely been "escrow agent for Joseph Braun and Harry Holtzman who are not the owners either"; the building belonged to the 454 West Realty Corporation "whose last known address was a post office box. The city believes Mr. Holtzman holds the four mortgages on the building."[50]

---

[49] *New York Times*, Feb. 22, 1964, p. 28, col. 5.

[50] *New York Times*, Jan. 23, 1965, p. 38, col. 1. Gelfand said, "the city had been informed that the owners were not in the position to remove the violations, and intended to 'walk away from it.' No one paid any rent, he said." This then was a building at the end of its tether. See "Slum-Makers are Shadowmen," *Journal of Housing*, 14 (1957), 232 (cited hereafter as *JH*). See also the case studies of landlords hauled into New York's Housing Court, in Community Service Society of New York, *Code Enforcement for Multiple Dwellings in New York City*, Part II, "Enforcement through Criminal Court Action" (1965), pp. 33–50.

These shadowy figures may be the landlords who "milk" their buildings; as the buildings sink toward utter ruin, the property rights are traded among a group of owners, some of them totally unscrupulous, others apparently mentally deranged. New York's "slum queen," Mrs. Auguste Redman, made 125 court appearances in the four years ending in 1961, was fined thousands of dollars, given two years probation, then finally sent to jail. The probation department recommended "commission to Bellevue hospital for psychiatric observation."[51] These dead-end landlords hide or run until the building no longer pays, either because its ruin is complete, because vandals have gutted it, or because its cumulative illegality finally becomes so gross that the building is fined to death, demolished by court order, or otherwise extirpated by law.[52] Thus, there is an important group of slum properties—those nearly at the end of their rope—which are not exorbitantly profitable; they are not profitable at all. In the slums, buildings may return big profits, small profits, or no profits, depending upon where they are situated in the life-cycle of a house, who the owner is, and the general state of the neighborhood. At least this is a plausible guess.[53] That some slum buildings are losers is plainly established. Woody Klein studied a particularly noxious building in New York: 311 East 100th Street. It was a dead loss to the owners.[54] David Satter reports that the worst buildings in Chicago's Lawndale district are unprofitable.[55] The worst buildings, then, are dead-end buildings owned by dead-end slumlords; neither is able to make even a dishonest dollar.

Legislative programs (some intentionally, some not) are calculated to make the small landlord fade away. In 1936, in the midst of the depression, enforcement of new amendments to New York's housing laws seemed to threaten certain city landlords with ruin. An Association of Harlem and Bronx Property Owners was formed; it fought

---

[51] See "Courts Beginning to Get Tough in Code Violation Cases in Cities Everywhere," *JH*, 18 (1961), 163.

[52] Demolition is discussed below, at pp. 68–72.

[53] Not enough is known about the economics of slum ownership. See Arthur D. Sporn, "Empirical Studies in the Economics of Slum Ownership," *Land Economics*, 36 (1960), 333, which found wide variation in profitability. For another discussion, see Alvin L. Schorr, *Slums and Social Insecurity* (London: Thomas Nelson, 1964), pp. 69–74. Since the text was written, an important new study has shed great light on the problem. George Sternlieb, *The Tenement Landlord* (New Brunswick: Rutgers Univ. Press, 1966).

[54] Woody Klein, *Let in the Sun* (New York: Macmillan, 1964), pp. 141–68, 273–74.

[55] David Satter, "West Side Story," *New Republic*, 155 (July 2, 1966), p. 15.

unsuccessfully in court and legislature for relief.[56] But in 1935, a law was passed which suspended enforcement of the Multiple Dwelling Law against an owner who, together with the owners of two-thirds of the property in an area designated by the local housing authority or state board as "suitable . . . for housing," agreed to convey his houses and lots "to a limited dividend housing corporation organized under the state housing law" (or to the housing authority itself) for clearance and rebuilding.[57] Another law suspending enforcement made a somewhat different point. In 1936, the state amended the Multiple Dwelling Act, excusing civil and criminal penalties for six months to owners who acquired ownership of tenements by foreclosure.[58] Savings banks had chosen to evict 4,000 families from noncomplying tenements on which they had foreclosed, rather than "take the risks of prosecution." The law was passed to give them and their tenants relief. Depression conditions created this crisis; but law, policy, and politics sharply distinguished between the individual owner (the classical landlord) and the reputable, corporate owner. As we shall see, the same distinction has been made in more recent programs.[59]

From Tenement House Laws to Housing Codes

The rush to enact restrictive housing laws and ordinances slowed down in the 1920's and decidedly so in the 1930's. A good deal of disillusionment had set in on the part of those who had actively backed tenement house laws. In the first place, the laws were hard to administer and enforce. The story is best known for New York. Constant complaints were heard that the staff was too small to do its job. This was to be expected. Reform movements that are oriented toward the passage of legislation measure enactment as success. Some relaxation of passion is afterwards hard to avoid. It is hard to maintain the same high pitch of enthusiasm for problems of administration, appropriation, and staff as for the enactment crusade.

Administration and enforcement are problems for all government agencies and programs. Yet tenement house laws seemed unusually

---

[56] Mabel L. Walker, *Urban Blight and Slums* (Cambridge, Mass.: Harvard Univ. Press, 1938), pp. 147–50.

[57] Laws N. Y. 1935, ch. 863. Regardless of ownership, enforcement was not suspended as to conditions "dangerous to the life or health of any occupant."

[58] Laws N.Y. 1936, ch. 809, amending Multiple Dwelling Law §304.

[59] See below, p. 176. Recently, however, the law has specially favored owners who are below the poverty line themselves; on this point, see below, at p. 179.

"impractical" and unusually difficult to enforce. Complaints of poor enforcement come from many jurisdictions and are curiously similar. Perhaps the tenement house laws were unenforceable even under favorable circumstances. The New York law of 1901 was well drafted and particularly cunning in its administrative provisions. Why then was enforcement imperfect? One conventional answer blames feeble enforcement on inadequate staff. But perhaps some defects in these laws made a comparatively large staff necessary.

The very fact that slum landlords formed a diffuse class of small businessmen was a stumbling-block for enforcement. It meant that regulation had to be imposed; compliance with forms, formalities, and complex regulation was not a standard business habit. Moreover, some provisions of the tenement house laws imposed costs on landlords or tenants without providing any means of meeting these additional costs. Provisions against overcrowding, for example, if vigorously enforced, would have compelled large slum families either to rent more space at a higher rent, move into larger but poorer housing, or split up their household groups.

Blanket prohibitions on overcrowding, then as now, were also hard to enforce because no attempt was made to understand the causes of overcrowding and to provide alternative solutions. For example, during the age of heavy immigration, many small landlords took in lodgers. This was a serious source of overcrowding. Yet the lodger system served a real function in "slums of hope." It helped the immigrant to adjust to an alien culture. Men lodged with their relatives or with fellow-countrymen who spoke their language. True, conditions were sometimes virtually intolerable. Some lodging houses were squalid dormitories for transients and immigrants. In a Milwaukee building in 1903, seventeen Hungarians lived in four rooms; when the building was inspected in the afternoon, some of the lodgers who worked on night shifts were asleep. The inspector thought it "quite probable that the same beds [were] occupied at night by another set of men who work during the day." But many of these men were residents in this country only temporarily; some expected to lead the life of a lodger only long enough to earn money to bring their families over; others wanted to save every penny possible and return home with substantial savings.[60] Landlords, in turn, often took in lodgers to help eke out low family incomes. In short, the lodging houses served important functions.

---

[60] Kunz, p. 297. On the lodging house problem, see also Abbott, *et al.*, pp. 341–62.

Reformers quite properly objected to conditions in the lodging houses. But what were the alternatives?

Other provisions of the tenement house laws interfered with customary practice. One section of the New York law of 1901 prohibited the encumbering of fire escapes. But tenants were used to treating fire escapes as part of their home; they resented any efforts to make them change. The provision could not be made to work. Sometimes the fire escapes were cleared off for the inspector, but encumbered again moments later. Moreover, city judges would not cooperate in punishing offenders. In 1906, a concerted effort to clear up the fire-escape problem failed because city "magistrates were apparently loath to impose fines on immigrants and workers for violations which they considered relatively trivial."[61]

Like the slum landlord, the "lax judge" has been a constant character in the drama of slum housing and another scapegoat of reform. In 1966, too, there was an outcry against him. In New York, the Community Service Society attributes the failures of code enforcement at least partly to the New York City Housing Court. At fault is the "court's failure to comply strictly with criminal procedure" and its "view that most defendants are not 'criminals' in the usual sense of the word." The Society has suggested that the court tighten its procedures and that it impose heavier fines and even jail sentences on offenders.[62] But the persistence of the lax judge—like the persistence of the evil slum landlord—invites a more-or-less sociological explanation. It seems apparent that the housing-case judge sees his role differently from that of the administrator. The judge has before him a series of concrete instances—specific individuals charged with specific acts. He does not necessarily feel that his duty requires him to advance at all costs the policies of the

---

[61] Lubove, pp. 161, 164. There were difficulties with the analogous provisions in New Jersey; tenants resented giving up the use of fire escapes for storage. Board of Tenement House Supervisors of New Jersey, *Second Report* (Legislative Document No. 24, 1905), p. 35.

[62] "Slumlords' Fines Called Too Low," *New York Times*, Jan. 27, 1965, p. 23, col. 1. The recommendations were based on the Society's interesting and thorough 1965 study, *Code Enforcement for Multiple Dwellings in New York City*, the second part of which dealt with enforcement through criminal court action. For other complaints about low fines, lax judges, or the slow pace of judicial enforcement, see "The Slum Operators: A Day in Court," *Chicago Daily News*, May 22, 1963, p. 1, col. 1; *New York Times*, Dec. 6, 1963, p. 38, col. 1; "[New York City Buildings Commissioner Charles G.] Moerdler Scores Judges on Housing," *New York Times*, April 9, 1966, p. 26, col. 2.

housing code; his role is that of the judge who dispenses justice in the particular case.[63] The landlord and the tenant in the fire-escape cases are individuals confronting the power of the government. Then, too, lower court judges may be drawn from the same economic and social strata of society as the landlords. They may be upwardly mobile men of immigrant stock, like the landlords. They may thus tend to see the landlord's point of view.[64] Campaigns against the landlord, moreover, are often responses to political pressures of the moment; but political pressures may have less effect on judges than on other elected office-holders. Especially is this true when the importance of any particular decision in a housing case is virtually nil. For these and other reasons, the lax judge has remained a problem of the housing laws.

Were the tenement house laws really successful? Did they have an impact on life in the slums? In certain gross respects, measurable change took place during the age of the tenement house laws. By 1915, in New York, "windows had been installed in 300,000 interior rooms of old-law tenements and several thousand school sinks had been replaced by water closets."[65] The death toll from slum fires had been greatly reduced; the filth had been, if not eliminated, substantially reduced. Hunger and disease had perceptibly abated. Yet the reformers remained dissatisfied; and what is more, their dissatisfaction took the form of psychological abandonment of their own device—the tenement house laws. In 1936, Edith Abbott wrote: "Gradually it became clear ... that the housing problem was almost as immovable as the Sphinx." She agreed that the tenements of Chicago were improving; but she refused to credit the change to "any important improvements in the tenement house ordinances of Chicago, nor to the enforcement of these ordinances." Change had been brought about by technological progress which affected the en-

---

[63] See "Slum Violations Get Easier Fines," *New York Times*, Aug. 19, 1965, p. 33, col. 1.

[64] Early in 1966, a considerable fuss in New York City was made over the fact that in-laws of Charles Moerdler, the Building Commissioner, owned slum houses with code violations. Moerdler insisted that he was capable of treating his relatives impartially, and the tempest subsided. No one was really surprised that a man like Moerdler might have relatives who owned slum property (with or without violations). But it would have been inconceivable for his relatives to be dope peddlers, prostitutes, common thieves, or even ex-convicts. *New York Times*, March 13, 1966, p. 1, col. 7.

[65] Lubove, p. 165, quoting from the eighth report of the New York Tenement House Department.

vironment of the poor. Nowadays every urban evil under the sun is blamed on the automobile, but to Edith Abbott the automobile was a blessing. It rid the slums of the horse, and along with it "the filthy stables and the dreadful manure heaps."[66]

The sources of dissatisfaction with the tenement house laws were various and in some ways puzzling. But the fact of disillusionment was clear. Disillusionment, whether or not justified, removed an important prop from the political and social underpinnings of the tenement house movement. Some housing reformers turned their attention to an ancient colleague, and rival, of the tenement house movement: the model tenement house. As we shall see, this movement was never crowned with full success. Some housing experts began to turn to a more radical solution: government-built houses for the poor. Indeed, the tenement-house laws themselves were adduced as causes for the breakdown in any private solution. Reformers, through experience, had "learned" that "private builders are not in business for pleasure"; when regulatory measures extract the profit from housing the low-income groups, this market is abandoned: "Now that building codes and other building ordinances are in effect, it is unlikely that private enterprise will ever again undertake to house the lower income groups in new dwellings."[67] "The best restrictive legislation," wrote Edith Elmer Wood, "is only negative. It will prevent the bad. It will not produce the good. Especially, it will not produce it at a given rental. And rental is a despot. A high standard of restrictive legislation will not be enacted, or if enacted, will not be enforced, when its enforcement will leave a considerable number of people homeless."[68] During the First World War, the federal government took some small steps to

---

[66] Abbott, *et al.*, pp. 476–77.

[67] Michael W. Straus and Talbot Wegg, *Housing Comes of Age* (New York: Oxford Univ. Press, 1938), p. 19. Straus and Wegg held out two hopes: innovations in building techniques, or "some subsidy."

There is a certain inconsistency between the two sources of disillusionment: that the codes were ineffective, and that they were so effective that they choked off low-income housing construction. In a sense, however, both statements can be true at once. "Reputable" low-income housing had become more difficult and expensive. The *laissez faire* housing of the nineteenth century was now formally illegal; businessmen would not and could not any longer put up great numbers of new buildings that would house the very poor, meet code standards, and still return good profits. Additions to the stock of low-income housing would of course continue to occur as long as poor people existed. But some of the increase would come through illegal means, and the new supply would tend to corrupt and disrupt the administration of existing housing laws.

[68] Wood, p. 20.

ease the shortage of houses for war-workers.[69] The program was hastily dismantled after the war, and the public housing movement was swept aside in the rush to "normalcy." Nonetheless, the cutting edge of the reform brigade had shifted away from tenement house regulation toward public housing. During the 1920's, a few concrete steps were taken in the states toward support of positive housing programs; in the 1930's the New Deal housing and resettlement programs suggested that the day was near when a profound housing solution was at last possible. The Wagner-Steagell Housing Act was passed in 1937. The housing-code movement continued to sleep.

But the public housing program in turn lost its glamour, as we shall later explore in more detail. The housing code came back into its own after the Second World War with the rise of urban renewal. The Housing Act of 1949 created federal urban redevelopment. This Act required the federal government in deciding whether or not to extend slum clearance and redevelopment aid to particular cities to consider whether "appropriate local public bodies" in such cities had undertaken "positive programs . . . for preventing the spread or recurrence . . . of slums and blighted areas through the adoption, improvement, and modernization of local codes and regulations relating to land use and adequate standards of health, sanitation, and safety for dwelling accommodations."[70] The roots of this requirement lie deep in the nature of urban redevelopment—a program which, as we shall see, has closer allegiances to business and political goals and to the social cost concept than to welfare. The new emphasis on housing codes was only part of a new emphasis on central city planning. It thus differed profoundly from the impetus behind the original tenement house laws. The resulting housing codes were, however, in many ways similar to the older tenement laws.

The code requirement has gradually become more explicit. The Housing Act of 1954 broadened the attack on blight by adding the concept of "urban renewal" to the older concept of "redevelopment." Renewal made use of a whole range of techniques; no longer was federal aid confined to bulldozing and rebuilding from scratch. The law now demanded from each city a "workable program" before federal renewal gold could flow in. The statute specifically mentioned a housing code as a possible element of a "workable program." The Housing and Home Finance Agency (HHFA) made the

---

[69] See below, pp. 95–96.

[70] 63 Stat. 414, §101(a) (1949).

requirement mandatory; finally, in 1964, the statute was amended to reflect this fact.[71] Consequently, there has been a great rush to enact housing codes.[72] Many major cities had long had housing codes; but the rest, and many smaller communities as well, are quickly falling into line. "Up to 1955, only 56 communities had housing codes. By July 1961, the number had increased to 493, and by July 1963 to 736."[73]

It is clear why the cities have adopted the codes; they must do so or forfeit federal money. But why has the federal government forced the codes on the cities? One reason may lie in the increased acceptability, sophistication, and presumed utility of land-use controls, of which housing codes are only one example. There are other reasons, too. The costs of urban renewal are vast; billions of dollars will be needed to reconstitute the cities. Federal subsidy is available to help do the job of clearing the worst of the slums; but costs would be reduced and the federal dollar could go further if marginal areas were upgraded through the use of lesser measures. "Over the long pull," it might be possible to "establish healthy cities with reduced requirements for . . . Federal aid."[74] The use of housing codes is one such technique. It may prevent or arrest blight in neighborhoods near the slums or with spots of blight scattered here and there. Countless millions of renewal dollars might be saved in the long run.

The new emphasis on housing codes is thus in part a tool for a kind of cut-rate urban renewal.[75] Through land-use techniques and

---

[71] See below, p. 162.

[72] On legal problems arising under the codes, see Joseph Guandolo, "Housing Codes in Urban Renewal," *George Washington Law Review*, 25 (1956), 1; Note, "Municipal Housing Codes," *Harvard Law Review*, 69 (1956), 1115; Note, "Administration and Enforcement of the Philadelphia Housing Code," *University of Pennsylvania Law Review*, 106 (1958), 437. A comprehensive and excellent survey is to be found in "Enforcement of Municipal Housing Codes," *Harvard Law Review*, 78 (1965), 801.

[73] HHFA, *17th Annual Report* (1963), p. 387; see, for example, the history of code adoption in Birmingham, Alabama, *JH*, 18 (1961), 71. In Buffalo, HHFA "ruled the city's old Multiple Dwelling Law inadequate and cut off aid"; the city then passed an "adequate code." *New York Times*, July 29, 1965, p. 58, col. 1.

[74] The President's Advisory Committee on Government Housing Policies and Programs, *Report* (December, 1953), p. 112.

[75] Housing codes can of course be used as part of a broader approach; F. Stuart Chapin, Jr., has suggested uniting zoning, subdivision control, building, housing, fire, and other codes into a single "urban development code" to "function as a positive influence in shaping growth." "Taking Stock of Techniques for Shaping Urban Growth," *Journal of the American Institute of Planners*, 29, No. 2 (May, 1963), 76, 85.

housing codes neighborhoods can be preserved and even upgraded; the creation of new Georgetowns and Oldtowns can be stimulated. Deterioration can be arrested. The use of housing codes to create or help create what are in effect new neighborhoods resembles the positive aspects of many housing programs as much as or more than it resembles the negative regulatory use to which, historically, these codes have been put. The historic regulatory use, to be sure, remains. The codes, it is felt, help quarantine neighborhoods against the creeping diseases of the cities. In theory the codes, if rigorously enforced, would mitigate the horrors of all but the very worst slums. The main thrust of the program, however, is to fight blight; and the main justification for the use of the codes is based on a social-cost approach which sees in blight a source of economic and social injury to the community. The welfare elements in the program (e.g., relocation requirements) have been distinctly secondary, both in the governing statutes and in their administration. Because code enforcement is relatively cheap and is useful as a conservation device, code enforcement stands in better odor today than at any time since the days of Veiller. Indeed, the Housing Act of 1964 authorized a new type of renewal project—the code-enforcement project—"to be comprised wholly or substantially of a program of code enforcement" but financed by the federal government.[76] And the 1965 act expressed a Congressional finding that there is a "need to study housing and building codes" (along with zoning, tax policies, and development standards) to determine how, with government aid, "local property owners and private enterprise" can "serve a greater share of the total housing and building need." Accordingly, HHFA was directed to study local "housing and building laws, standards, codes, and regulations," with an eye to making them simpler in structure and easier to enforce.[77]

Explicit theories voiced in the literature to justify use of the codes break no new ground. Joseph Guandolo, then Associate General Counsel of HHFA, wrote in 1956 that

> Slums and blight are brought about by owners of property who are unable or unwilling to maintain or improve their property at decent levels, by unconscionable, profiteering landlords squeezing bootleg profits out of wretched housing, and occa-

---

[76] 78 Stat. 785 (1964); Melvin Stein, "The Housing Act of 1964: Urban Renewal," *New York Law Forum*, 11 (1965), 1, 3–5; *JH*, 22 (1965), 207. The "workable program" provision is also discussed below, p. 162.

[77] P.L. 89–117, §301(a) (1965).

sionally by tenants who are indifferent to their squalid environments. But . . . the ultimate causation factor is the local
government itself [which] . . . fails to enforce effectively . . . adequate police power measures to control bad housing, improper
environments and overcrowding.[78]

The reader will note the historic emphasis on the evil landlord and
the faith in the efficacy of controls if enforcement problems could
only be somehow surmounted. Petulant complaints against local
government have, if anything, increased with the passage of time.
The entrance of the professional city planner onto the arena has, to
be sure, made a difference in the rhetoric of housing; the planner has
placed his stamp quite notably upon the vocabulary of social costs.
Planlessness and chaos are now among the leading evils, along with
the more conventional sorts. We can see this planners' influence
in many statutory definitions of a "blighted area." The Wisconsin
Blight Elimination and Slum Clearance Act, for example, after
reciting the usual symptoms of blight, adds these as tell-tale signs
of decay:

> predominance of defective or inadequate street layout, faulty lot
> layout in relation to size, adequacy, accessibility or usefulness,
> . . . diversity of ownership, tax or special assessment delin-
> quency exceeding the fair value of the land, defective or un-
> usual conditions of title. . . .[79]

Some of these signs no doubt refer to the consequences of "premature subdivision," that is. arrested developments on the fringe of
the cities.[80] Both in and out of town, however, the definition of
blight owes much to the principles and ideals of experts in urban
design and land-use controls.

The contents of modern housing codes, however, do not differ
essentially from those of the tenement house laws. This fact may be
somewhat obscured by the manner in which, in some cities, "housing-code" elements are lumped together with elements of building
codes, plumbing codes, electrical codes, and the like. We can analytically reserve the term housing code for ordinances and statutes

---

[78] Guandolo, p. 3.

[79] Wis. Stat. §66.431(4) (e).

[80] Described in Philip H. Cornick, *Premature Subdivision and Its Consequences*
(New York: Inst. of Public Administration, 1938).

which set up standards for "minimum facilities and equipment which are required in each dwelling unit" for "maintenance of the dwelling unit and of facilities and equipment" and for "conditions of occupancy of the dwelling unit."[81] In fact, there were never any pure housing codes; the tenement house laws typically contained fire and safety provisions as well. Building codes can and do overlap with housing codes. A provision for a minimum number of windows in a dwelling might be contained in either sort of code. Minimum plumbing standards could be in either, or in a plumbing code. But peculiar to a housing code are standards applicable only to dwellings *qua* dwellings (e.g., forbidding habitation in cellars, even though these cellars were built in perfect conformity to the building code), relating to the maintenance rather than to the erection of the building (e.g., insisting that the roof not leak), or to the social conditions or behavior of the tenants (e.g., forbidding overcrowding).

Since the days of Veiller, there has been, naturally, considerable upgrading of standards. As before, codes seek if possible to set up hard and fast standards which can be objectively measured and thus, in theory at least, easily enforced. Some standards can be policed through the use of building or occupancy permits. The Milwaukee Housing Code asks that "every habitable room shall have at least one window facing directly to the outdoors. The minimum total window area, measured between stops, for every habitable room shall be 10 per cent of the floor area of such room." But other sections of the same code set up maintenance standards incapable even in theory of precise enforcement by objective standards or regulation through building or occupancy permits. Thus, "every interior partition, wall, floor, and ceiling shall be capable of affording privacy . . . and maintained so as to permit them to be kept in a reasonably good state of maintenance and repair." And the Milwaukee Code directs many of its sections against tenants. For example, "every occupant of a dwelling or dwelling unit shall dispose of all his rubbish in a clean and sanitary manner by placing it in . . . rubbish containers."[82] Such provisions are as little likely to be enforced as the provision

---

[81] Gilbert Barnhart, *Local Development and Enforcement of Housing Codes* (Washington, D.C.: Housing and Home Finance Agency, 1953), p. 6.

[82] Milwaukee, *Code of Ordinances*, ch. 75, §75–6(1), §75–7(5), §75–9(2). Comment, "Federal Aids for Enforcement of Housing Codes," *New York University Law Review*, 40 (1965), 948.

against obstruction of fire escapes in the New York law of 1901. Probably some of these provisions were inserted to provide a kind of balance between landlord and tenant—to show that tenants, too, have duties and responsibilities under the law.

The provisions of the codes are arrived at through a process part political, part idealistic, and part economic. The influence of tenants, owners, reformers, bankers, and politicians may be felt to a greater or lesser degree. The codes must be politically palatable. They must attempt to strike some sort of balance between laxity and stringency. As Warren Lehman has pointed out, standards which are too low simply "clutter up the books"; standards which are too high can be "used as weapons . . . by prospective purchasers to soften sellers . . . by building contractors and suppliers as a means of drumming up business . . . as weapons to assure party regularity," or "simply for graft." The too-harsh code also leads to the vice of "unequal enforcement."[83] Not everyone would agree that unequal enforcement is necessarily evil; it has been recommended and used in programs of selective neighborhood conservation and rehabilitation, as in St. Louis.[84] But graft, corruption, and venality are hardly commendable under any theory. Perhaps some of the fault lies in the moralizing tendency of tenement house laws and housing codes and in the use of evil landlords and lax politicians and judges as scapegoats. These may be more than labels. They may be, as we have argued, self-fulfilling prophecies.[85]

Recent programs call for a vast increase in the pace of enforcement of housing codes. The federal code-enforcement program has been slow in getting started; at this writing, it is still too early to judge its total impact.[86] So far, tenement house laws and housing codes have neither cleared the slums nor convinced housing experts that they can do so. Enforcement has been a persistent headache.

[83] Lehman, pp. 180, 188-91.

[84] William W. Nash, *Residential Rehabilitation: Private Profits and Public Purposes* (New York: McGraw-Hill, 1959), pp. 96–104. On selective enforcement in Milwaukee, see William L. Slayton, "Urban Renewal Short of Clearance," in Coleman Woodbury (ed.), *Urban Redevelopment: Problems and Practices* (Chicago: Univ. of Chicago Press, 1953), pp. 313, 319–22, 345–53.

[85] For the phrase and concept, see Robert K. Merton, *Social Theory and Social Structure* (Glencoe, Ill.: Free Press, 1957), p. 421ff.

[86] At the end of April, 1966, programs calling for the expenditure of $5,268,534 had been approved by HUD; applications for six times this amount were pending. See "First Rehabilitation Loans, Grants Approved in East, Midwest, West Regions of HUD," *JH*, 23 (1966), 253.

The perception of failure of housing codes has called for and will call for alternative solutions. Some of these solutions ask for more public effort; others for more voluntary means. Some programs, too, have attempted to mix private and public efforts, achieving slum reform by mobilizing more or less nongovernmental groups to take advantage of the restrictive codes and other housing laws.

(2) PRIVATE ENFORCEMENT OF SLUM CONTROL LAWS

Nongovernmental efforts to enforce minimum housing standards are more than a century old. Before the age of the tenement house laws, missionaries and humanitarians worked among the poor, and their work included modest efforts to improve the physical conditions of life. The most they could have hoped for was a little paint or soap or minor repairs; structural changes in the tenements were impossible without powerful weapons of law that were as yet unavailable. Some pressures could be brought to bear, though, on errant landlords. Later in the century, propaganda and persuasion had an impact in the notorious case of New York's Trinity Church which owned and operated a group of unsavory tenements. But propaganda campaigns against slum landlords rarely accomplished much. Economic interests of landlords were too powerful to be outweighed by small gains in public good will, even if the landlords had been convinced of the error of their ways. Those landlords who were drawn from the same class as their tenants were at any rate beyond the reach of middle-class persuasion. And if an occasional "respectable" landlord becomes conscience-stricken, his natural response is no doubt to sell his buildings to someone with less conscience. The result is that filtering-down process of landlords already alluded to.

In recent years, privately initiated programs of code enforcement have come into greater prominence. These programs lean heavily upon government at one level or another, but they are private in the sense that the initiating party or group is nongovernmental. The programs often appear in the context of a movement to upgrade a city, or some part of it, to fight blight, or to supplement urban renewal. Sometimes code enforcement is defensive in nature, such as programs to ward off even greater government intervention into the housing market by showing that private persons can "do the job." The "job" is maintaining a decent supply of decent houses under negative housing laws without any necessity for more positive programs, such as public housing. A showing that private persons can do the job delights the heart of real estate brokers and conservative builders.[87] A notable program of code enforcement and rehabilitation in Charlotte, North Carolina, began as a response by realtors to the public-housing program which "seemed a threat to their businesses." The program was apparently successful in both its aims; housing was in fact improved, and "public housing was officially declared unnecessary by Housing Authority officials in 1955."[88] The model tenement house movement (to be later discussed) also toys with the notion that private interests, with only slight help from government, can efficiently solve the housing problem. In the 1960's, San Antonio home-builders organized a demonstration project "to construct low-cost houses for low-income families." The city supported them by agreeing to sell city lots at a bargain price, to "relax codes and ordinances for the demonstration project, and to provide certain planning and engineering services."[89]

The San Antonio plan (called SARAH), interestingly enough, made use of a technique quite the reverse of many other private plans of enforcement. Relaxation of code requirements is unusual; extra strictness is more common in these plans. SARAH, however, preferred the carrot to the stick. In any event, the use of variable enforcement of housing codes calls for some comment.

When a network of regulation is dense and enforcement is not uniform or automatic, variable enforcement may be used as a lever to achieve ends quite different from those contemplated in the original laws. This is a general trait of "over-severe" laws. It has a certain utility. Some regulations survive because—whether so designed or not—they are violated so easily and so often that government can use their enforcement as a technical tool of great flexibility. Laws and ordinances against vagrancy and disturbing the peace have something of this character. Ordinances against loitering,

---

[87] In many of the political struggles against public housing or urban renewal, the opposition, in addition to decrying "socialized housing," insist that some variant of the "Baltimore Plan" (see below, pp. 57–58) would work; see, for example, the experience in Portland, Maine, told in *JH*, 7 (1950), 266–67.

[88] Nash, pp. 87–96.

[89] Robert D. Katz, "Low-Income Housing Demonstrations," *JH*, 22 (1965), 416, 417.

commonly adopted by city governments, may be technically violated
by anybody who stands on a street corner. Ordinances of this kind
are valuable to the police, who can, for example, hold suspects on a
loitering or vagrancy charge, when in fact they wish to investigate
these suspects in connection with more serious crimes.[90] Some anti-
loitering ordinances have been declared unconstitutional; but since
those against whom they are used rarely bring suit, most of the
ordinances go unchallenged. Indeed, a Missouri case of 1908[91] which
cast down an anti-loitering ordinance "might just as well not have
been decided." More than fifty years later an "almost identical"
ordinance was employed by St. Louis police to make over 1,000
arrests a year, mostly in lower-class neighborhoods, "to clear the
streets of derelicts and indigents."[92]

Variable code enforcement can similarly be used to single out a
particular neighborhood or class of owners and impose a housing
standard not demanded of other neighborhoods or owners. So blunt
a use is often not legitimate; it is simply a demand for a pay-off.
But variable enforcement has been used in local renewal programs.
These programs are taken to be demonstrations of the potency of
private enterprise. They may also serve two additional functions.
First, an enforcement program can reduce the costs of urban renewal. Such a program, to the extent it is privately carried out, is
cheaper to government than full public participation; it stirs up
nontax resources. Second, it can be a device to get people interested
in renewal and willing to support it.

Either of these impulses can be considered as a value in itself
or as a means of setting up the familiar *cordon sanitaire* about
blighted areas. A famous example of private action was the so-called
"Baltimore Plan."[93] It was widely praised as a slum clean-up program
"achieved strictly through the enterprise of private home builders

---

[90]Wayne LaFave, *Arrest: The Decision to Take a Suspect into Custody* (Boston:
Little, Brown, 1965), pp. 354–60.

[91] *City of St. Louis* v. *Gloner*, 210 Mo. 502, 109 S.W. 30 (1908).

[92] Comment, "The Constitutionality of Loitering Ordinances," *St. Louis University Law Review*, 6 (1960), 247, 249, 252.

[93] See Barnhart, pp. 29–34. For discussion (and criticism) of Baltimore's efforts,
see "Baltimore Plan for Slum Clearance Is Not *ALL* the Homebuilders Association
Claims It Is," in "Letters to the Editor," *JH*, 5 (1948), 141–42; and "Baltimore Adds
Housing-code Enforcement to Its Program," *Architectural Forum*, 93 (October,
1950), 176.

in cooperation with property owners and city officials."[94] But far
from being private, the plan called for massive code enforcement
on a block by block basis by a whole battery of municipal agencies.
A special Housing Court was established to deal only with housing
and sanitation violations. Private agencies were, however, attracted
to participate in the program; neighborhood committees were set
up; civic and business leaders were encouraged to lend a hand.
A Paint Manufacturers Committee "donated paint for general
beautification and decoration purposes." An organization called
Brotherhood Service, Inc. was formed mostly by members of the
Church of the Brethren. They bought and rehabilitated a slum house
"as an example of what physical improvements could be made to provide a clean and comfortable home out of a converted substandard
dwelling."

The Baltimore program, as described by its admirers, was more
subtle and complex than a pure enforcement program. It was more
than sanctions and promises of sanctions. It leaned heavily toward
"education" in the broadest sense. It assumed that some blight conditions result from ignorance, others from malice; the malice was to
be punished, and the ignorance was to be cured by education. It
assumed that some slumdwellers were potential members of the
middle class, uninformed about proper living habits or unable to
follow them. Punishments were imposed on erring landlords, but
only as a last resort. Loans were made to "worthy owner-occupants."
The model house was designed to educate those who simply did not
know what opportunities were open; free paint and soft loans were
available to induce people to make a beginning. The Baltimore
Fight Blight Fund "found that a majority of cases it handled involved families who wanted to make required repairs but did not
know how to go about financing them. Careful rearrangement of
family budgets solved all but a few of the cases handled."[95]

The Baltimore Plan and similar code-enforcement drives in other
cities, whatever their relationship to the urban renewal program,
do have at their core a healthy welfare motivation. Those who devise such plans want to help the people of the slums—or help them
to help themselves. Whether the techniques used are adequate is

---

[94] "Baltimore Plan for Slum Clearance Is Not *ALL* the Homebuilders Association Claims It Is," p. 141.

[95] Nash, p. 113.

another question. Many of the strategies of Baltimore reduce themselves to the customary Geiger counters for searching out members
of the submerged and potential middle class. The hard-core family
must be abandoned; the hard-core building must be destroyed.
Moreover, rents often rise after a campaign, since costs must be
somehow absorbed. Code-enforcement campaigns probably work
best not in hard-core neighborhoods, but in fringe areas, and not
as tactics that lead to unslumming, but as a means of isolating and
containing the blighted parts of town. In any event, the line between
a private campaign, in the style of Baltimore, and the community
programs of code enforcement under more recent versions of the
Urban Renewal law is thin indeed. Private enforcement, it turns out,
costs money; and the Baltimore idea has consequently been swal-
lowed up by forms of rehabilitation in which public funds are used
to prod, cajole, and encourage private owners, and if this fails, are
used to do the job themselves.[96]

Enforcement programs are certainly possible in which private
persons initiate actions of enforcement. In theory, tenants might
make greater use of well-known legal techniques to bring pressure
to bear on landlords in the courts. Courts might, at the insistence of
slum tenants, issue injunctions to force landlords to make repairs.
Tenants might resist rent actions in court, claiming that bad conditions of the premises excused tenants from the duty to pay rent.
Legal scholars in recent years have become quite intrigued with the
possibility of reviving and extending old remedies. A literature is
gradually accumulating which points out legal remedies and defenses available to slum tenants or suggests the use of new ones.[97]
Of course, impoverished people rarely defend themselves in court
against rent actions or eviction; and they do not sue landlords of
their own accord, even if it were clear (which it is not) that the law
everywhere provided a full battery of appropriate remedies. In New
York, a tenant has for many years been able to resist rent and eviction actions if the landlord's failure to repair amounts to "construc-

[96] See the description of Baltimore's Harlem Park project, Richard L. Steiner,
"Baltimore Rehabilitation Experience," *JH*, 22 (1965), 99.

[97] See, for example, Robert S. Schoshinski, "Remedies of the Indigent Tenant:
Proposal for Change," *Georgetown Law Journal*, 54 (1966), 519; Comment, "Sub-
Standard Housing and the Law in the District of Columbia," *Howard Law Journal*,
12 (1966), 137; Carl Schier, "Protecting the Interests of the Indigent Tenant: Two
Approaches," *California Law Review*, 54 (1966), 670.

tive eviction."[98] Not much use seems to have been made of this right by individual tenants of the slums. Private action to enforce code standards in practice means private *collective* action. Group leadership or some action organization working in the slums is an absolute prerequisite, at least until the apathy and futility of generations is overcome.

The most talked-about kind of collective enforcement action is that self-help movement called the rent strike. Rent strikes have appeared in a number of cities—New York, Washington, D.C., Cleveland, Providence, and Newburgh, New York. Prominent rent strikes occurred in New York City in 1963–64.[99] Rent strikes have been organized by civil rights groups, such as CORE and SNCC; they have occurred in the most fetid and rebellious Negro slums. The rent strike is a simple device; the tenants organize themselves and refuse to pay rent until conditions in their building are improved. In New York, Jesse Gray has been a prominent leader of the movement through an organization called the Community Council on Housing, which at one time had 325 buildings under strike.[100] Gray, an effective leader, had a flair for the dramatic; he once asked his followers to bring a "harvest of rats, dead or alive" to Civil Court to "dramatize . . . the misery of slum dwellers who were refusing to pay rent until landlords did something about rodents, vermin, broken windows, cold radiators, and stinking hallways."[101] In New York, at least, the success of the rent strike movement has been tied to the momentum of civil rights agitation and to the Negro protest movement in general. Gray failed in his first attempt in 1959 to arouse interest in a rent strike. A few years later "the moral climate was more propitious"; Negroes were aroused and were less frightened of eviction notices than previously.

The reaction of white community leaders to the rent strike has

[98] New York Real Property Actions Law, §755.

[99] "Withholding Rent: New Weapon Added to Arsenal for War on Slumlords," *JH*, 21 (1964), 67, 70–72, "Rent Withholding and the Improvement of Substandard Housing," *California Law Review*, 53 (1965), 304, 323–27, 331–32. On Newburgh, see *New York Times*, May 2, 1966, p. 15, col. 1.

Martin Luther King "took over" a West Side (Chicago) slum in February, 1966. *New York Times,* Feb. 26, 1966, p. 14, col. 3. A rent strike occurred in Brooklyn in the same month. *New York Times*, Feb. 9, 1966, p. 33, col. 2.

[100] *New York Times*, Aug. 11, 1964, p. 25, col. 2. On a Lower East Side rent strike, led by Mrs. Margaret Bloom, "a petite housewife," see *New York Times*, Mar. 20, 1964, p. 66, col. 1.

[101] *New York Times*, Dec. 31, 1963, p. 32, col. 2.

been in general cautious, compliant, and somewhat guilt-ridden. Officials have made mild complaints, judges have issued an injunction or two, but rent strikers have not gone to jail. The rent strike "punishes" the slum landlord whose political power is small and whose public image is degraded. The rent strike itself was probably illegal at the time it began in New York, though the law was not entirely clear.[102] Sympathetic judges and members of the city administration began to search for ways to ratify the strike or to divert its energies to more palatable ends. In December, 1963, the city announced a program of "reinspecting 35 Harlem tenements . . . in a move to speed repairs and end a spreading rent strike."[103] One judge directed tenants to bring their rent into court to be spent on bringing the building up to code.[104] Others ruled in favor of tenants on one basis or another.[105] The city also sought legislation to legalize the rent strike.[106] This effort was crowned with success in 1965. The new law can be invoked by one-third of the tenants of a building who organize and convince a judge that "dangerous conditions" exist in their building. Rents are deposited with the court, and the money is applied to repairs.[107] Ironically, the first group to use the rent-strike law was made up of "tenants of a luxury East Side apartment house," whose landlord of record was the Chase Manhattan Bank.[108] But these were tenants who read newspapers and who do not need Jesse Gray to arouse them to make use of their rights. In the history of welfare, an ironic and persistent fact is that middle and upper classes are prone to exact advantage from

---

[102] See Comment, *California Law Review*, 53 (1965), 304, 323–27.

[103] *New York Times*, Dec. 6, 1963, p. 38, col. 1.

[104] *New York Times*, Dec. 31, 1963, p. 1, col. 7.

[105] See *Gombo* v. *Martise*, 41 Misc. 2d 475, 246 N. Y. Supp. 2d 750 (1964), where the judge went so far as to hold that tenants in bad buildings were simply not liable for rent. The decision was summarily reversed, 44 Misc. 2d 239, 253 N. Y. Supp. 2d, 459 (1964).

[106] *New York Times*, Dec. 6, 1963, p. 38, col. 1.

[107] "Rent Strikes Made Legal in City by Two New Laws," *New York Times,* July 20, 1965, p. 1, col. 1, p. 21, col. 1. The second law gives a landlord six months to correct violations before rent can be withheld; but under it, "no organizing of tenants is required—one tenant alone can stage a rent strike. Also, the rents are not paid to the courts for repairs, but are simply withheld by the tenant." This is Multiple Dwelling Law §302-a. The first of the two laws is the more stringent, and it was a "surprise" that Governor Rockefeller signed it. For the text, see Real Property Actions Law, Art. 7A, §769ff.

[108] *New York Times,* Aug. 4, 1965, p. 37, col. 4. The suit was settled out of court. *New York Times,* Aug. 5, 1965, p. 31, col. 8.

programs set up ostensibly for the poor. The rent-strike law in operation may well be different, but only if Negro militancy breaks through the barriers of passivity and red tape.

Rent "withholding" has also been used by welfare agencies as a way of exerting pressure on erring landlords.[109] A clause in Veiller's *Model Housing Law* declared that no rent could be recovered by the owner of a dwelling so long as the building lacked a certificate of compliance with the housing laws.[110] This clause found its way into some of the subsequent codes.[111] The clause was probably little used because tenants were unlikely to be aware of it or to know whether their building had a certificate or not. In Connecticut, the Bureau of Labor Statistics reported in 1910 that not a single tenant had claimed immunity from rent under a provision of the state's tenement house law, despite the fact that five out of six cities subject to the law issued no certificates at all.[112] Staffs of welfare agencies have the necessary know-how, however, to make use of such a provision. Apparently rent withholding began in Cook County (Chicago) in 1961. The public aid department refused to continue to be "unwillingly the largest subsidizer of slums in the community." The department investigated buildings, turned its findings over to the courts, and withheld rent payments to relief clients who lived in buildings that had the worst records of code violations and that had been placed under injunction. In a period of two and one-half years,

> a total of 74 buildings have felt the pinch; 691 welfare recipient cases have been involved for an average monthly rent withholding of $42,814. Rent payments have been restored only in those buildings where the landlord has complied in the elimination of all violations. Other buildings have been vacated, demolished, or placed in the hands of court-appointed receivers.[113]

---

[109] "Withholding Rent: New Weapon Added to Arsenal for War on Slumlords," p. 67; "Rent Withholding and the Improvement of Substandard Housing," pp. 304, 327–31, 333–34.

[110] Lawrence Veiller, *A Model Housing Law* (1st ed.; New York: Russell Sage Foundation, 1914), §142, p. 268.

[111] Laws Mich. 1917, No. 167, §100, at 338. Veiller considered the provision necessary but somewhat drastic; he was willing to allow it to be omitted as a "concession." Veiller, *A Model Housing Law*, 1st ed., pp. 268–69. Some housing laws and codes took the hint. Laws Cal. 1915, ch. 572, §86, at 974.

[112] Bureau of Labor Statistics of Connecticut, *24th Report* (1910), p. 206.

[113] "Withholding Rent: New Weapon Added to Arsenal for War on Slumlords," p. 68.

By April, 1965, the amount withheld reached $67,761.51 in 108 buildings.[114] It was hardly a "victory" for the cause of good housing to tear down a few buildings; but some tenants were benefited, at least in the judgment of Chicago's housing authorities, since *their* buildings were brought up to code. Technically, rent withholding was no more legal in Chicago than a rent strike. In theory, Chicago tenants who lacked rent money were liable to be evicted. Of course, the matter was not that simple. Attempts to evict could lead to a confrontation in court between the welfare department, other city agents, and the landlord.

Withholding, however, is just one more device to punish the evil slumlord. Indeed, it carefully selects those with the least consciences, the worst buildings, and the most desperate tenants; and it forces their hand. But a genuine withholding program can only work, that is, result in code compliance, for buildings which can be salvaged—not for the worst, but for the borderline cases. Rent withholding does prod some landlords into making improvements. The difficulty is to know when this is the normal result of pressure. In other cases rent withholding simply tips the scale toward demolition, thus decreasing the housing supply without corresponding gains for the tenants. In New York, the so-called Spiegel law of 1962 has made formal place for rent withholding in the order of battle in the war against the slums. Under this law, a public welfare agency may

> withhold the payment of . . . rent [to the landlord] . . . where he has knowledge that there exists . . . any violation of law in respect to the building . . . occupied by the person entitled to . . . assistance which is dangerous, hazardous, or detrimental to life or health.[115]

---

[114] Testimony of Victor Spallone, Supervisor of Housing Consultants, Cook County Department of Public Aid, April 2, 1965, at a hearing of the Legislative Committee on Slum Housing (mimeographed statement, supplied by Mr. Spallone).

[115] N. Y. Soc. Welfare Law, §143–b(2). By §143–b(5) violations of the kind described are made "a valid defense" to any action for nonpayment of rent. The constitutionality of the law was upheld in *Milchman* v. *Rivera,* 39 Misc. 2d 347, 240 N. Y. S. 2d 859 (1963). The Court of Appeals did not rule on the question, as the case became moot, 13 N. Y. 2d 1123, 196 N. E. 2d 555 (1964). But the view taken in *Milchman* will probably prevail despite the doubts cast on §143–b in *Trozze* v. *Drooney,* 35 Misc. 2d, 1060, 232 N. Y. S. 2d 139 (1962), a decision of the City Court of Binghamton. The legal questions raised by the law are fully discussed in Peter Simmons, "Passion and Prudence: Rent Withholding under New York's Spiegel Law," *Buffalo Law Review,* 15 (1966), 572.

Not all welfare-minded people greeted the Spiegel law with joy. The Community Service Society of New York opposed it on a number of grounds. The powers "granted to welfare officials" under the act were "so broad and undefined that landlords would be understandably reluctant to rent to welfare clients."[116] There is some indication that this has happened in a few areas; but that this effect will be serious has not been proven. In general, the economic and social impacts of various punitive tools of housing law remain to be measured. But at least in theory, the withholding technique uses tenants as pawns in a battle with landlords. Ultimately, the vice of rent withholding may lie in the war hysteria that surrounds its usage: the struggle with the evil slumlord.[117] The device is too untried and sporadic in its use for a firm judgment.[118] But it hardly promises a fresh

---

[116] Community Service Society, *Housing Legislation in New York State*, Report of The Committee on Housing and Urban Development, Department of Public Affairs (September, 1964), p. 80. The Report also commented that it was "degrading and demoralizing to recipients of public assistance to be singled out for special treatment of this kind"—a rather weak and far-fetched objection.

[117] An amendment to the law, Laws N. Y. 1965, ch. 700, provided that no rent recovery or eviction action could be maintained with respect to the period during which "there was outstanding any violation of law relating to dangerous or hazardous conditions . . . reported to the appropriate public welfare department." N. Y. Soc. Welfare Law, §143–b (5) (b) and (c). The Legislative Representative of the City of New York had argued for this amendment, since the prior law (as interpreted by the courts) allowed recovery of rent, once violations were corrected. There was "thus no penalty for prolonged exploitation by landlords and they [were] afforded no worse treatment than the landlord from whom rent was withheld because of temporary conditions beyond his control or under circumstances which did not render him culpable.

"The proposed amendment would make it clear that the landlord is not legally entitled to payment of rent withheld for the period during which a violation which is dangerous, hazardous or detrimental to life or health existed. It would restore to the public welfare official the discretion to differentiate between those landlords who are not guilty of censurable conduct and those who have exploited their tenants for extended periods. . . ." *McKinney's Session Law News*, No. 7 (Aug. 10, 1965), pp. A–298, A–299. Note the emphasis on the evil slumlord.

[118] A quite different program of rent withholding occurred during the Depression. Welfare departments in Chicago and certain other cities stopped paying rents for their clients, so that the pitiful funds of the clients could be used for food and fuel. The result was to place the burden unilaterally and exclusively on the landlords—many of them small-holders—though tenants suffered, too, because buildings deteriorated and some irate landlords tried to freeze out welfare tenants who were not paying rent. Many small landlords were driven into bankruptcy by rent withholding. The plan arose out of desperation and is not to be judged too harshly. Rent can be delayed; evictions take time; food and fuel are necessities every day. Notice, however, that, whatever other motives were involved, the departments were plainly favoring grocers *as a group* over landlords *as a group* and perhaps this was due, at least in part, to feelings about the morality of landlords. A description of this dismal episode is to be found in Abbott, *et al.*, pp. 443ff.

start in slum law; rather, it is the latest in a series of weary attempts to take the profit out of slums. It is no more likely to achieve this result than any other such device. The worst buildings have no profits left to spare. This comment applies equally to the rent strike. Some of the militants realize this, at least obliquely. In a remarkable address to the 1965 CORE Legal Conference in New York City, a lawyer named George Schiffer anticipated as one result of rent strikes further abandonment of buildings by landlords. He proposed that these buildings be run by tenants' cooperatives or a nonprofit "citizens' company" which would, of course, rehabilitate them.[119] But the flaw in his logic is that these abandoned buildings cannot be run even at cost and still meet decent standards. If they could, their owners would not be so quick to abandon them. The argument assumes that the landlords are greedy and rapacious and that the tenants will not be profit-mad. The tenants, once in power, may not be rapacious in the same sense as the landlord; but they will not be magicians either. The problem of money will remain to plague these buildings and the unfortunate souls who inhabit them.

(3) TWO TRANSITIONAL DEVICES:
RECEIVERSHIP AND DEMOLITION

Two devices—receivership laws and demolition programs—may be looked upon as falling somewhere between programs of regulation and programs which attempt to find alternatives to the slums. New York's receivership law is the most prominent of its type.[120] Under this law, the city may take over slum houses whose owners have let them go to ruin or which contain hazardous conditions. A receiver is appointed who collects the rent, manages the building, and makes the necessary repairs, using rent money to do so. If the rent money is insufficient for this purpose, the department of real estate advances what is necessary from a special fund supplied by the taxpayers. The houses are turned back to private management once code violations have been eliminated, repair charges met, and the receiver paid. Receivership is therefore a "method of compelling the loosen-

---

[119] George Schiffer, "Ending the Landlord Tenant Relationship in the Slums" (Mimeographed, Feb. 5, 1965). I am indebted to Ezra G. Levin, of New York City, for providing me with the text of this address.

[120] Illinois passed a receivership law in 1965. Ill. Ann. Stats. 24 §11–31–2.

ing of private purse strings and the expenditure of private capital in slum areas."[121]

The city occupies and in a sense owns houses taken into receivership. From a certain standpoint, receivership is makeshift public housing; but the ultimate aim is code compliance. The law clearly contemplates that its buildings will end up once more in the private domain. Judah Gribetz, Deputy Commissioner of the New York City Department of Buildings in 1964, reported that by April 1, 1964, 327 buildings had been the subject of receivership proceedings in New York City; but in only 32 cases had a receiver actually been appointed. Most of the other cases were still pending. Seventy-one cases, however, had been discontinued because of compliance with the law. These figures on voluntary compliance indicated that some success was achieved by receivership. New York's department of buildings "conferred with owners, mortgagees, or others interested in a receivership building," to work out a solution to its problems; and the department took "pride in the number of buildings in which we compel private compliance."[122] Under the law, the department can use a stick as well as a carrot. Although the receiver's lien is "subject" to existing mortgages, the mortgagees (if duly notified and accorded procedural safeguards) are not "entitled to any of the rents, issues and profits of the property, nor, in any action to foreclose his mortgage or lien, to a discharge of the receiver . . . until the lien of the receiver in favor of the department of real estate shall have been fully paid."[123] Thus the department can reach out and bruise the creditors of the building, who are often "respectable" businessmen and may not want bad publicity and trouble. "In several cases, initiation of receivership action has resulted in the sale of buildings by neglectful property owners to responsible individuals, who immediately undertake required repairs."[124] In other words, receivership brought with it a kind of "filtering-up" process of landlords. In Chicago, too, where

---

[121] Judah Gribetz, "New York City's Receivership Law Seen as Essential Code Enforcement Weapon," *JH*, 21 (1964), 297–98; *New York Times*, June 18, 1963, p. 25, col. 2. The receivership law is New York Multiple Dwelling Law §309.5. It was upheld as constitutional in *Re Department of Buildings of the City of New York*, 14 N.Y. 2d 291, 200 N.E. 2d 432 (1964), noted in *Michigan Law Review*, 63 (1965), 1304.

[122] Gribetz, p. 299.

[123] New York Multiple Dwelling Law §309–5(e).

[124] Gribetz, p. 299.

the Chicago Dwellings Association, a nonprofit agency affiliated with the Chicago Housing Authority, acts as receiver, many buildings had been brought up to code by the receiver, while in other cases the owner had been prodded into line.[125]

There is, however, another less attractive aspect to the picture. The New York receivership law was born out of hatred and desperation. It had been proposed by Mayor Wagner for several years before final passage in 1962. Debate over the law figured in the mayoral campaign of the year before; it was advanced for political reasons as a means of "taking the profit out of the slums" and dealing with "ruthless and irresponsible landlords."[126] Once passed, the receivership law was sparingly used until the rent strike movement lit a fire under the city. Thus, mediately or immediately, the receivership law and its administration owed much to the campaign against the slum landlord. Under these circumstances, the filtering-down of landlords is at least as likely a result of the receivership law as the filtering-up. Under threat of receivership, rotting buildings even more rapidly change hands; successive shadow-owners milk the property and depart with what profit they can; their investments are at best short term. Gribetz reported in 1964 that "not a single building, of the 103 in which compliance was obtained or in which a receiver was appointed, was erected after 1929"; in fact 77 of the buildings were old-law tenements built prior to 1901. "In effect, we attempt to prolong the life, or make more liveable, tenements that passed out of style a generation ago."[127] But these facts expose a serious weakness in the receivership program. The correlation between the age of a building and proneness to receivership means that these buildings have inherited grave physical defects; it would, therefore, take substantial infusions of money to repair them and eliminate their code violations. The horrors of life in these tenements are the result of generations of decay and disregard of the housing laws. The present crop of owners cannot be held responsible for all of these deficiencies, even if the tenants were blameless in the matter. Nor can an owner realistically make the necessary changes and still show a profit on his investment. He may have bought the house at a price which reflected its income-producing qualities—somewhat tempered

---

[125] Letter Report on the Receivership Program, Chicago Dwellings Association, May 6, 1966.
[126] Klein, pp. 123, 128, 130.
[127] Gribetz, p. 299.

by the necessity for a quick, high rate of return precisely because of
the risks of running afoul of the law or incurring great expense.
If so, then the rate of return is high only in relation to an assumed
"true" value or a hypothetical "original" investment. Many receivership buildings are dead-end buildings; their landlords had
gambled and failed. Faced with receivership, the landlord may simply shrug his houlders, abandon the building, and write off his investment. We have seen evidence that this happens from time to
time. Some buildings find receivership a one-way street; they enter
and do not leave. The cost of repairs may be such that the city cannot economically do the job and ever turn the property back—it
would not pay the owners to discharge the receiver. Nor will the city
be able to maintain the property in a state of repair without raising
the rent; but if the rents go up, the tenants howl. The city is not
happy, then, to find itself the owner of "public housing" that con-
sists of the most wretched tenements in town. It is costly, inefficient
housing; it saddles the city with property that brings it one headache after another. Mayor Wagner's Real Estate Commissioner told
him in 1964 that receivership was "a good way to go broke."[128] In
one building, the city spent $31,611 improving a structure assessed
at $17,000.[129] In another, the city spent $39,350 for repairs on a fire-
gutted building assessed at $10,000—and went to court to raise the
rent over tenant protests. These and many other receivership cases,
according to a story in the *New York Times,* involve "dismal, rat-
infested and frequently dangerous buildings" which "offer such a
grim picture financially that their owners have, in effect, abandoned
them and their tenants."[130] Under Mayor Lindsay, New York City
has virtually abandoned the receivership program.

The city can make still another response of abandonment; it can
order a building demolished. Demolition of unfit buildings is an
old technique of slum reform. Nearly all the housing codes and
tenement house laws provide for demolition of buildings from
which all hope has fled. Dangerous buildings or buildings imperil-
ing public health could sometimes be abated as nuisances even before
there were tenement house laws.[131] The nuisance concept was ex-

[128] *New York Times,* Feb. 15, 1964, p. 26, col. 2.
[129] *New York Times,* Apr. 30, 1964, p. 27, col. 1.
[130] *New York Times,* Nov. 6, 1964, p. 32, col. 1.
[131] See *Ferguson* v. *City of Selma,* 43 Ala. 398 (1869), under an ordinance empow-
ering the city to remove as nuisances "decayed and dilapidated houses or structures
calculated to produce disease of any kind, or unfit for human habitation."

plicitly one of social costs; a public nuisance is a land use which hurts the common good in some fashion. Housing reformers adopted both the term and the concept into their laws. For example, Veiller's model housing law and the statutes which were based on it provided that "any dwelling or . . . structure" which in itself or in respect to its "plumbing, sewerage, drainage, light or ventilation" was "detrimental to life or health" could be declared a "public nuisance" and "abated."[132] Under the New York Multiple Dwelling Law, "Whatever is dangerous to human life or detrimental to health, and whatever dwelling is overcrowded with occupants or is not provided with adequate ingress and egress or is not sufficiently supported, ventilated, sewered, drained, cleaned or lighted in reference to its intended or actual use," is a "nuisance" and is "unlawful."[133] Housing reformers have tended to view the worst tenements as centers of pestilence and to conceive of their destruction as ends in themselves. This emphasis on the social costs of buildings as buildings leads to a certain callousness in the execution of demolition policy. Jacob Riis tells proudly of the work of the Department of Health of New York City in the 1870's in "ousting the 'cave-dwellers' and closing some five hundred and fifty cellars south of Houston Street, many of them below tide-water, that had been used as living apartments. In many instances the police had to drag the tenants out by force." This was not a case of demolition; but the principle is the same. Anything that thins out the housing supply leads to suffering or at least to extreme inconvenience for tenants. There were no "relocation" programs in the days of Jacob Riis, nor was there any public housing. Tenants "dragged out by force" had to fend for themselves. The poor suffered both by virtue of their situation and by virtue of programs ostensibly designed to alleviate that situation.

In many cities, demolition programs have been carried out in waves in response to particular economic or social conditions or to particular crises. Demolition powers normally are not systematically used. Who demands demolition? Neither landlord nor tenant demands it; and the civil service does not usually move unless pushed. On the other hand, no major interest stands in the way, so that a

---

[132] Veiller, *A Model Housing Law*, 2nd ed., §113, p. 237; under §112, pp. 234–35, "infected and uninhabitable dwellings" could be ordered vacated. See, e.g., Laws Minn. 1917, ch. 137, §117, p. 212, §118, p. 213, for adoption of these provisions.

[133] N.Y. Mult. Dwelling Law, §309–1.

demolition campaign is both politically safe and excellent public
relations. There have been many such campaigns. In Milwaukee, the
mayor appointed a "tough" building inspector, Leon M. Gurda,
in 1927 with instructions to enforce the building code. By 1937,
5,300 shacks had been demolished.[134] During the depression, many
substandard buildings were abandoned or given up for taxes; in
other cases, landlords boarded them up because they would not pay.
Under these conditions, it became relatively easy to mount a program of demolition. The New York Tenement House Department,
in 1934, worked out agreements with owners of dilapidated, half-
empty tenements to provide "free demolition and a reduction in
taxes on the building amounting to as much as 75 per cent in return
for permission to demolish the offending structures." The demolition "hands" were provided by workers on the federal dole. From
1935 to 1939, a total of 3,611 buildings containing 30,362 dwelling
units were demolished in New York City by the WPA Demolition
Project.[135] Conversely, during periods when there are or are perceived to be severe housing shortages, it is difficult to make much
use of demolition. Demolition policies were virtually abandoned
during the Second World War. At all times except during the depression, when the destroying of houses, like the killing of little pigs,
could be defended as a good way to raise prices and reduce excess
supply, demolition has been a radical, self-defeating tool. It is, after
all, usable only for buidings *in extremis.* When the city uses it on
its own buildings in receivership, it faces the headache of relocation
and the protests of tenants. Whether the city or a landlord owns
the building, the tenants want repairs, not eviction. Nonetheless, the
city is no more anxious to keep a losing building than a landlord
would be. Up to the end of April, 1966, 17 per cent of the buildings
under receivership in Chicago had been ordered to undergo demolition.[136]

Demolition is or may be appealing because it seems to punish
the landlord. Destruction cuts off his rent—the ultimate sanction.
If the costs of rehabilitation are greater than market value, the landlord has no rational alternative to expropriation. The tenant of
course receives no compensation and has no option. Eviction is the

[134] Frank Zeidler, *A Liberal in City Government* (n.d., unpublished manuscript),
Chapter IV, p. 11.

[135] Ford, *et al.,* II, pp. 515, 592.

[136] Letter Report on the Receivership Program, Chicago Dwellings Association,
May 6, 1966.

handmaid of demolition. Evicted tenants have to live somewhere, and since destruction of houses in and of itself causes no increase in the housing stock, but rather the converse, it follows that the overall condition of the poor is made worse by demolition. Especially is this true over time if the number of family units seeking housing increases and demolition is not tied to any program of fresh construction. The unhappy consequences of demolition would be reduced or eliminated if public housing, or new housing for the middle classes on the fringe of the city, increased the supply of low-income housing concurrent with the demolition program. This may in fact have happened, at least sometimes in some places; but cities did not historically investigate this possibility. Demolition programs were executed without any census of the housing available to those displaced.[137] Rather, reformers seem to have felt that the social costs imposed by slums on society could be lessened by thinning out buildings and destroying the most horrible examples. From Mulberry Bend to urban renewal, destruction of slums has been hailed as an end in itself. When Knickerbocker Village was constructed by Fred P. French in the early 1930's, with the blessings and subsidy of government, Al Smith "swung a golden sledge hammer against a golden wedge" to mark the demolition of the infamous slums on the site.[138] But a study of 386 families displaced showed that more than 80 per cent of them "continue to live in Old Law Tenements, declared to be unfit for human habitation by the Tenement House Commission as early as 1900"; and only a small number were able to move into Knickerbocker Village, because the rents were too high.[139] This is a story which continues to have relevance in the days of urban renewal. Demolition programs are more popular than ever. In Chicago, a "specific program to rid . . . neighborhoods of . . . dangerous buildings" was instituted by Mayor Richard J. Daley in 1955; and the

---

[137] Demolition might be a gain to poor tenants if dwellings which were dangerous, e.g., about to collapse, were exchanged for new, overcrowded but not dangerous houses. Perhaps this is the normal consequence of demolition. The city destroys the worst houses and the poor tenants relocate themselves in somewhat better housing, but overcrowding increases. Even so, the burden of demolition falls on low-income tenants; and this seems rather unjust.

[138] Eugene Rachlis and John E. Marqusee, *The Land Lords* (New York: Random House, 1963), p. 186.

[139] Leo Grebler, *Housing Market Behavior in a Declining Area* (New York: Columbia Univ. Press, 1952), p. 27. But Grebler's study of the lower East Side indicates that the net impact of this form of demolition was very small compared to the impact of demolition for public housing, highways, and other public improvements.

tempo has in recent years been radically increased. In 1962, 337 buildings were demolished; in 1965, 956 were leveled.[140] Under the Housing Act of 1965, federal grants may be made to cities "to assist in financing the cost of demolishing structures . . . unsound or unfit for human habitation," as part of an urban renewal program.[141]

Like code enforcement, then, demolition has become part of the total urban renewal approach. It retains its attractiveness, too, as a punishment for dead-end landlords. Moreover, it is a cheap and apparently moral response to the public outcry. In Chicago, what could be more effective an answer to the screams from the slums than a crackdown on landlords? And what could be cheaper? It costs so much less to tear down than to build. Urban-renewal demolition, on the other hand, embodies a central irony of housing reform. It proceeds from a social-cost approach, makes use of the welfare approach in its propaganda, and ends with a clear net gain not to the poor but to merchants, city officials, and apartment dwellers.

In any event, demolition for new construction far outweighs demolition for code enforcement in American cities. Schools, highways, expanding businesses, and urban renewal have caused many more houses to be torn down than building inspectors have.[142] This trend is likely to continue. For one reason or another, thousands of low-rent houses—many of them in poor condition—will be destroyed. Some of this destruction will be deliberate. Urban renewal will continue to focus its attention on blighted areas. Highways will be deliberately routed through low-income areas. These areas protest highway demolition less effectively than areas of the prosperous. Moreover, cleaning out slums by building highways looks like killing two birds with one stone. In any event, clearance and demolition will continue. Whether planned or unplanned, demolition is only half of a program for the slums. It is more drastic than code enforcement, but less of a solution than rebuilding. If the slums are torn down, with what shall they be replaced? We turn now to the programs of positive alternatives.

---

[140] Report, Department of Buildings, City of Chicago, *Demolition of Dangerous and Hazardous Structures* (1965) (typescript).

[141] P.L. 89–117, §311 (1965); the amount of such grants is not to "exceed two-thirds of the cost of the demolition."

[142] Total public demolition in New York City displaced 15,000 families per year by 1960. Bernard J. Frieden, *The Future of Old Neighborhoods* (Cambridge, Mass.: M.I.T., 1964), p. 135.

CHAPTER III

Replacing the Slums: The Alternatives

(1) PRIVATE ACTION ENCOURAGED

The earliest attempts to provide alternatives to slum life were private and philanthropic. Slum life appeared to many good souls to be rotten to the core. Tenements could not help but brutalize and degrade those who lived in them; social rehabilitation was hopeless so long as the slums remained. Clearing the slums was impossible—certainly beyond the reach of private action and philanthropy. Of course, missionaries and kind-hearted souls did work with the poor in their homes; but many were convinced that the only salvation was to abandon the evils of the city. American thought has always harbored a general distrust of great cities as "pestilential to the morals, the health and the liberties of man."[1] Certainly the city was crowded, dirty, dangerous, and unhealthy. During epidemics, members of the gentler classes left town if they could.[2] The poor were trapped in their quarters.

The vices of the slums were obvious. Virtues, if there were any, were difficult to comprehend. It was hard for middle-class Protestants to grasp the texture of slum life, hard to sympathize with the foreign ways and "clannishness" of the poor, hard to treat with respect their Catholic and Jewish faiths. But though reformers may have overlooked the benefits and functions of slum life (such as they were), they were probably justified in feeling powerless to resolve the problem. Therefore, it made sense for them to focus their energy on

---

[1] Thomas Jefferson, quoted in Morton G. White and Lucia White, *The Intellectual Versus the City* (Cambridge, Mass.: Harvard Univ. Press, 1964), p. 28.

[2] Charles E. Rosenberg, *The Cholera Years* (Chicago: Univ. of Chicago Press, 1962), pp. 28, 109–10.

rescuing at least a few souls from the slums. The New York Society for Improving the Condition of the Poor exhorted immigrants in 1850 to "escape . . . from the city—for escape is your only recourse against . . . beggary."[3] The Five Points House of Industry, whose name commemorates the most notorious slum district in early New York, labored in the 1850's and 1860's to resettle worthy members of the poor. Conversion to the "true faith" seemed particularly hopeless in the slums:

> The adults of the neighborhood are mostly Catholics. . . .They seem inaccessible to any good influence, and it is only by removal and a change of circumstances, that we have much hope of seeing these barriers broken down, and a willingness manifest to listen to the truths of the Gospel.[4]

It was only natural that resettlement agencies should concentrate on children. Children were still not totally corrupted by their environment. They might yet be saved for American ideals and morality. American reformers have always been sentimental about the innocence of children and hopeful of their redemption—this by way of contrast to their sometimes harsh judgments on errant adults. Campaigns to save children can mobilize mass support fairly easily— children are hard to hold guilty of drunkenness, crime, and bad faith.

The need was there. Gangs of undernourished, homeless children roamed the streets of the major cities; sickly, pathetic children worked and starved in the tenements and factories. The very existence of this army of innocents reproached society for its sins. Charles Loring Brace organized the Children's Aid Society in 1853 to help the children of New York City and to place at least some of them in rural foster homes.[5] The Society pitched its appeal, as usual, to the

---

[3] Quoted in Roy Lubove, *The Progressives and the Slums: Tenement House Reform in New York City 1890–1917* (Pittsburgh: Univ. of Pittsburgh Press, 1963), p. 7.

[4] Quoted in Carroll Rosenberg, "Protestants and Five Pointers: The Five Points House of Industry, 1850–1870," *New York Historical Society Quarterly* (1964), p. 346; see also Miriam Z. Langsam, *Children West: A History of the Placing-Out System of the New York Children's Aid Society 1853–1890* (Madison, Wis.: State Historical Society of Wisconsin, 1964), pp. 44–55.

[5] See Jeremy Pollard Felt, *Hostages of Fortune: Child Labor Reform in New York State* (Syracuse, N.Y.: Syracuse Univ. Press, 1965), pp. 1–7; Jacob Riis, *How the Other Half Lives* (New York: Hill & Wang, 1957), pp. 135–58.

socially cost-conscious as well as to the kindly-of-heart. The children
of the poor

> grow up passionate, ungoverned; with no love or kindness ever
> to soften the heart. We all know their short, wild life, and the
> sad end. These boys and girls, it should be remembered, will
> soon form the great lower class of our city. . . . They will, as-
> suredly, if unreclaimed, poison society all around them.[6]

The Society gathered children, organized them into "companies,"
and sent them West to be resettled on good, clean, airy, Protestant
farms. Children were generally welcome on these farms, as an inexpensive source of labor. Most of the children had probably bettered
their lot on the farms. Some were adopted by the farmers they worked
for. They were at least rescued from the massive city death rate.
Some children were treated cruelly, however. Ultimately, New York
felt moved to subject the program to state control and curtail the
abuses of placing-out.[7] And in any event, child resettlement was a
means of saving only a remnant. Placing-out reached only a small
number of children. Thousands and ultimately millions more were
sentenced to life in the slums. By the twentieth century there was no
denying that the city was here to stay; the country was in no position
to absorb surplus humans from the city. Indeed, most traffic went
the other way.

A more ambitious program was that which attempted to replace
the evils of slum buildings with new buildings—model tenements.
Since so many of the vices of the slums seemed to have physical
sources, better housing design might alleviate some of the worst
conditions. Unfortunately, the model-tenement movement has provided housing history with more than its share of black irony. Perhaps the most notorious instance was the infamous "dumb-bell"
tenement. In 1878, the *Plumber and Sanitary Engineer,* a trade
journal, sponsored a contest inviting designs for tenements to be
built on New York's characteristic "shoestring" lot (25′ × 100′). "The
design which best combined maximum safety and convenience for

---

[6] Quoted in David Schneider, *The History of Public Welfare in New York State 1609–1866* (Chicago: Univ. of Chicago Press, 1938), p. 332. See also Robert H. Bremner, *From the Depths* (New York: New York Univ. Press, 1964), pp. 39–41.

[7] N. Y. Soc. Welfare Law, §374; Laws N. Y. 1898, ch. 264.

the tenant, and maximum profitability for the investor, would win."
The dumb-bell design was the winner. This was

> essentially a front and rear tenement connected by a hall.
> Situated on a pinched 25 x 100 foot lot, the dumb-bell was
> usually five or six stories high and contained fourteen rooms to
> a floor, seven on either side running in a straight line.
> . . . of the fourteen rooms on each floor, ten depended for light
> upon the narrow air shaft. This was an indentation at the side
> of the building about twenty-eight inches wide and enclosed on
> all sides. It proved to be not only inadequate for the purpose
> of providing light and air, but a positive hindrance to the
> health and comfort of tenants . . . a fire hazard [and] . . . a re-
> ceptacle for garbage and filth of all kinds.[8]

Even its contemporaries realized that the dumb-bell design was no
way to house the urban poor; no building which harbored two
dozen families in a six-story building, and which took up to 75 to 90
per cent of its narrow lot, could bring much benefit to New York.
Yet the dumb-bell design caught on; by the turn of the century
hundreds of tenements were built according to this plan. The narrow shafts were fire hazards, conveyors of noise and stench, garbage
cans for the filth of the building. One of the achievements of the law
of 1901 was that it put an end to the building of these tenements.

By the late nineteenth century, many housing reformers felt that
architecture could not "reconcile the tenant's welfare and the investor's profit."[9] Attention began to shift to the next best thing;
sound housing for the poor built to yield a modest but respectable
profit. Purely philanthropic housing ventures (that is, model tenements which are no-profit rather than limited-profit) were uncommon in the nineteenth and early twentieth century. Edith Wood,
writing in 1919, knew of only two: Charlesbank Homes in Boston,
founded in 1911, and Mullanphy Apartments in St. Louis. She con-

---

[8] Lubove, pp. 29, 31. See also James Ford, *et al., Slums and Housing* (Cambridge, Mass.: Harvard Univ. Press, 1936), I, pp. 162–63, II, pp. 907–11.

[9] Lubove, p. 31. Ernest Flagg agreed that the 25′ x 100′ lot made the problem
insoluble; but he felt that the "philanthropic method of reform can accomplish
practically nothing. What if a hundred or five hundred landlords erect model
tenements . . . such relief would be only a drop in the bucket. . . . Relief can
only be brought about through the pockets of the landlords. Show them how
they can build good houses for less than it now costs to build bad ones. . . ."
Ernest Flagg, "The New York Tenement-House Evil and its Cure," *Scribner's
Magazine,* 16 (July, 1894), 108, 117.

cluded that "pure philanthropy cannot be described as the American method of solving the housing problem."[10] Practically speaking, then, the privately owned model tenement was one erected to yield a limited but definite profit or acquired to be run on a similar basis.

One kind of model home stressed rehabilitation of the tenants by the management. Miss Octavia Hill, an Englishwoman, had conceived the notion of "obtaining possession of houses to be let ... to the poor," in the belief that "the spiritual elevation of a large class depended to a considerable extent on sanitary reform." John Ruskin supplied her with capital. He convinced Miss Hill that "a working man ought to be able to pay for his own house" and that the project ought "to yield a fair percentage on the capital invested."[11] Miss Hill worked assiduously to "educate" her tenants; she kept only those who paid their rent and who responded to her moral and social advances. Miss Hill's aim was essentially missionary; housing reform was secondary. She has had a following in this country. The Octavia Hill Association was chartered in Philadelphia in 1896 and faithfully followed the precepts of Miss Hill. "The educational and moral influence" of the Association was described in 1900 as dependent "to a considerable extent upon the regular visits of the rent collector,"[12] who acted as a kind of social worker. In 1917, the Association owned 179 houses with 244 families and was the agent for 224 houses with 460 families.[13] The Association to this day restricts its dividend to 4 per cent, though it is not legally obligated to do so. The houses of the Association remain in excellent condition, and its rents are moderate.[14] In 1965 the Association charged a median rent of $44.00 a month; it operated 290 dwelling units, many of them refurbished houses as much as 200 years old.[15]

By the end of the nineteenth century, a considerable model tenement-house movement had begun; and in a number of cities there

---

[10] Edith Elmer Wood, *The Housing of the Unskilled Wage Earner* (New York: Macmillan, 1919), p. 93.

[11] Octavia Hill, *Homes of the London Poor* (London: Macmillan & Co., 1883), pp. 17, 18; Enid Hester Chataway Moberly Bell, *Octavia Hill* (London: Constable, 1942), pp. 73–77.

[12] *Charities Review*, 9 (1900), 478.

[13] Wood, p. 111.

[14] William W. Nash, *Residential Rehabilitation: Private Profits and Public Purposes* (New York: McGraw-Hill, 1959), pp. 114–24.

[15] Octavia Hill Association, Inc., *69th Annual Report* (Philadelphia, 1965).

were projects of one sort or another—some more sociological (or, if you will, more paternalistic) than Miss Hill's, some less.[16] In New York a number of companies were formed as early as the middle of the nineteenth century to build decent houses for the poor. These companies limited their dividend rate to a specific percentage. The most famous of these builders of model tenement houses was Alfred T. White, the apostle of "philanthropy and 5 per cent." His houses, built in Brooklyn, were clean and provided the tenants with sanitary facilities far beyond what most of them could have been accustomed to. His standards of maintenance were high, and he prohibited boarders and lodgers. He had many imitators, both within New York and without.

The model tenement-house movement, first of all, arose out of a genuine impulse to aid the poor. Furthermore, it was a more hopeful step than the restrictive laws since it attempted to provide a real alternative to the rat-infested, overcrowded buildings of the slums. Then, too, the homes were not charitable gifts to the poor; they were not designed to degrade the poor. Except for extreme followers of the Octavia Hill plan, they did not meddle excessively in people's lives. Moreover, they were designed to be self-supporting. Indeed, this last was a crucial point. Ideologically, the model tenement can be viewed as an answer to the implicit criticism of the social system that arose from the very existence of slum conditions and, more particularly, from the failure of such enterprises as the dumb-bell tenement and the apparent demonstration that private enterprise could never solve the problem of the slums. In a business society, businessmen had to be able to show that sound financial principles and the exercise of morality could turn a profit; they had to demonstrate that reputable men of affairs, if persuaded and encouraged, could outdo government and do good without committing the sins which government commits when it interferes in economic affairs. Catherine Bauer reported that a Harlem co-op built in 1927, under the sponsorship of

---

[16] There is considerable literature on the model tenement house movement. See Ford, *et al.*, II, pp. 572–90, 671–701; Wood, pp. 91–132; Lawrence Veiller, *Housing Reform* (New York: Russell Sage Foundation, 1910), pp. 63–73, for extensive coverage of the pre-New Deal developments; Lubove, pp. 34–39.

Some industrial employers built homes or even towns for their employees. Many were purely business ventures but some were subsidized either from philanthropic motives, or as a fringe benefit, or to stabilize the work force. Wood, pp. 114–16; John W. Reps, *The Making of Urban America* (Princeton, N.J.: Princeton Univ. Press, 1965), pp. 414–38.

John D. Rockefeller, Jr., refused "to take advantage of the [New York statutory] provision for tax exemption on such housing" in order to preserve "civic self-respect."[17] Some housing projects were constructed under business sponsorship. In addition to outright "company towns," there were ventures more comparable to model tenements. For example, in 1917, oil industrialists of Bayonne, New Jersey, formed the Bayonne Housing Corporation, to build wage-earners' houses "on sound business principles . . . rented to yield a moderate return." John D. Rockefeller was one of the stock-holders. "Garden-apartment" buildings were erected in 1924 in which tenancy was restricted to wage-earners and dividends were limited to 6 per cent.[18] On the other hand, the chance of profit opened the door to hope of widespread investment. The editors of the *Charities Review* hailed the news of some proposed new model tenements in 1899 and remarked that, "when we stop urging the charitable features of a number of things, in which philanthropic people may be interested, and present them as business propositions, the chances of social progress will be increased. Philanthropy is a strong motive force, but the prospect of sound business investment is stronger."[19] Another writer stated that, "it is well to get from the government all you can, but it is not desirable to depend solely upon government for reform. . . . Individualism seems minute, but it is mighty."[20]

The model tenement-house movement did not exist in isolation. It may be fruitfully compared, for example, with the semiphilan-thropic small-loan movement which stood in the same position to-ward loan sharks as the model tenement-house movement did toward slumlords. The small loan societies wanted to provide the honest poor with cheap, sound loans at decent rates. The Provident Loan Society, a limited dividend company, was established in New York in 1894 by a group of reputable businessmen; the next year New York passed a general statute authorizing the formation of like societies in urban areas under state supervision.[21] The movement spread. A

---

[17] Catherine Bauer, *Modern Housing* (Boston: Houghton Mifflin, 1934), p. 84.

[18] Andrew J. Thomas, *Industrial Housing* (Bayonne, N. J.: Bayonne Housing Corp., 1925), p. 10 and passim.

[19] *Charities Review*, 10 (1899), 103.

[20] Alice Rollins, "The Tenement-House Problem," *Forum* 5 (1888), 206, 213.

[21] David Gallert, Walter S. Hilborn, and Geoffrey May, *Small Loan Legislation* (New York: Russell Sage Foundation, 1932), pp. 13, 24–25.

Provident Loan Society was established in Wisconsin in 1905.[22] The idea of reforming this or that aspect of society through limited-dividend, semiphilanthropic ventures was attractive to those who wished to avoid government intervention—more accurately for those who did not mind a governmental role provided it was cheap and self-effacing. And the limited-dividend movement was certainly cheap. It called for no state money as such. The state was asked merely to authorize the formation of semiphilanthropic companies through appropriate legislation. Private capital would do the rest.

The logic of limited-dividend housing was simple enough. Model housing companies would provide good housing for the poor. At the same time, they would yield a sufficient return to encourage investment even by "hard-boiled businessmen." Thus the free market should eventually be able to solve the housing problem, except for those people who by virtue of ignorance or inability to bargain could not effectively make use of the market. Similarly, the loan-shark problem would evaporate if reasonably priced money were made available to the poor by sound businessmen. The Provident Loan Company, in Wisconsin and elsewhere, in fact did a good business and made a profit. Ultimately, the small-loan business came under direct government supervision. Small-loan laws began to be enacted in the twentieth century. A Uniform Act was drafted under the sponsorship of the Russell Sage Foundation between 1916 and 1923. Versions of this act were widely adopted. The Uniform Act provided for state licensing of small-loan companies and prohibited small-loan lending, at more than a given rate of interest, without a license. The act further set up standards of business behavior for companies. For example, the law required that, upon repayment, the loan papers had to be cancelled by indelible marks to prevent fraud. The law also fixed maximum interest rates.[23] Whatever other economic consequences came about, by making the small-loan business "respectable," the semiphilanthropic companies encouraged investment in small-loan companies, since psychological costs were reduced for proprietors in the small-loan business. Licensing helped the reputable lenders; it increased their prestige and gave them legitimacy and a

---

[22] *Milwaukee Daily News*, Feb. 15, 1905, p. 10, col. 2; Lawrence M. Friedman, "The Usury Laws of Wisconsin: A Study in Legal and Social History," *Wisconsin Law Review* (1963), pp. 515, 563–65.

[23] See, in general, Gallert, Hilborn, and May; Laws Ill. 1917, p. 553, was among the first of the "uniform" laws to be adopted.

voice in their own regulation. It secured them a legal base to force co-operation on all members; it made possible the elimination of marginal, disreputable competition. The upper interest limits in small-loan laws were and are higher than those of state usury laws. The Wisconsin act, which sets no limit, makes explicit the policy of encouraging reputable lenders to enter the business. The law empowers the state banking department

> To determine and fix by general order such reasonable maximum rate of interest . . . as will induce efficiently operated commercial capital to enter such business in sufficient amounts to make available reasonably adequate credit facilities to individuals pressed by lack of funds to meet necessities.[24]

Rates under small-loan laws have to be realistic; they must allow a profit despite the high costs of handling small loans. These costs have always existed, but usury laws ignored them and fixed maximum rates for *all* loans, large and small, despite the difference in unit costs. This oversight partly reflected the fact that the small lender was a disreputable and hated figure whose opinions did not have to be taken into account; usury laws were laws of passion, not of economics. Once a body of reputable lenders arose, their opinions had to be taken into account; rates which would drive semiphilan-thropic lenders out of existence could not be tolerated.[25] On the whole, the laws have succeeded in taming the small-loan business. It would be premature to say that no loan sharks exist; or that the poor are never victimized by individuals and agencies of credit and loan. But a regular, orderly, and respectable market for consumption loans to relatively poor people does operate. Abuses have probably been reduced.

The model tenement-house movement has had a checkered history, which, significantly, does *not* parallel the history of the small-loan movement. In some cases, "model" tenements turned into slums as bad as ordinary free-enterprise tenements. The movement failed to

---

[24] Wis. Stat. §214.07(2).

[25] Similarly, in the case of many once-hated public utilities, a kind of exchange has taken place. The business gives up some autonomy. In return, the state affords respectability and a "fair" return on investment. See Gabriel M. Kolko, *Railroads and Regulation* (Princeton, N.J.: Princeton University Press, 1965); also see Lawrence M. Friedman, "Freedom of Contract and Occupational Licensing 1890–1910: A Legal and Social Study," *California Law Review,* 53 (1965), 487, for an analogous analysis of occupational licensing laws.

generate enough capital to make a real impact on the slum problem. And it failed to act as a transition to a stage where "small housing" would be regularized, tamed, and licensed like small loans. The success (if it was that) of philanthropic loan societies lay in the fact that they prepared the ground for a nonphilanthropic, but orderly solution of an economic problem. Clearly, nothing of the sort happened in the case of the model tenement. Many model tenements were, at least initially, quite successful. They served their purpose; they were cheap, sanitary, and wholesome places to live. Some, like the Philadelphia houses of the Octavia Hill Association, still stand and still provide low-rent houses at decent standards. But the *movement* itself failed; it did not solve the slum problem, and, like the tenement house laws, did not succeed in keeping the love and admiration of housing experts. Also, in at least a few noisome instances the model tenements themselves failed, concretely and badly, and turned into festering slums. One such well-documented case was the notorious "Big Flat" of nineteenth-century New York City.[26]

The Big Flat was a six-story building built in 1855 by the New York Society for Improving the Condition of the Poor. It was originally called the Workmen's Home. Land and building cost slightly over $90,000. The building occupied most of six city lots, from Mott Street to Elizabeth Street; it was, at the time, the largest multiple dwelling in the city. Originally, there were 87 apartments in the building, each with three rooms and a "closet large enough to be used as an extra bedroom." Each apartment had at least two windows; those facing the street had three. Rents ran from $5.50 to $8.50 a month.

From the start maintenance was a problem. Water pressure, for example, failed on the upper floors. The design contained hidden flaws of another sort, too; halls which ran from street to street, originally designed for the convenience of the tenants, attracted "a disorderly crowd of idlers into the public portions of the house." In 1867 the house was sold to the trustees of the Five Points House of Industry. The building was converted into a Workingwomen's Home—a place for poor but decent working-women to live. There were parlor and library facilities. The building was expected to be

---

[26] The following account is taken from Robert H. Bremner, "The Big Flat: History of a New York Tenement House," *American Historical Review*, 64 (1959), 54–62; see also Veiller, pp. 67–68.

self-sustaining, though rents were very cheap. But the home was not successful. It was never fully rented. Some of the working-women tenants were in fact prostitutes. In disgust, the trustees sold out in 1873; later the building changed hands a few more times, each time for a higher price. The private owners raised rents and allowed nature to take its course; the house sank to the level of the worst tenements of the area. By 1886 the Big Flat was a "pest-hole," filled with garbage and filth, overcrowded, and disorderly. The Board of Health had to remove the toilets from the upper floors, which were primarily used as garbage holders; as a result, all the tenants (some 500 in number) used the "twenty-eight privy-like compartments originally intended for the tenants on the first two floors." The top-floor tenants were primarily Jews from Eastern Europe who worked merciless hours in their rooms at their sewing machines. The ground floor rooms were given over to prostitutes and cheap saloons; in the early 1880's, police raided six opium dens that were operating there in the lower depths.

The final owner was the New York Steam Company, attracted by the value not of the building but of the site. Land values finally brought the Big Flat to heel. The building was torn down and replaced by a carriage factory. Jacob Riis hailed the death of the Big Flat as a sign of the progressive influence of business which "has done more than all other agencies together to wipe out the worst tenements."[27] But dispossession and demolition were small help to the tenants of the Big Flat; they "benefited little from its destruction. In all probability they moved into buildings equally as bad, and perhaps worse than the one they had vacated."[28] If they did find decent housing, it would have been at a much higher price.

The story of the Big Flat speaks for itself. Poor design and miscalculation destroyed it. As a home for poor but honest working-women, the house failed because poor but honest women did not want to live in the neighborhood. Rent is not the only factor in choice of a dwelling. There are expenses and benefits which affect rent but are not part of the usual calculation. People buy neighborhoods and are willing to pay for neighborhoods; bad neighborhoods impose high costs on them, while good neighborhoods give them valuable satisfactions. The honorable working-girls presumably had

[27] Riis, p. 206.
[28] Bremner, "The Big Flat," p. 62.

alternative places to live that they could afford or at least tolerate. The cheap rent of this dismal slum was not worth the price to them. Thus, a model tenement, to succeed, must take the neighborhood and the conditions around it into account; there are places in which no one will live at any price unless they have no alternative at all or cannot recognize the vice of the location. Builders of model tenements want tenants from the submerged or potential middle class—they want the respectable poor, the honest working-girls, the upward-striving workmen, the unfortunate but honorable widows. Yet unless people of this sort are absolutely destitute, they will not live in the heart of the slums. This fact has not changed since the days of the Big Flat. In the 1950's, the Washington Urban Redevelopment Corporation, a private organization in Washington, D. C., had a project to rehabilitate and rent a slum area at modest rentals; the project failed because

> families who could afford rents of $77.50 a month were unwilling to live in a row of houses surrounded by shabby dwellings, inhabited by families who were their economic if not their social inferiors. They had been initially attracted to the units because they were clean, attractive, and reasonable. Initial pleasure was soon overcome by vivid impressions of the neighborhood after dark.[29]

After it failed as a working-girl's home, the Big Flat was rented to two classes of people. Some were inhabitants of slums of hope— recent Jewish immigrants who had no choice in the matter and who looked on their degraded condition as temporary.[30] The others were the "dregs of society"—drunkards, drug addicts, prostitutes, who

---

[29] Nash, p. 126.

[30] "The Jew is merely waiting his opportunity. He cares neither for the reputation of the street nor the standing of his neighbors; hence those streets which were formerly of a bad character are now largely Jewish streets." Robert A. Woods (ed.), *The City Wilderness* (Boston: Houghton, Mifflin, 1898), p. 41.
   Indulgence in racial, religious, and national stereotypes (offensive to present tastes) was quite characteristic of the writings of welfare workers in older generations: "As a whole the Lithuanians are a primitive and childlike people, but worthy and capable under proper leadership," Robert A. Woods and Albert J. Kennedy, *The Zone of Emergence,* abridged and edited by Sam B. Warner, Jr. (Cambridge, Mass.: Harvard Univ. Press, 1962), p. 65. "With all his conspicuous faults, the swarthy Italian immigrant has his redeeming traits. He is as honest as he is hot-headed. . . . The Italian is gay, light-hearted and, if his fur is not stroked the wrong way, inoffensive as a child." Riis, p. 41.

had no desire for and were not suited for any other kind of neighborhood. The reputable owners reacted to their disappointment by withdrawal. They abandoned the building to private owners who, as they knew full well, would milk the property, that is, charge as much rent as they could and give minimum maintenance.

The neighborhood problem is not easy to overcome. Tenants, like loan applicants, can be screened; it is possible to detect the submerged and potential middle class. But the effect of a total neighborhood is as great as that of a culture or class; and the neighborhood cannot be moved. To conquer a neighborhood, vast amounts of capital have to be supplied. To be effective, reconstruction must take place in large enough units to change a whole area. This amount of money was never available from private philanthropists. Model tenement-house buildings were costly. The original investment in the Big Flat was quite substantial; the sale of the building in 1875 brought in $225,000; in 1888 the value of the site alone was $96,000. And this was only one building. Philanthropic capitalists simply did not respond to the call with sufficient investment. No strong, politically active group of reputable businessmen developed to organize the "business" of running houses for the poor. As it turned out, the bulk of the business remained where it was—in the hands of an enormous, unorganized, diffuse group of owners. It never became professionalized and never achieved the outward signs of reputability. Occupational licensing, or status as a "public utility," are signs of businesses that have "gone straight"—businesses that have limited entry to a closed group of respectable men who police the field and exclude marginal and unduly competitive operators. The proposal has been made that housing ought to be treated as a "public utility,"[31] but nothing concrete has been done. Registration of tenements (as under New York's tenement house law of 1901) did not imply occupational self-government, as it does for plumbers and doctors; it was a way of simplifying law enforcement for local government. Thus, nothing emerged to arrest the cycle of stigma and response in low-income housing. In any event, licensing of tenement houses and the creation of a middle- and

[31] See Lawrence K. Frank, "To Control 'Slumland' Abuses," *JH*, 20 (1963), 271. Frank proposed that all privately owned rental housing "be designated as a public utility, subject to regulation by municipal or state commissions, fully empowered not only to set rents but to supervise the operation of privately owned property and to prevent . . . exploitation and profiteering."

upper-class business of running homes for the poor had the most chance to succeed in a city like New York where tenements were high-rise and required serious capital investment. In cities like Chicago or Milwaukee the slums were small, ramshackle houses, often owned by the occupants or their descendants; a rationalized big business of housing was even less likely. And the technology and economics of housing have been such that no low-cost, mass-production product has emerged, which is capable of servicing the poorest of the poor. Bread and salt are in every man's reach; but a decent home is not.

Despite its failures and shortcomings, the model tenement-house idea has retained a great deal of vitality. Both on ideological and economic grounds, many students of the housing problem—Jacob Riis for one—have favored a solution in which private enterprise does "the lion's share."[32] Model tenements and limited-dividend housing ventures continued to be built in the late nineteenth and early twentieth century. The Bayonne Housing Corporation built its garden apartments in 1924; in the same year a vast project financed by the Metropolitan Life Insurance Company was opened. Yet the vice of the model tenement and of limited-dividend housing—insufficient investment—became glaringly obvious in the course of time. Lawrence Veiller pointed it out in 1910:

> During . . . forty years, through the efforts of philanthropically inclined persons, there have been built in the Borough of Manhattan 25 groups of model tenements equivalent to 89 separate houses, providing accommodations for 3,588 families or 17,940 persons. In the same period of time the speculative builder has built approximately 27,100 tenement houses, most of them of very objectionable type, unsanitary buildings. . . . In these buildings are housed approximately 253,510 families or over one million and a quarter of people (1,267,550). . . .
>
> In other words, for every 13 people who have been provided with model tenenents, 1000 others have been condemned to live in insanitary ones.[33]

---

[32] Riis, p. 216. Riis believed it was the duty of the rich to help solve the slum problem—still another reason why private reform was desirable.

[33] Veiller, pp. 71–73. Veiller's solution, of course, was "the enactment and enforcement of proper housing laws." In his opinion, the New York law, by upgrading standards, had in effect made "model" tenements for more than a million and a quarter people; thus "wise legislation" had provided 99-3/10 per cent of the "improved living conditions" in New York in the age of the tenement house laws.

Moreover, the nature of the "successes" could be challenged on the ground that the model projects, on the whole, had "not housed the class originally aimed at by their sponsors." Two authors pointed this out in the 1930's:

> [It] is almost universally true that no decent low-cost housing has ever reached the class whose need was greatest. . . . The people housed in [model] projects are of the clerical, professional and skilled worker class with average incomes in the $2,000–$3,000 bracket. . . . [If] any new and decent housing [is] to be built for workers with incomes appreciably under $2,000, some additional aid would be necessary.[34]

A study of the way in which nine limited-dividend and philanthropic projects picked their tenants was published in 1937; from this study, a similar conclusion can be drawn. These projects were for white-collar workers and members of the upper working-class; typically, prospective tenants were carefully screened, and people with very low incomes were systematically excluded. Indeed, one model project, "built by a philanthropist as a demonstration in good housing for Negroes," had tenants who were "of the higher income group among Negroes generally" and even included "teachers, lawyers, and nurses."[35] Reformers had to agree that the unsubsidized model tenement could not succeed in solving the problem of housing the poor. The model-builders wanted, said Catherine Bauer, "to provide good dwellings, on an 'economic' basis, at a price which everyone could pay, and without disturbing or even questioning any part of the current social-economic system"; it was an "impossible job."[36] Either model housing had to be abandoned as a solution, or some further incentive had to be provided. Some subsidy—or at least cost reduction—was necessary. In practice, cost reduction meant some sort of resettlement of the poor in the country or on the urban fringe. Land costs could be reduced by this means, but other costs would remain more or less fixed, short of some technological breakthrough.

Twentieth-century statutes have searched for and tried out a variety of relatively inexpensive subsidies. In 1926, during the

---

[34] Michael Straus and Talbot Wegg, *Housing Comes of Age* (New York: Oxford Univ. Press, 1938), pp. 22–23.

[35] Beatrice G. Rosahn and Abraham Goldfeld, *Housing Management: Principles and Practices* (New York: Covici Friede, 1937), p. 247.

[36] Bauer, p. 83.

administration of Governor Al Smith, New York enacted the influential Nicoll-Hofstadter law.[37] The law created a six-man State
Board of Housing, which was charged with the duty of studying
housing conditions. In areas where the Board found it impossible
for pure private enterprise to solve the housing problem, the Board
could authorize housing construction by limited-dividend corporations. Two kinds of corporations were authorized in the act; one was
called "public" and the other "private." Both were, however, private
in the source of their funds, and both were subject to public control.
The public company had the right of eminent domain; the private
company did not. The public company could not dispose of its
property, except to another public company; the private company
was under no such restriction, although the Board had to approve
any transfers. Both types of companies were excused from payment
of state fees and taxes; and municipalities were authorized to exempt
the companies from local taxation. This, of course, was a valuable
subsidy; and the right of eminent domain was a subsidy, also, in
that it enabled the companies to assemble tracts of land much more
efficiently than private operators could. New York City, by local law,
granted to buildings approved by the State Board of Housing a
ten-year tax exemption. Under the act, a few major projects were
constructed. One very notable one was a cooperative, financed by the
Amalgamated Clothing Workers, with mortgage funds from the
Metropolitan Life Insurance Company. The soul of the enterprise
was Abraham Kazan.[38] The cooperative was extremely successful,
until the Great Depression wiped out at one time both its waiting
lists and the ability of many tenants to pay rent.

The depression, however, led to a sudden burst of interest in
limited-dividend housing laws. The federal government, as part of
the Emergency Relief and Reconstruction Act of 1932, had authorized the Reconstruction Finance Corporation (RFC) to "make loans
to corporations formed wholly for the purpose of providing housing
for families of low income, or for reconstruction of slum areas, which
are regulated by State or municipal law as to rents, charges, capital

---

[37] Laws N.Y. 1926, ch. 823. For a general discussion of this law, see Dorothy
Schaffter. *State Housing Agencies* (New York: Columbia Univ. Press, 1942), pp.
252ff; Louis H. Pink, *The New Day in Housing* (New York: John Day, 1928), pp.
105–14.

[38] See Eugene Rachlis and John Marqusee, *The Land Lords* (New York: Random House, 1963), pp. 131–63; Timothy McDonnell, *The Wagner Housing Act*
(Chicago: Loyola Univ. Press, 1957), p. 24.

structure, rate of return, and areas and methods of operation."[39]
At the time the act was passed, New York was the only state that
qualified. Not surprisingly, a sudden interest in New York's law as
a legislative model swept the country. "Housers all over the country
rush[ed] to their state capitols, copies of the New York State Housing Act in their hands."[40] In 1932 and 1933, Texas, Arkansas, California, Delaware, Illinois, Kansas, Massachusetts, New Jersey, North
Carolina, and South Carolina all passed limited-dividend housing
laws.[41] But the only substantial project to benefit from an RFC loan
was in New York. This was Knickerbocker Village which was built by
the Fred P. French Company—1,593 apartments on the site of one of
New York's worst slums.[42] Under the Public Works Administration
(PWA), which succeeded the RFC in its limited-dividend lending
program, only seven loans were actually made, out of 500 applications from 197 cities in 39 states! The seven projects "began operations by charging average gross rents of $10.38 per room per month
. . . rents . . . so high that they excluded many low-income families
for whom the dwellings were intended." In 1934, the PWA suspended its program.[43]

Limited-dividend laws remain on the books in many states;[44]
but little low-income housing is built under these laws. Pennsyl-

---

[39] 47 Stat. 709, 711 (1932).

[40] Straus and Wegg, p. 26.

[41] Laws Ark. 1933, ch. 89; Laws Cal. 1933, ch. 538; Laws Del. 1933, ch. 61; Laws
Ill. 1933, ch. 622; Laws Kans. 1933, ch. 225; Laws Mass. 1933, ch. 364; Laws N.J.
1933, ch. 78; Laws N.C. 1933, ch. 384; Laws S.C. 1933, ch. 143. All of these were
modeled directly on the New York law of 1926. Laws Tex. 1932, ch. 42 (which
went into effect three months after the federal legislation) was independently
drafted.

[42] Land acquisition costs alone were more than $3,000,000; the RFC had agreed to
lend $8,075,000. See Ford, *et al.*, II, pp. 704–8; Rachlis and Marqusee, pp. 182–92.
The only other RFC housing loan was for $155,000 to finance rural farm homes
in Ford County, Kansas. McDonnell, p. 28.

[43] Robert Moore Fisher, *Twenty Years of Public Housing* (New York: Harper,
1959), pp. 84–85.

[44] Pa. Stat. Ann. 35 §1601ff; Cal. Health and Safety Code, §34800ff; N. Y. Priv.
Housing Finance Law, §70ff; the Mitchell-Lama Act of 1955 (Limited-Profit Housing Companies Laws, N. Y. Priv. Housing Finance Law, §1ff) has been used for
middle-income housing. Even before 1955, New York state was interested in the
"lower middle class" and its housing problems. See Herman T. Stichman, "New
York Gives Housing Aid to Lower Middle Income Families," *JH*, 8 (1951), 163.
Possibly the 1965 rent supplement program will stimulate use of limited-
dividend housing corporations. It is still too early to tell.

vania and California both report that their statutes are dead letters as far as housing the poor is concerned.[45] The subsidies are simply not great enough. To grant greater subsidies would be incompatible with the fact that private profit is to be made from these houses. Major subsidies would raise a demand for outright public owner-ship. Subsidies for limited-dividend companies have not gone be-yond those perceived as "incentives" rather than subsidies, even though economically speaking they are in fact subsidies.[46] Yet at the same time, rents must be low or the housing will turn into middle-income housing. The New York Act of 1926 set specific ceilings on rents. No project was to be approved by the State Housing Board "unless it shall appear practicable to rent the accommodations to be constructed at a monthly rental not to exceed, per room in the county of New York, twelve and one-half dollars; in the counties of Kings and the Bronx, eleven dollars; in other counties within the city of New York and in cities of the first class throughout the state other than New York City [Buffalo], ten dollars; and elsewhere in the state . . . nine dollars, provided that bath rooms shall not be counted as a room."[47] These maxima were above the level that could be paid by the poor. Limited-dividend housing has been and still is primarily middle-income housing. One of the newest and most widely hailed federal programs of the 1960's—the section 221 (d) (3) below-market-interest-rate program which authorizes loans below

---

[45] Telephone communication, July 11, 1966, William A. Good, Chief, Housing and Redevelopment Division, Department of Community Affairs, State of Penn-sylvania; letter, July 12, 1966, from Edmund A. Tworuk, Coordinator, Community Development, State of California, Department of Housing and Community Devel-opment.

[46] Tax exemptions and the power of eminent domain are subsidies as much as money grants are. They encourage investment by reducing costs. Yet psychologi-cally these devices are *not* perceived as equivalent to cash subsidies, at least not by everyone. Thus Governor Al Smith, in the introduction to Pink, *The New Day in Housing,* pp. viii, ix, praised his own limited-dividend housing plan as "rational, economically sound, and thoroughly American. Many European governments con-fronted by similarly grave situations have resorted to outright gifts, loans or sub-sidies in various forms. . . . These methods are alien to our practice. The plan which has been inaugurated here and which already has proved eminently suc-cessful does not invoke these aids. It does not put government into the real estate . . . business. It is . . . private business with a public purpose." Tax exemp-tions for property owned by churches and charities are also a subsidy. This sub-sidy has not raised the same political and legal problems that an outright money grant in the same amounts would raise.

[47] Laws N. Y. 1926, ch. 823, §13. Of the acts of 1933, only Illinois and New Jersey had maximum rent provisions.

market rates to nonprofit and limited-profit corporations—is also primarily for the lower middle class and even, in large cities, for the general middle class. The federal government's rent-supplement program of 1965 contemplates nonprofit and limited-profit sponsors for its housing; the Johnson Administration visualized the tenants as members of the lower middle class before Congress restricted the program to those eligible for public housing.[48]

The high cost of land and the neighborhood problem could be avoided by building on the outskirts of town. Here cheap land might be found and a pleasant neighborhood created from scratch. Resettlement of the poor on the urban fringes is also attractive to those who fear and hate the corruptions of city life. Some attempts at resettlement were made by builders of model tenements. Low-cost housing—sometimes taking the form of row houses or bungalows—was built at some distance from the center of town, perhaps in a lower middle-class neighborhood. The houses of Robert Treat Paine, built in Boston before 1890, were of this type. (Even these "mean and unfortunate structures" were designed for the "substantial workingman."[49]) The New York City houses of Alfred T. White, considered unusually successful, were built in Brooklyn where land prices were cheaper than in Manhattan.[50] Yet resettlement has not played a major role in housing reform, neither for private low-income housing nor for public housing where resettlement would seem, on the surface, an attractive alternative to building in the ghetto.

Resettlement has been a far more productive notion for the architects and planners of new towns, garden cities, and garden subcities. There is a distinguished list of these built over the last several decades. The City Housing Corporation, a limited-dividend company organized in 1924, built Sunnyside Gardens, a "garden-city" development on Long Island. Sunnyside Gardens, completed in 1928, was a salutary contrast to the products of the typical real estate boom on the edge of the city—"endless rows of cramped shoddy wooden houses and garages [which] covered the land and destroyed natural

[48] On the rent supplement, see below, pp. 176–77. A.M. Prothro and Morton W. Schomer, "The Section 221(d) (3) Below Market Interest Rate Program for Low and Moderate Income Families," *New York Law Forum*, 11 (1965), 16; Charles Abrams, *The City Is the Frontier* (New York: Harper, 1965), pp. 127–29.
[49] See Sam B. Warner, Jr., *Streetcar Suburbs: The Process of Growth in Boston 1870–1900* (Cambridge, Mass.: Harvard Univ. Press, 1962), pp. 101–5.
[50] Lubove, p. 38.

green spaces."[51] Sunnyside Gardens, however, was not designed for the poor, but for the working class and the lower middle class. Its "population was a cross-section of those of moderate means. . . . They were not the very poor."[52] The model towns and communities descended from Sunnyside Gardens have been of the self-same nature. They may have done a lot for America in general; but the very poor have been consistently excluded from these garden dwellings. It is not a criticism of these new towns to point out that they did not accomplish something they never intended to do; but it is worth reminding the readers that new towns in America are for those who can pay the price.

At least three major reasons can be adduced for the failure of resettlement for the poor to take hold. First, the urban, working poor have been peculiarly tied by their jobs to the central city. They must be able to walk to work or take convenient public transportation. The rich owned carriages in the nineteenth century and own automobiles in the twentieth; and they can afford to use relatively expensive commuter trains and interurbans. Distance severely limited resettlement throughout the nineteenth century and well into the twentieth century. Indeed, it is still an important factor. The cheapest land is located where not one but two cars are necessary—for work, school, and shopping. The problem is not insurmountable, of course. Employers might locate plants in outlying areas to take advantage of available cheap labor, and to some extent they do. More important, purely from a welfare standpoint, it might be cheaper to provide mass transportation (or even second-hand cars) for poor people than to buy land near the central city. Yet transport lines in outlying areas have tended to follow class lines, although admittedly the geographical diffuseness of suburbia makes mass transit less economical. And, naturally, a howl of righteous wrath would rise up if it were seriously proposed to buy such a "luxury" item as a car and supply it free to the poor. By conventional morality, only the middle class and those higher up have

---

[51] Clarence S. Stein, *Toward New Towns for America* (New York: Reinhold, 1957), p. 21.

[52] *Ibid.*, p. 34. The Russell Sage Foundation opened Forest Hills Gardens in 1910 for "persons of modest means"; but this too was an experiment in urban design, not in housing for the very poor. It was conceded that the plan would "not reach the so-called laboring man, or even the lower paid mechanic"; moreover, "no town can long remain 'model' without 'model' inhabitants." Grosvenor Atterbury, "Forest Hills Gardens," *The Survey*, 25 (1910), 563.

earned the right to drink, to be wasteful, and to own luxury goods. For the poor to do so, especially on government money, is immoral.

Second, resettlement poses enormous political problems. Suburban areas were originally the province of the wealthy. Their capacity and willingness to resist any influx of the poor is obvious. The American dream unfortunately includes the right of the upwardly mobile to segregate themselves by hook or by crook from those with less money.[53] Land for low-income housing, whether public or private, must be located in an undesirable area, or else project plans will be sabotaged through ordinance and outrage by unwilling neighbors.

Third, resettlement programs *have* been carried on, but not for the poor. The garden-city and new-town movement has already been mentioned. In general, resettlement land on the edge of town has been preempted by the middle class which has been running away from life in the slums and near-slums. The great belts of space about the cities have been reserved for the expansion of the expanding middle class. Massive resettlement of this kind began when the pace of urbanization increased in the nineteenth century; and it has greatly accelerated in the twentieth. The movement has been heavily subsidized by government. The Homestead Act of 1862 was a rural forerunner of the modern subsidy. More recently, government has undertaken to make credit available through various mortgage-aid programs. Interest payments and real estate taxes are deductible from the federal income tax.

The most spectacular developments in suburban subsidy have taken place since 1945. The government, in a dramatic burst of legislation, guaranteed free education, business loans, on-the-job training, and easy credit for housing to veterans of World War II.[54] Gratitude and payment for the lost years spent in the armed forces were official reasons for the program; but gratitude and moral consideration, in this cold-blooded world, have often needed tougher allies in the legislative chamber. There was also a desire to blunt the impact of returning soldiers on the job market and a desire to stimulate jobs in civilian industries, such as housing construction. In essence, the veterans' benefits were an immense, postponed out-

---

[53] See Lawrence M. Friedman, "Suburbs and Slums in Perspective," *Wisconsin Law Review* (1964), pp. 523, 526–29.

[54] Servicemen's Readjustment Act of 1944, 58 Stat. 284, Title II, p. 288 (education), Title III, p. 292 (business loans) (1944).

pouring of the welfare state in a characteristic American form: "across-the-board" and not restricted to those who showed a "need."[55] The veterans' program of benefits naturally included housing loans.[56] The middle class, sadly depleted during the depression, had won back millions of new members during the days of full wartime employment. These millions—voters all—were among the main beneficiaries of veterans' legislation; resettlement in private single-family homes on the outskirts of the cities was one of their major new benefits. Public housing, too, which had been converted to defense housing during the war, received a new burst of life as "veterans' housing." At that moment in history, resettlement became technically possible: cars and highways were available or could be made available to free the factory workers and the white-collar workers from their dependence on the central city. But the prime resettlement areas were generally reserved for the veterans and the middle class. There would have been space for the poor as well, but the power of income segregation and, increasingly, race-segregation shut them inside the walls of the central city.

(2) PUBLIC HOUSING AND PUBLIC RESETTLEMENT

The basic purpose of public housing is quite simple: to serve as an alternative to slum housing, the government will itself build decent, respectable houses and apartments and rent or give these to the poor. Public housing, however, is a recent development in American history. Federal money for public housing assumed real importance only during the Great Depression of the 1930's. State- and city-backed housing programs can be traced back a decade or so further. They have not been significant factors in housing history, except in a handful of states.

Before the First World War, few people favored a direct public role in the building of houses. Lawrence Veiller, for example, thought municipal tenements would be improper, inefficient, and open to all the mischiefs of local politics. Private enterprise would be "driven out of the field," and only city governments would build

---

[55] Under the Servicemen's Readjustment Act of 1944, substantially any veteran was entitled, for example, to tuition, books, and fees up to $500 a year at any university which would accept him, and to a subsistence allowance of $50 a month for a man with no dependents, $75 for a man with dependents. 58 Stat., p. 289. These allowances were raised to $65 and $90 a month, respectively, in 1945.

[56] 58 Stat., p. 291 (1944).

houses for the poor.[57] Veiller's remarks were directed exclusively to the subject of city-owned housing; federal tenements were totally unthinkable in 1910. The question, moreover, was academic. Government was not able or willing to provide the enormous investments which would have been required.

The first federal program of importance arose during the "emergency period of World War I" and was justified by fear of a critical shortage of houses for workers in shipyards and defense industries.[58] Under the authority of the Shipping Act of 1916, the United States Shipping Board Emergency Fleet Corporation was organized in 1917. In 1918 the Board was authorized to buy land, to make housing loans, to requisition housing, and also to build its own facilities for "employees and the families of employees of shipyards in which ships are being constructed for the United States."[59] The Corporation lent money to limited-dividend companies incorporated by shipbuilders for the purpose of building housing. The companies defaulted in repaying their loans, and the government took over in 1920. At the direction of Congress, these houses were disposed of to other agencies. The government lost $42 million on the deal.[60]

In 1918, the United States Housing Corporation was established under authority of a federal act which authorized the President to provide housing for "war needs."[61] The Corporation was empowered to buy land, make loans, and requisition housing facilities; it could also build houses on its own. Its class of beneficiaries was broad: "such industrial workers as are engaged in arsenals and navy

---

[57] Veiller, pp. 77–86. Some municipalities did, however, run "lodging houses" or "shelter houses" for the homeless or for transients, e.g., New York's Municipal Lodging House, opened in 1909, which contained "six dormitories with 912 beds." The Lodging House is pictured in Ford, *et al.*, II, p. 761. On municipal and charitable lodging houses, see Pink, pp. 167–83. Of course, cities also had jails and institutions for the old, sick, and insane.

[58] Fisher, p. 74. The account of the rise of public housing leans heavily on this source. Two good, succinct accounts are Robert K. Brown, *The Development of the Public Housing Program in the United States* (Atlanta: Georgia State College of Business Adm., 1960); and Stefan A. Riesenfeld and Warren Eastlund, "Public Aid to Housing and Land Redevelopment," *Minnesota Law Review*, 34 (1950), 610. See also Harold Robinson and Lewis H. Weinstein, "The Federal Government and Housing," *Wisconsin Law Review* (1952), p. 581; McDonnell, *The Wagner Housing Act;* Straus and Wegg, *Housing Comes of Age;* on war housing see, in addition, Ernest M. Fisher, "Housing Legislation and Housing Policy in the United States," *Michigan Law Review,* 31 (1933), 320, 323–25.

[59] 40 Stat. 438 (1918).

[60] Robert Fisher, p. 76.

[61] 40 Stat. 550 (1918).

yards of the United States and in industries connected with and essential to the national defense, and their families." The Corporation built accommodations for approximately 6,000 families and 7,000 single persons. When the war ended, however, the federal government abandoned its brief essay in public housing with almost indecent haste. Congress ordered all units sold in 1919.[62]

These two wartime programs were planned to meet emergency needs. They were for the benefit of a definite class (government and defense workers) who were not necessarily poor. In one sense, then, the program was not a striking departure from past practice. Federal and local governments had for a long time built some housing, such as barracks for soldiers, prisons, and mental institutions. Yet, in another sense, the program foreshadowed greater involvement of government in housing construction. The scope of government had reached a point where massive public expenditures for housing programs were no longer out of the question.

By the 1920's, many housing experts had come to believe that government should play an active and direct role in clearing the slums and housing the poor.[63] The great age of the tenement house laws was drawing to a close. Awareness was growing that the housing problem could not be solved by restrictive laws alone, without massive rebuilding. Government subsidy or government construction was an absolute necessity. Reformers were convinced that the defects of existing tenements in structure and design made rehabilitation completely impractical on the great scale needed. But housing experts did not propose government expropriation or purchase of existing housing. As housing experts saw it, the problem was not high rentals and maldistribution of the housing stock; rather, supplies of decent housing for the poor were inadequate to the need. Edith Wood proposed, in 1919, a comprehensive plan to ensure "a sufficient supply of workmen's houses of acceptable standard and cost," financed by government and making use of all available techniques, including "municipal housing . . . in the form of tenements or suburban cottages."[64]

Housing specialists did not convince the federal government of the 1920's to take steps toward a housing program of any sort, let alone public housing. Ideologically the time was not ripe for a

---

[62] Robert Fisher, p. 78. 41 Stat. 224 (1919): "All property shall be sold at its fair market value as soon as can be advantageously done."

[63] E.g., Wood, pp. 257–60.

[64] Wood, p. 275.

federal program. The most important housing law of the decade was a state law: the New York State Housing Law of 1926. Other significant developments took place in the states. In North Dakota (1919-1923), the state embarked on an experimental home-building program. The homes, urban and rural, were to be sold to residents of the state.[65] The home-building plan was part of the program of the National Nonpartisan League, which gained power in North Dakota. Few houses were ever built, however. Maladministration, high costs, and the political misfortunes of the League brought discredit and an early death to the program.

Massachusetts had a more durable experience. Massachusetts had long concerned itself with the housing problem. A law of 1911 established a Homestead Commission[66] which was charged with reporting a bill "embodying a plan whereby homesteads or small houses and plots of ground may be acquired by mechanics, factory employees, laborers and others in the suburbs of cities and towns." An advisory opinion, handed down by the Massachusetts Supreme Court, expressed the view that the plan was unconstitutional.[67] The judges reminded the legislature that many working-class people had acquired homes through "industry, temperance and frugality" and ought not to be taxed to raise money for their fellows "whose temperament, environment or habits have heretofore prevented them from obtaining a like position." That did not end the matter, however; the Commonwealth continued to take a vital interest in housing, the Commission continued to propose bills, and constitutional amendment removed some of the sting of the court's opinion.[68]

A law of 1917 authorized the Homestead Commission to buy:

a tract or tracts of land for the purpose of relieving congestion of population and providing homesteads, or small houses and

---

[65] Laws N.D. 1919, ch. 150; Schaffter, pp. 552—67. The whole legislative program of North Dakota, of which the Home Building Act was a part, came before the U.S. Supreme Court in 1920 and was sustained. The court said that "the judgment of the highest court of the State declaring a given use [of the proceeds of taxation] to be public in its nature, would be accepted by this court unless clearly unfounded." *Green* v. *Frazier,* 253 U.S. 233, 242, 64 L. Ed. 878 (1920).

[66] Laws Mass. 1911, ch. 607.

[67] Opinion of the Justices, 211 Mass. 624, 98 N.E. 611 (1912).

[68] Mass. Const., Amendments, Art. XLIII (1916) gave the state power to take land and build upon it, to relieve congestion and provide homes; but no such land or buildings could be sold at less than cost. Amendments, Art. XLVII (1918) declared that the "maintenance and distribution at reasonable rates" of "necessaries of life and the providing of shelter" were "public functions" during times of war or emergency.

plots of ground, for mechanics, laborers, wage earners of any kind, or others . . . and [to] hold, improve, subdivide, build upon, sell, repurchase, manage and care for such land and the buildings constructed thereon.[69]

The 1917 law called for a pilot project only; it authorized an expenditure of not more than $50,000. The Commission built a project called Lowell Homesteads. But no more work was ever authorized; the Commission itself was abolished in 1919, and its functions were transferred to the Department of Public Welfare.[70]

The Justices of the Massachusetts Supreme Court had complained that the Commission's plan was "not a plan for pauper relief." This was completely accurate. It was a "homestead" plan in the truest sense of the word. It was a landmark in the history of public housing in one sense; but in another sense it represented one of the oldest strands of American history. Its roots lay in the famous Homestead Act of 1862[71] and in other legislation designed to ensure the settlement of the country by a class of honest, small-scale landowners. The program was for the benefit of working people with steady incomes: lower middle class or submerged middle class. It was a resettlement program; it chose the suburbs because land costs there made it possible to build single-family homes. California, too, embarked on a program of housing assistance in the 1920's. This was for veterans only—a worthy and politically potent group.[72] None of these state programs was conceived primarily as welfare in the sense of aid to the helpless poor. The programs looked for the "honest mechanic," or the war veteran, for the good citizen whose income was low, to be sure, but who, with a little help, could acquire land and a house for himself. Even the "socialistic" North Dakota plan did not contemplate permanent government ownership of its houses, but merely their sale at bargain prices to the sturdy farmers and town-dwellers of the state; it, too, was a kind of Homestead Act. These housing laws may rather be compared to many others which embody a revolt of the middle class against the rich. A law of Wisconsin in 1911, for example, created a State Life Fund—nonprofit

---

[69] Laws Mass. 1917, ch. 310; see further Schaffter, pp. 9–33; John I. Robinson, "Public Housing in Massachusetts," *Boston University Law Review*, 18 (1938), 83.

[70] Laws Mass. 1919, ch. 350, §87, p. 418.

[71] 12 Stat. 392 (1862).

[72] Schaffter, pp. 180ff.

life insurance sold by the state.[73] This insurance was not for the pauper. The state insurance fund was an attempt to reduce costs which, in the opinion of many, the rich unfairly imposed on the middle class in regard to necessities of life. Much American social legislation has been of this type. The goal is to allow access to some goods or opportunities to a broad group just below that group which has access through power or wealth unaided by public subsidy. Housing history has many examples. The various "middle-income" housing programs are among the most recent.

The public-housing laws of the 1920's were middle class at least in ideology; they were not concerned with providing housing for a more or less permanent class of the poor. Their roots lay in such programs as the Homestead Act. To be sure, there were some who had other goals in mind for public housing. Particularly during the depression, a conception of public housing arose which was radically different from the homestead model. Charles Ascher wrote in 1934 of low-cost housing projects which would be "more than the provision of cheap shelter"; they would "presage a new mode of life," with "community laundries, organized adult education and recreation, forums, libraries, pre-school child training and care, [and] consumers' cooperatives."[74] This vision of public housing was more radical than the vision underlying the Massachusetts and North Dakota programs. It seemed to accept a permanent program of government housing—built by government and run by government—perhaps permanently occupied by a stable class of workingmen or the poor. In the 1920's, such a view had no broad appeal or hope of success. In the 1930's, during the Great Depression, it seemed to prevail. Yet in some ways, as we shall see, New Deal programs of public housing had some kinship with the homestead branch of housing history.

The depression had a devastating effect upon all aspects of American life. Housing was no exception. The effect was complex, however. Few private homes and apartments were built in the blackest days of the depression. Yet a housing shortage did not initially develop. Great numbers of unemployed men could not afford to pay their rents; they doubled up with relatives, drifted back to impoverished farms, or improvised shacks and shanties in "Hoovervilles."

---

[73] Now Wis. Stat. §210.05; originally Laws Wis. 1911, ch. 577.

[74] Charles Ascher, "The Housing Authority and the Housed," *Law and Contemporary Problems,* 1 (1934), 250, 254.

Marriage plans were frequently postponed, and the birth rate declined. High vacancy rates were common in apartment buildings, both slum and nonslum. Landlords boarded up decaying buildings or destroyed them; cities took over thousands of tax-delinquent properties. Some buildings were actually abandoned by their owners and occupied by armies of squatters.[75] Whole neighborhoods fearfully deteriorated.

Housing was available, and rentals were low. Yet since construction had virtually ceased, the quantity and quality of the housing relative to the population had declined. Therefore, "with the first signs of economic recovery, families undoubled, marriages increased, vacancies were reduced, and rents began to rise." At that point the housing shortage was felt to be "critical."[76] Thus, in the first stage of the depression, stagnation in the housing business and the dreadful conditions of the poor were the major housing problems. Later on, a shortage of good housing at decent prices was perceived as a major problem, too.

One significant fact of the depression was that millions of people had left the middle class for the subsistence level or worse. People who had become used to a good standard of living were reduced to ignominious poverty. In the spring of 1933,

> Approximately 15 million people were out of work. . . . Essential public services were being suspended. Thousands of families were losing their homes and their farms. . . . Four million families representing 18,000,000 persons were receiving relief from public funds. In some states 40 percent of the population were on relief; in some counties of these states even 90 percent. This meant that nearly one family out of every six in the United States was dependent.[77]

This state of affairs for the first time created a tremendous pressure for government housing—not merely for loans, not merely for a plan to prime the economic pump, but for a program of public building designed for the needs of the decent poor. The creation of a huge,

---

[75] Edith Abbott, *et al.*, *The Tenements of Chicago 1908–1935* (Chicago: Univ. of Chicago Press, 1936), pp. 443–468.

[76] New York State Constitutional Convention Committee, *Problems Relating to Bill of Rights and General Welfare* (New York: 1938), p. 641.

[77] Josephine C. Brown, *Public Relief 1929–1939* (New York: Henry Holt, 1940), pp. 145–46.

new, submerged middle class may have finally set up irresistible
pressure for public housing.

Of course, such a program could take many different forms. It
could take the form of a resettlement program of building new
towns on the fringes of the cities. It could take the form of slum
clearance and reconstruction within the city. Housing could be free,
it could be sold on the installment plan, or rents could be charged.
Rents in turn could be based on ability to pay or upon the cost of
the housing or some fraction of cost. Building design and locus of
administration were unknowns. And there were no real precedents
or models. The program would have to be worked out from scratch;
its contours would be determined by the social and economic forces
at work at the time, with relatively little guidance from the relevant
legal past.

One terribly salient force in molding the shape of the public-
housing law was the widespread unemployment. Government programs of the early New Deal period had to justify themselves by
producing jobs. Housing was not only a "means of providing emergency employment"; it was also "one of the few potentially self-
liquidating forms of public works."[78] Under the National Industrial
Recovery Act (1933), the President had authority to create an emergency Administration of Public Works (PWA); and "with a view to
increasing employment quickly," the President was empowered
"through the Administrator or through such other agencies as he
may designate or create (1) to construct . . . any public-works project." Public works projects could include: "construction, reconstruction, alteration, or repair under public regulation or control of
low-cost housing and slum-clearance projects."[79] The PWA Administrator, Harold L. Ickes, established a Housing Division in
June, 1933. The Division had power to make loans to limited-
dividend corporations; but it could also buy or build projects on its
own. In a 1937 report, Ickes listed "five principal objectives and policies of the Housing Division"; the first was "to deal with the unemployment situation by giving employment to workers, especially
those in the building and heavy-industry trades."[80] This tremendous

---

[78] Bauer, p. 240.

[79] 48 Stat. 195, pp. 201, 202 (§202, 203). See Robert Fisher, p. 82. Straus and
Wegg, *Housing Comes of Age*, published in 1938, is a full discussion of the PWA
housing program.

[80] Robert Fisher, p. 83.

stress on employment could not help but affect the nature of the
public housing that emerged in the 1930's. First of all, it ruled out
government nationalization, by seizure or purchase, of all or part of
the housing stock—a course of action which was ideologically unacceptable anyway—and made it certain that government would
build its own houses or pay others to build. Second, it militated
against any rent subsidy, rent certificate, or dole. To give tickets to
the poor which could only be spent for rent would undoubtedly
stimulate housing construction; but this stimulation would be slow
and indirect.

Initially, the government hoped to do its work through limited-
dividend companies. This hope was not realized. There were many
applications for loans, but few of them had merit. PWA soon shifted
its emphasis to construction.[81] Few states had enabling acts creating
housing authorities which could build public housing. So PWA
began to build houses itself. But the federal program received a
serious setback in 1935. A federal district court, in *United States* v.
Certain Lands in City of Louisville, held that the federal government could not use its power of eminent domain to acquire slum
property and to clear it, in order to build public housing. The
power could be exercised only for a public use; and it was not a
proper "governmental function to construct buildings in a state for
the purpose of selling or leasing them to private citizens for occupancy as homes."[82] The government never appealed this decision.
The outlook for New Deal programs before the Supreme Court
looked dismal in 1935; the government probably decided to let
sleeping dogs lie. As a result, PWA was forced to build on vacant
land. This meant abandonment of federal slum clearance. On the
other hand, state courts did not face comparable legal obstacles to
slum clearance carried on by operating agencies which were arms of
the state government. In 1936, the New York Court of Appeals held
that state use of eminent domain for purposes of slum clearance was
indeed a "public use." The court ticked off a mournful list of social
and economic costs imposed by the slums on society—crime, disease,
delinquency, and tax loss—all "unquestioned and unquestionable"

---

[81] Straus and Wegg, pp. 33–47.

[82] 9 F. Supp. 137, 141 (D.C.W.D. Ky. 1935), affirmed by a divided court in 78
Fed. 2d 684 (C.C.A. 6, 1935); dismissed on motion of the Solicitor General, 294
U.S. 735 (1935), 297 U.S. 726 (1936). See also *United States* v. *Certain Lands in
City of Detroit,* 12 F. Supp. 345 (D.C.E.D. Mich. 1935).

public evils. "Legislation merely restrictive in its nature has failed.
. . . The cure is to be wrought . . . through the ownership and operation by and under the direct control of the public itself." Local
government could therefore use its powers of eminent domain "to
protect and safeguard the entire public from the menace of the
slums."[83] There were and are political forces which oppose central-
izing welfare programs in Washington. Pressures for local rule,
aided by the two court cases, added force to the argument for decentralized control over public housing.

PWA met with more than legal obstacles; the number of jobs
which it created and the speed at which it created these jobs were
both sources of disappointment. All in all, PWA was responsible
for the construction of a sizeable but not really critical number of
dwelling units. More than 10,000 substandard units were destroyed,
and 21,639 units in 49 projects were added to the national stock of
low-income housing. But relative to what was needed, this was no
great amount, and the jobs generated hardly justified the effort.
Organization of projects, clearance of the site, and the actual building occupied far too much time in an impatient era. PWA's major
role, in a sense, was that of forerunner. It set the stage for passage
of the Wagner Housing Act of 1937.

> From June 1933 to September 1937 . . . the temporary PWA
> public-housing program . . . helped to focus attention on sub-
> standard housing problems and the use of federal funds to deal
> with them. It built up the first large inventory of low-rent
> public-housing projects. It operated these projects according to
> principles later adapted to the program under the United States
> Housing Act of 1937. Finally, the PWA Housing Division stimu-
> lated the passage of enabling legislation in a majority of the
> states. Local authorities created under it were ready to partici-
> pate in a decentralized program allegedly stressing local initia-
> tion, financing, construction, and management of the projects.[84]

In addition, some of the specific provisions of the Wagner Housing
Act were anticipated in the George-Healey Act of 1936, which
waived federal jurisdiction over PWA projects, authorized agree-

---

[83] *New York City Housing Authority* v. *Muller,* 270 N.Y. 333, 1 N.E. 2d 152
(1936). The court conceived of the case as one of first impression; the Louisville
case, in its view, held only that such projects were beyond the power of the federal government.
[84] Robert Fisher, pp. 86, 89.

ments with local government for payments in lieu of taxes ("based upon the cost of . . . public or municipal services to be supplied"), and set rental policy for tenants in the projects.[85]

Nonetheless, public housing in the United States is virtually synonymous with housing built under the great Housing Act of 1937. This law was the culmination of a long legislative struggle. That it was passed in 1937, rather than in 1933, is not without meaning. A major program of public housing was no part of the first phase of the Roosevelt New Deal. The precursors, as we have seen, were outgrowths of a public-works campaign. Roosevelt himself was lukewarm toward the Housing Act. Ultimately he embraced it, but with a certain touch of reluctance. Public housing for low-income groups was not one of his "musts," at least initially. He had to be coaxed.

The coaxing came from a number of sources. Labor—in particular the building trades—showed great enthusiasm, for obvious reasons.[86] In 1936, Senator Wagner read into the Congressional Record a resolution of the American Federation of Hosiery Workers which pointedly mentioned labor's "double interest in the construction of low-rent dwellings." Labor was the "representative both of the unemployed building and material workers and of low-income families in need of better housing."[87] In addition, the New Deal had opened the doors of government to a class of reformers naturally sympathetic to the general principles of public housing. Economic and social planning was regarded with more understanding than in the 1920's. Reform-minded men and women had more influence in Washington than before. Liberal pressure groups lobbied for the act. The key legislative figure in the passage of the housing act was Senator Wagner of New York. But he had wide and powerful help.

Passage of the bill was perhaps delayed less by concrete opposition

---

[85] 49 Stat. 2025, 2026 (1936). Tenants with incomes of more than five times the rentals were declared ineligible; rentals were to be fixed at amounts sufficient to pay "administrative expenses" and to repay "within a period not exceeding sixty years, at least 55 per centum of the initial cost of the project, together with interest."

[86] McDonnell, pp. 116–23.

[87] *Cong. Rec.*, 80 (May 7, 1936), 6772. The resolution endorsed the pending Wagner-Ellenbogen bill and remarked that the bill might make possible an "arrangement with the Government" allowing rent reductions in the union's own project, Carl Mackley houses, "to the point where most hosiery workers can live in the project and the financial problems of the undertaking can be solved." See *Cong. Rec.*, 81 (June 7, 1937), 5346, for other resolutions of labor groups.

than by problems of administration (Would Ickes or Hopkins be the new czar of housing?)[88] and by considerations of legislative tactics; but concrete opposition was also manifested. The National Lumber Dealers' Association wrote to Senator Vandenberg complaining of government interference with the business of housebuilding; the mere threat of public housing, they claimed, retarded construction.[89] Many members of Congress were conservative and reluctant to vote for a measure that would so emphatically put Congress and the country in the business of building and operating housing. The usual cries of socialism went up.[90] The law was denounced as "a scheme whereby a preferred few may live at the expense of the taxpayers of the Nation through the instrumentality of Government paternalism."[91] More to the point was the concept, as expressed by Senator Walsh, for example, that government ought not to compete with "private property."[92] This was a period when business was struggling to survive the stagnation and low profits of the depression. The National Association of Real Estate Boards (NAREB) favored federal support for mortgage insurance in order to stimulate home-ownership and home sales; but they bitterly opposed public housing. Public housing would "discourage ownership by setting up competition which individuals cannot meet," or it might make "tenement occupancy so attractive that the urge to buy one's home will be diminished."[93] Whatever one may think of this argument as fact or logic, the voice of NAREB was loud, and it echoed in Congress. The New Deal's huge legislative majorities did not mean that opposition could be utterly ignored. In order to pass the bill, it was necessary, or felt to be necessary, to confine the program to the construction of housing only for those who could not afford what private enterprise was willing and able to build. Yet insofar as we can speak of the potential tenants of public housing

---

[88] Since Ickes and Hopkins represented rather different philosophies within the New Deal, the identity of the "czar" was not without some importance. Moreover, there had been a good deal of dissatisfaction with the ways Ickes ran the PWA housing program. Ickes was "ironhanded, puritanical"; his tactics alienated the local authorities and brought about "conflict, delay, and confusion." Charles Abrams, *The Future of Housing* (New York: Harper, 1946), p. 251.

[89] *Cong. Rec.*, 80 (June 15, 1936), 9350.

[90] E.g., remarks of Senator Walsh, *Cong. Rec.*, 81 (August 3, 1937), 8079.

[91] Remarks of Cong. Taylor of Tennessee, *Cong. Rec.*, 81 (August 18, 1937), 9247.

[92] McDonnell, p. 166.

[93] Quoted in McDonnell, p. 139.

as at least an indirect pressure group, influence flowed not from the destitute, the descendants of the destitute, the children of Five Pointers, the Negro ghetto dwellers, or the abject poor; it flowed from the submerged and potential middle class. The ideal housing act, then, would be one which would accept the new poor and reject the old poor; it would shut the doors on those with the ability to get housing privately, but would not open the doors to people on the dole and likely to stay there. It would also provide employment for workers. For legal and political reasons and to disarm conservative opposition, a decentralized program was desirable. Local initiative would govern as much as possible; states and communities would be allowed to opt out if they wished.

These were precisely the provisions of the federal Housing Act of 1937. The preamble[94] declared first and foremost an intention to "promote the general welfare" by assisting local government "to alleviate present and recurring unemployment." Another aim was "to remedy the unsafe and insanitary housing conditions and the acute shortage of decent, safe, and sanitary dwellings for families of low income, in rural or urban communities, that are injurious to the health, safety, and morals of the citizens of the Nation." The act created the United States Housing Authority—a "body corporate" within the Department of the Interior—to take charge of the federal program (§3a).[95] The Authority would not itself build and manage public housing. Local housing authorities had that function.[96] The federal government promised first, and most importantly, financial support; second, it promised a measure of control over the nature and governance of local housing programs. At the time of the passage of the Housing Act, the states were, in general, unprepared to receive and administer the federal money; but this

---

[94] 50 Stat. 888 (1937).

[95] After 1947, the Public Housing Administration handled the public housing program; PHA was a subdivision of the Housing and Home Finance Agency (HHFA). Under the new Department of Housing and Urban Development (HUD), public housing functions are handled by the Housing Assistance Administration (HAA).

[96] PHA was not barred from owning and managing housing projects; but it did not plan and build them. (During the World War II emergency, authorization to USHA to develop defense housing projects was granted. Fisher, p. 106.) PHA might acquire projects in a number of ways, e.g., by a takeover in the nature of a foreclosure, 42 U.S.C.A. §1413. In 1937, the PWA projects were transferred to USHA. As of Dec. 31, 1964, there were still 1,871 federally owned dwelling units out of a total of 714,228, most of which were inherited from PWA. HHFA, 18th Annual Report (1964), Table IV-2, p. 259.

defect was soon remedied. The Wagner Housing Act was followed
by wholesale passage of enabling acts in the states.[97] By the mid-
1960's, virtually every state had such legislation; and in no state
were there no units of public housing at all.[98]

Three types of financial support to local authorities were authorized in the Wagner Housing Act: first, loans "to assist the development, acquisition, or administration of low-rent housing or
slum-clearance projects" (§9); second, "annual contributions to public housing agencies to assist in achieving and maintaining the low-
rent character of their housing projects" (§10a); and third, "capital
grants" as an "alternative" to annual contributions (§11a).[99] Of
these, the provision for annual contributions was the financial heart
of the act. The federal agency and the local housing authority were
to agree on a "contract," under which the federal government would
agree to make uniform yearly payments to the local housing authority for a given number of years not exceeding 60 (§10e). The amount
of the annual contribution was limited to a sum "equal to the annual yield, at the going Federal rate of interest at the time such
contract is made plus 1 per centum, upon the development or acquisition cost of the low-rent housing or slum-clearance project involved" (§10b). The Authority was authorized to enter into contracts
for annual contributions amounting in the aggregate to "not more
than $5,000,000" per year for the first year; for the following year
(1938–1939) additional contracts for up to $7,500,000 were au-

[97] E.g., on Pennsylvania, see Sidney Schulman, "Housing Legislation in Pennsylvania," *Temple Law Quarterly*, 13 (1939), 166, 178; Laws Wis. 1935, ch. 525.
The constitutionality of these housing authority laws has been almost universally
sustained. *Willmon* v. *Powell*, 91 Cal. App. 1, 266 Pac. 1029 (1928); *New York City
Housing Authority* v. *Muller*, 270 N.Y. 333, 1 N.E. 2d 152 (1936).
[98] By December 31, 1964, every state had *some* public housing. In a few states,
however, the only public housing was federally owned. HHFA, *18th Annual Report* (1964), p. 259. Oklahoma was one such state; moreover, it had no enabling
act until 1965. Laws Okla. 1965, ch. 251; Okla. Ann. Stats., 63 §1051ff. Since then,
a public housing authority has begun operations in Oklahoma City. Utah, however, still lacks any state-sanctioned program.
[99] "Capital grants" may be dismissed from consideration; as of 1959, not a
single such grant had been made. Robert Fisher, p. 106. Loans were to bear interest at a rate not less than "the going Federal rate at the time the loan is made,"
plus one half per cent (§9). The "going Federal rate of interest" was defined as
"the annual rate of interest specified in the then most recently issued bonds of the
Federal Government having a maturity of ten years or more" [§2(10)]. In no
event was the total of loans (or loans and grants) to exceed 90 per cent of "development or acquisition cost" of a project. The loans had to be repaid within a
period fixed by the Authority, but no more than 60 years.

thorized; and for the next year (1939–1940) additional contracts up to $7,500,000 were also authorized. Beyond 1939–1940, a fresh Congressional mandate was necessary for new commitments. The "faith of the United States" was "solemnly pledged" to pay the annual contributions contracted for (§10e).

The system of annual contributions was somewhat extraordinary in that it assumed to bind the federal government to a series of long-term contracts. Politically, it was a useful way of organizing a housing program. It called for relatively small annual appropriations; this made the passage of the bill more palatable to fiscal conservatives. Had outright capital grants been made, huge sums of money would have been necessary at the outset. As it was, the government bought public housing on the installment plan.

Though complex in detail, the basic scheme of the Wagner Housing Act was simple. Local public-housing authorities face two major expenses: (1) acquisition and development costs, which are the costs of buying land, demolishing what is on it, and building new buildings; and (2) the yearly cost of operating the building, paying for expenses and maintenance, fixing the windows, supplying heat, and paying the equivalent of property and other taxes.[100] Any homebuilder faces both types of costs. Acquisition and development costs may be met out of cash or through borrowing. Most people borrow money on a purchase-money mortgage; a few people pay cash for land and buildings. These people have "paid off" their houses and remain liable only for taxes and upkeep. The others make mortgage payments every month, with part of the money going toward the interest on their borrowed money and the rest toward the principal. People distinguish in their thinking between the two kinds of costs.

Under the Wagner Housing Act, the federal government would bear acquisition and development costs, and project tenants would cover the operating expenses by paying rent. In order to buy, destroy, and build, local authorities would raise money by floating bonds on the private money market or by borrowing directly from the federal government. The tenants would be charged only enough rent to pay for current expenses; interest costs and amortization of principal would be met by the federal government through pay-

---

[100] Public housing agencies are exempt from local taxation, but *must* pay 10 per cent of annual shelter rents in lieu of property taxes unless state law provides for less or the local government agrees to take less. 42 U.S.C.A. §1410(h). On payments in lieu of other taxes, see 42 U.S.C.A. §1410(i).

ments made under the annual contribution contracts. These
contracts were designed to provide enough money to retire the
"mortgage," and no more.

This plan was cheap in the short run; in other ways, too, it
admirably reflected the intersection of various forces working for
and against passage. Under the Housing Act program, tenants were
not to be given charity; they were going to "pay their own way."
They could well imagine that they were paying the "true" rent for
their units, that is, the current operating expenses. The requirement of a rental sufficient to meet expenses would, furthermore,
tend to restrict public housing to the honest, working poor. Dependent families, families with no incomes, and problem families
would be usually too poor for public housing. Senator Wagner remarked during debate that "there are some people whom we cannot
possibly reach; I mean those who have no means to pay the rent.
. . . [O]bviously this bill cannot provide housing for those who cannot pay the rent minus the subsidy allowed."[101] The projects would
mainly be filled with deserving but underpaid workers—innocent
victims of economic reverses, who needed a "break" to tide them
over the lean years. In the initial period, housing specialists believed
that public housing "should exclude recipients of relief and be only
for self-supporting families who lived in substandard or overcrowded dwellings."[102] Later this barrier broke down; relief families were freely eligible, and welfare income was treated as un-
tainted. In 1949, the federal act was amended to declare that local
agencies must "not discriminate against families, otherwise eligible
for admission . . . because their incomes are derived in whole or in
part from public assistance."[103] This provision has now been repealed;[104] but welfare tenants are, in practice, freely accepted as
tenants in big-city housing projects, and in many of them they constitute a sizeable proportion of the tenants.[105] Even so, the ideal remains strong that in a healthy housing project and in a healthy
society members of the deserving, working poor predominate. This

---

[101] *Cong. Rec.*, 81 (August 3, 1937), 8099.
[102] John Ihlder, "How Should Rents be Set for Relief Families in Public Housing," *JH*, 2 (1945), 197.
[103] 63 Stat. 422 (1949).
[104] 75 Stat. 164 (1961).
[105] The rent to be charged these tenants is something of a problem, which was
agitated as early as 1945. See Ihlder, p. 197. See also Conn. Stat. §8-48. Typically
the matter is handled by local authority regulation.

is one reason why in some cities, such as Chicago, housing managers go to some lengths to keep good, stable tenants whose incomes exceed the permissible amount.[106] The requirement that projects pay their own way encouraged, in addition, a businesslike attitude among managers. Some managers in the 1940's were proud of their records of 100 per cent rent collection, even though it sometimes took diligent use of threats and evictions to achieve this goal.[107]

On the other hand, though the abject poor were to be excluded, only "families of low income" would be eligible, families who could not "afford to pay enough to cause private enterprise in their locality or metropolitan area to build an adequate supply of decent, safe, and sanitary dwellings for their use" [§2(2)]. This requirement was echoed in the various state statutes as well. In Illinois it is the "duty" of a local Authority not to "accept any person as a tenant in any dwelling in a housing project if the persons who would occupy the dwelling have an aggregate annual income which equals or exceeds the amount which the Authority determines . . . to be necessary in order to enable such persons to secure safe, sanitary and uncongested dwelling accommodations" in their community "and to provide an adequate standard of living for themselves."[108] To make sure that only this kind of family actually received benefits, the Wagner Housing Act restricted tenancy to families whose net income did not exceed five times the rental or six times for families with three or more minor dependents [§2(1)].[109] In this way, government would not be in "competition" with private enterprise. Indeed, in 1949, Congress specifically provided that no annual contribution contract could be entered into

> unless the [local] . . . agency has demonstrated . . . that a gap of at least 20 per centum . . . has been left between the upper rental limits for admission to the proposed low-rent housing and

---

[106] Based on interviews with Chicago project managers.

[107] E.g., "Buffalo Housing Managers Compete for 100 Per Cent Rent Collections" ("Some managers attach the three-day [eviction] notice to the tenant's door, for public view"), *JH*, 2 (1945), 79; *JH*, 3 (1946), 154 (Philadelphia project manager refers delinquents to the constable for collection after the tenth of the month); *JH*, 4 (1947), 49–50 ("hardboiled" tactics in Wilmington, North Carolina, and New Orleans); *JH*, 6 (1949), 57.

[108] Ill. Ann. Stats. 67½, §25.

[109] Similar formulae appear in the typical state statute, e.g., Wis. Stats. §66.402, but a few have a more general type which does not use a rent-income ratio e.g., La. Rev. Stats. Tit. 40, §481.

the lowest rents at which private enterprise unaided by public subsidy is providing . . . a substantial supply of decent, safe, and sanitary housing.[110]

Not surprisingly, this statute was later amended to except the elderly and families displaced by urban renewal. A commentator waspishly remarked that the provision merely created "a guaranty that there will always be a segment of the population for whom neither public housing nor private enterprise will provide housing."[111] Most families, writes Daniel Seligman, "just have to go back to the slums when they bump the limit."[112] Actually, the provision was merely designed to underscore Congress' fear of "competition" with business. It is not that easy to determine what the lowest going rent is for decent housing. It was hoped that the provision would fence in and protect the national policy.

The Wagner Housing Act also harnessed public housing to slum clearance. This may be viewed as something of a compromise. The depression seemed to some to be a golden opportunity for slum clearance. Vacancy rates were high, and populations of central cities were nearly stationary. Many houses were boarded up; mortgage defaults and tax delinquencies were frequent. Why not proceed with vigorous demolition of substandard buildings? Slum clearance appealed to those housing reformers whose main concern was with the social costs of the physical aspects of the slums. Their views conflicted with those whose primary concern was the welfare of tenants. The latter stressed the building of low-rent housing; this housing was most economically built not in the slums, but in outlying districts where land values were cheapest. Moreover, to buy out slum land rewarded slum landlords and cost the government huge sums for "fictitious" land values. A "spirited contest" was "waged in housing circles . . . concerning low-rental housing versus slum clearance."[113] In the Housing Act, slum clearance and low-rent housing were tied to each other—straddling, if not satisfying, two opposing views. The law required a so-called "equivalent elimination agreement" to

---

[110] 63 Stat. 422 (1949); 42 U.S.C.A. §1415(7)(b)(ii).

[111] "The Housing Act of 1949," *Illinois Law Review*, 44 (1949), 685, 697.

[112] Daniel Seligman, "The Enduring Slums," in Editors of *Fortune* (periodical), *The Exploding Metropolis* (New York: Doubleday, 1957), p. 107.

[113] Mabel L. Walker, *Urban Blight and Slums* (Cambridge, Mass.: Harvard Univ. Press, 1938), p. 128.

appear as a mandatory term in the contract for annual contributions. This was a provision for the

> elimination by demolition, condemnation, and effective closing, or the compulsory repair or improvement of unsafe or insanitary dwellings situated in the locality or metropolitan area, substantially equal in number to the number of newly constructed dwellings provided by the project.[114]

Exceptions were allowed only for places suffering from critical shortages of "decent, safe, or sanitary housing available to families of low income" (§10a). The "equivalent elimination" provision, in effect, removed any possibility that public housing would become a large-scale resettlement program, moving the poor into the suburban fringe. Projects would tend to be located in slum areas where substandard houses would be cleared and vacant land used for public housing.

The provision also guaranteed that public housing would not result in any substantial net increase in the housing stock. This may have made apparent sense during the early days of the depression; housing was standing idle, and any increase in supply would arguably only depress prices in the private sector. Was it wise, in the long run, to tie public housing to slum areas heavily inhabited by the dependent poor? During the depths of the depression the precise effect of equivalent elimination was not obvious. There were plenty of poor people of all qualities who were well scattered throughout major urban areas; they were numerous enough to fill any program. Only later was the impact of slum clearance on public housing really felt.

The size and power of the submerged and potential middle class underlay the success of the Housing Act; the act as written reflected the ideas of those who wished to make sure that the unworthy poor won no undeserved benefits. Dependency was not to be encouraged. The houses to be built were to be sturdy, functional, cheap, and without frills. The federal government was allowed to support only projects without "elaborate or expensive design or materials," and which did not cost more than the "average construction cost of dwelling units currently produced by private enterprise, in the lo-

---

[114] See John I. Robinson and Sophia R. Altman, "Equivalent Elimination Agreements in Public Housing Projects," *Boston University Law Review*, 22 (1942), 375; the provision was trenchantly criticized in Abrams, *The Future of Housing*, pp. 268–69.

cality" [§15(5)]. That public housing should not have "frills" was almost taken for granted. No one stopped to consider that attractive urban architecture benefits everyone if it benefits anyone. Few people realize this even today. Congress, however, was cost-conscious; it did not want to foster colonies of dependent people; it did not want its public housing, any more than its jails, to be luxurious. Congress wanted public housing to act as a way station for the temporarily dispossessed; it was to be a "slum of hope," but without peeling plaster and nauseous privies. Conservative members of Congress trembled at the thought of what would result if no cost limitations were put in the law—if the federal government were allowed to pay and pay and pay. A government that was unrestrained by the profit motive and the healthy discipline of competition, and hypnotized by the radical dreamers of the Administration, would run wild. Senator Harry Byrd of Virginia sponsored a cost-limitation provision to prevent "extravagance." No project could share in federal money if it cost more than $4,000 per family dwelling-unit or more than $1,000 per room, excluding land, demolition, and non-dwelling facilities; in cities of more than 500,000 population, limits of $5,000 and $1,250, for unit and room respectively, were possible.[115] These limitations, along with a bureaucratic propensity toward timid architecture, virtually ensured that public housing would be minimum housing in looks and in life-style; it would be physically better and safer than the slums, but it would never grace the landscape and bring pleasure to the eye. That was the price one paid for keeping government in bounds.

Public Resettlement: A New Deal Digression

The New Deal's program of resettlement appeared to be a graphic example of what happened when government went wild—at least in the opinion of its critics. A careful recent study of the subsistence homesteads, the greenbelt towns, and the agricultural communities that formed the program lists 99 communities built under New Deal auspices, containing 10,938 dwelling units, at a unit cost of $9,691 and a total cost of $108,095,328.02.[116] Three garden cities

---

[115] 50 Stat., p. 896 (1937). For the debate see *Cong. Rec.*, 81 (August 4, 1937), 8186–90. The limitation is now contained in U.S.C.A. §1415(5). The per-dwelling-unit limitation has been dropped, so that big apartments can be built, and inflation has naturally pushed the per-room limitation considerably higher.

[116] Paul K. Conkin, *Tomorrow a New World: The New Deal Community Program* (Ithaca, N.Y.: Cornell Univ. Press, 1959), p. 337.

were built: Greenbelt, Maryland, near Washington, D.C.; Green-
dale, Wisconsin, near Milwaukee, and Greenhills, Ohio, near Cincinnati. Each cost more than $10,000,000. The names of these towns
point to one of the major components of the program: the garden-
city ideal developed by professionals in urban and regional planning
and design. The subsistence homesteads, on the other hand, in their
very name contained a significant reminder of the original Homestead Act which offered free land to potential farmers.

The professional-planners' aspect of this New Deal program
stressed strong government direction of community life, rational
planning, and harmonious spatial design. The homestead aspect
stressed economy, frugality, and ultimate private ownership of small
holdings with minimum government subsidy. The resettlement program owed a great deal to the back-to-the-land movement, to a desire to clear the noxious city slums, and to the perhaps romantic
notion that unemployed men could live on small homesteads and
grow enough for themselves to eat. Although resettlement did not
officially conflict with public housing, a few voices were sometimes
raised to suggest that resettlement was a preferable ideal and should
be encouraged at the expense of public housing. Congressman Lord
of New York saw no "rhyme or reason" to build houses in New
York City "when we do not have employment for those who are
already there." Government "should buy up tracts of good land outside the cities"; people resettled there "can raise a good share of
their living on an acre or two of land, keep some hens, a pig, some
goats, or a cow, and be almost independent."[117] The greenbelt
towns, on the other hand, were the most daring examples of public housing attempted under the New Deal and an example of serious social and economic planning.

Both kinds of settlement—homesteads and planned communities
—were constantly and severely criticized and were in difficulty from
the very start. The homesteads were an unhappy mixture of rural
and urban traits. The rural poor were hard-pressed to adjust to
their new homes, while the urban poor suffered from lack of jobs
and inability to farm. Planned communities were not always wel-
comed by their neighbors. The garden city of Greenbrook, New
Jersey, was nipped in the bud by local citizens who

> objected to the loss of tax revenue . . . to the location of the
> project, to the type of architecture planned (they feared . . .

---

[117] *Cong. Rec.*, 81 (August 21, 1937), 9639.

concrete-slab construction . . .), to the low class of people they
believed would live in the project, and to the purchase of such a
large amount of land (needed for a greenbelt).[118]

The local citizens obtained an injunction which ended Greenbrook
and very nearly ended the entire program.[119] Proposed projects interfered with race segregation as well as with income segregation.
During the planning of a Negro resettlement project near Dayton,
Ohio, adjacent townships protested bitterly. Negro children would
enter white schools and play with white children, and their property,
so they said, would decline in value. A Negro project planned for
Indianapolis was smothered by "obstructionism" which "prevented
the acquisition of any suitable site."[120] In all the projects, costs were
high; administrative blunders made the program vulnerable to
criticism. Neither high costs nor great blunders were, perhaps, inex-
cusable in projects that were experimental and struck out in new
directions. The notion of company towns owned by the government
was difficult for many politicians and constituents to swallow. Small
homes, in the American ethos, were destined to end up in fee simple
ownership; anything else was an "un-American scheme," said one
Congressman. Senator Harry Byrd of Virginia, who adhered with
great persistence to his limited themes in the course of a thirty-year
career, complained of the "stench" of "gross inefficiency and Russian
communism" which hovered over the projects.[121] Particularly obnoxious were the greenbelt towns, the collective farm projects, and
the long-term leases on some of the projects. Powerful voices insisted
that all of the New Deal homesteads belonged in private hands; and
that is where they are today. At Congressional insistence, they were
disposed of; a weary Administration, preoccupied with a major war,
had no will or courage to resist. Many of the houses now belong to

[118] Conkin, p. 174.
[119] The Court of Appeals of the District of Columbia in *Franklin Township* v.
Tugwell, 85 Fed. 2d 208 (1936), declared, on the authority of the famous case of
Schechter Poultry Corp. v. *U.S.*, 295 U.S. 495 (1935), that the Emergency Relief
Appropriation Act of 1935 embodied "a clearly unconstitutional delegation of
legislative power." This invalidated the legislation on which the Resettlement
Administration rested. The Attorney General ruled, however, that the decision
"despite its sweeping language, applied only to the Greenbrook project." No appeal was taken—the administration was having enough trouble in the Supreme
Court!—and the decision was simply ignored, except that Greenbrook itself was
permanently buried. Conkin, p. 175.
[120] Conkin, p. 201.
[121] Conkin, pp. 163, 226; for more by Byrd, see *Cong. Rec.*, 81 (August 2, 1937),
7964–67.

the middle class—either to the descendants of the original owners, since risen in the world, or to the middle class inheritors of this as of so many other programs for the poor. Some of the planned communities are now "prosperous suburbs." At Arthurdale, in West Virginia, one of the most famous, or infamous, of the settlements,

> outbuildings that were designed as barns or chicken-coops for rural self-reliance now house automobiles and, here and there, an outboard motorboat on a trailer. . . . [M]any of the attractive stone houses are owned or rented by members of the faculty at the University of West Virginia in nearby Morgantown.[122]

Beyond the Wagner Act: Public Housing Since 1937

Quite the contrary course, as is well known, was taken by the public housing program. It resolved its ambiguities in the opposite direction by gradually abandoning and being abandoned by the submerged and potential middle class. More and more, public housing was given over to the dependent poor, the bearers of the culture of poverty. The original Housing Act of 1937 contained the seeds of this development. This is quite apparent—in hindsight. But few recognized the fact at the time; and the precise chain of events that followed was certainly not foreseeable. War and prosperity utterly changed the conditions of American society; in so doing, the political basis of public-housing law was fundamentally altered.

The gross events are easily described. The public-housing program began with a great deal of enthusiasm. By February, 1938, funds had been earmarked for work in 50 cities in 19 states—cities ranging in size from New York to Decatur, Indiana, which had a population of 5,000. Some saw in the program the "beginning of a new era in the economic and social life of America."[123] Housing projects began to be built at a rapid rate. In 1939 New York state authorized construction of state-financed housing as well.[124] But the

---

[122] "New Deal Antipoverty Projects Now Are Prosperous Suburbs," *New York Times*, Feb. 6, 1965, p. 12, col. 3. On Arthurdale, see Conkin, pp. 237–55, and on the disposition of the homesteads, pp. 227–33.

[123] The phrase is from a letter from President Roosevelt to Nathan Straus, Administrator of USHA; quoted in Straus and Wegg, p. 189; the figures quoted are at p. 188.

[124] Laws N.Y. 1939, ch. 806; see Riesenfeld and Eastlund, pp. 626–27. The New York Constitution of 1938 specifically authorized such action (Art. XVIII). For background, see New York State Constitutional Convention Committee, pp. 620–57.

pace of the program was interrupted by World War II. The drive for public, low-rent housing was diverted into defense and war housing.[125] This was natural enough. So, too, was the rush to build housing for veterans and to use existing stocks of public housing for veterans late in the war and early in the postwar period.[126]

Some of the states, e.g., Massachusetts, also developed special low-rent programs of housing for veterans after the war.[127] Federal law still requires local housing authorities to give "consideration" to their "responsibility" to veterans and servicemen in filling slots in public housing. An outright preference for veterans is found in some state statutes as well, in Nevada, for example.[128] Public housing for veterans was mostly a temporary program to take care of a special need. A more important and more permanent postwar program for veterans made credit available to finance private housing.[129] Veterans might thereby pursue the American dream and leave slum tenements for their own suburban homes. During the war, the income level of the population rose dramatically; after the war, prosperity continued. The mass political appeal of public housing was therefore seriously, probably fatally, impaired. The submerged middle class emerged from its long bitter years of breadlines. The government's "resettle-ment" program—for veterans only, at first—opened up the urban fringes to the reborn middle class. In the city core, they were re-placed by Negroes and the dependent poor. Through a kind of political law, however, powerful subsidies generate pressure for countersubsidies. If the government made money available for pro-grams to move the middle class into the suburbs, by the same token pressures built up to do something for the city. These pressures were not, however, the product of the new urban poor, but of others with material and intellectual commitments to cities. The "something" turned out to be urban redevelopment and renewal, which arrived federally in 1949. But the poor of public housing were not major beneficiaries of urban renewal. If anything, they suffered from a diversion of funds.

---

[125] See, e.g., the Defense Housing Act, 54 Stat. 1125 (1940).

[126] See, for example, Veterans' Emergency Housing Act, 60 Stat. 207 (1946).

[127] Harold Robinson, "Massachusetts Has Funds, Powers to Build 30,000 Homes," *JH*, 5 (1948), 210.

[128] 42 U.S.C.A. §1410(g)(2); Nev. Rev. Stat §315.510.

[129] This was true of state programs, too; see Harold Robinson and John Robin-son, "State Spending for Veterans' Housing," *Wisconsin Law Review* (1949), p. 10; Harold Robinson, p. 210; *JH*, 5 (1948), 12.

Public housing remains a living government program. The federal contracts are still in effect; the projects still stand; new ones are built. As of December 31, 1964, more than 2,100,000 people lived in public housing; 3,634 projects were in operation; 574,679 housing units were under PHA management.[130] As of January 1, 1966, the New York City Housing Authority reported projects under construction or in planning which would add 11,969 dwelling units to the Authority's stock of houses at a total estimated cost of more than $200,000,000.[131] Yet these figures are somewhat deceiving. The pace of new construction is slow. Much of it is specialized for people who are not only poor, but also old. Politically, public housing lost much of its fire after World War II. In 1956,

> Public-housing advocates registered intense dismay when Congress . . . limited the federal program to 35,000 units a year. . . . But . . . even this small quota was not taken up. . . . [B]etween 5,000 and 10,000 units "washed away," . . . a measure of the low estate to which public housing has fallen.[132]

In the early 1950's, the House of Representatives defeated public housing "repeatedly," but the "other body" (the Senate) revived it in a reduced form. The "famous socialized public-housing project . . . is as dead as a doornail," cried Representative Smith of Virginia in 1955.[133] In a banner year, 1951, there were 65,201 PHA-aided housing starts. In 1964, there were 22,712. In 1965, the Administration thought it would be bold to ask for an authorization of 60,000 units.[134] Public housing does not make much of an impact on the total housing picture at this rate. The total figure for privately owned, nonfarm housing units begun in 1964 was 1,530,000. PHA housing starts in that year were less than 2 per cent of this figure.[135] By way of contrast, in 1959 public housing constituted 45 per cent of residential construction in Great Britain, and this was its worst showing since 1946.[136]

---

[130] HHFA, *18th Annual Report*, p. 236.

[131] New York City Housing Authority Fact Sheet (Jan. 1, 1966), p. 8.

[132] Seligman, p. 105. See also "29,000 Public Housing Units under contract by June 30 Deadline," *JH*, 12 (1955), 227. The act of 1949 spoke of commencement of 135,000 new units a year, 63 Stat. 428 (1949); see, by way of contrast, 69 Stat. 638 (1955).

[133] *Cong. Rec.*, 101 (July 29, 1955), 12107.

[134] "Federal Bulldozer's Fallacies," *JH*, 22 (1965), 190.

[135] HHFA, *18th Annual Report*, p. 386.

[136] Paul Wendt, *Housing Policy, the Search for Solutions* (Berkeley: Univ. of California Press, 1963), pp. 50–51.

Meanwhile, the destruction of low-income housing in the United States proceeds at a rapid rate. Urban renewal, business expansion, code-enforcement demolition, highways and public improvements tear down many of the homes of the poor. Many of these houses may be considered unfit for human beings to live in; yet somehow they do live in them. Destruction of the houses frequently leaves a gap in the low-income housing supply; demolition is not always accompanied by a plan for new housing construction, though a ritual cross-town shuffle called "relocation" is required by law in urban renewal projects. Relocation can be genuine, and it can be humane. In recent years, more attention has been paid to relocation than before. But relocation cannot *create* new housing; it can only find what exists. Relocation can smooth transitions for poor people; it can provide market information for people not used to a market. But it does not *make* houses, any more than an employment service makes jobs. If no new houses are available at low rents for the displaced poor, they will generate new low-rent areas, e.g., through overcrowding and conversion of bigger flats. New slums will replace the old.

Programs have been proposed which do aim at increasing the housing supply; these will be discussed at a later point. At present, however, it is enough to point out that these programs do not ensure any *major* increase in supply. Meanwhile, conventional public housing, in the Wagner Act sense, is stagnant and unloved. Some voices that might be expected to defend it are silent and sullen. The fact is that public housing has lost its major supporters. Just as housing experts abandoned the tenement-law movement, public housing, too, is no longer the darling of reform. In the opinion of the experts, public housing has been misdesigned, misconceived, and misdirected. It has neither conquered the slums nor helped the poor. Whether these opinions are right or wrong, they are profoundly damaging to the cause of public housing.

Public Housing and Its Problems

Public housing *design* has been troublesome since the postwar period. Many early projects consisted of one-, two- or three-story buildings. Some looked like developments of little houses. This was particularly true of projects in smaller communities during the earlier years of public housing. The Housing Division of PWA had a four-story maximum rule, except for New York City.[137] Middletown

---

[137] Straus and Wegg, p. 69.

Gardens, in Delaware City, Indiana, was a "112-unit low-rent housing community built on an 80-acre outlying tract: 15 acres in houses,
33 in gardens, 7 a recreation grove, 4 a ball field, 21 untouched tim-
ber."[138] Such projects were conceived of as "slums of hope"—way-
stations on the road to middle-class status. Indeed, it was reported
in 1944 that one-quarter of the families in Middletown Gardens
were able to save enough money to buy their own homes.[139] In the
cities, low-rise projects, though never architectural masterpieces, do
blend in with their surroundings. They have achieved in some cases
a kind of mellowness with age. They contribute far more to the
urban landscape than the prevailing big-city mode of construction
which is grimly institutional, high-rise, and barren to the eye.

Economic factors have dictated the rise of the high-rise. Sprawling
developments were not feasible in major cities. New York began
with six-story elevator buildings and went higher and higher. As
long ago as 1948, the city's director of development described the
process:

> With land costs increasing and with soil conditions requiring
> costly piling operations, it became apparent that perhaps six
> stories were not enough to realize full economy. . . . With some
> trepidation, and with social workers all over the country watch-
> ing us, we went to 10 and 11 stories. It worked fine. On the next
> job we went to 13 stories.[140]

Many in New York are now over 20 stories high. In Chicago's
Cabrini-Green project, the original two-story row-houses are over-
shadowed by 19-story giants. Land costs and the need for economies
of scale have been the villains. Once the Great Depression ended,
space was at a premium in and near the city core; vacant land was
not readily available. It is cheaper to build up than sideways.

The high-rise is not necessarily an architectural evil. Builders and
designers have strong feelings about "open space"; they like a low
density of coverage of land.[141] Tall buildings on grassy malls have

---

[138] "High Income Tenants Urged to Purchase Homes," *JH*, 2 (1945), 9.

[139] Purchase of Homes by Tenants of Middletown Gardens, Muncie, Indiana,"
JH, 1 (1944), 47.

[140] John P. Riley, "Cost Reductions Pioneered in New York Public Housing,"
JH, 5 (1948), 105, 106.

[141] Thus, at least in New York, renewal projects have been built at lower densi-
ties than nearby private projects of comparable quality. There is a "double standard" which separates zoning law and renewal requirements. See Bernard J.
Frieden, *The Future of Old Neighborhoods* (Cambridge, Mass.: M.I.T., 1964),
pp. 140–41.

an open, airy, orderly appearance that pleases designers; but the tenants, as Jane Jacobs reminds us, may find the project design sterile and useless.[142] A study made in 1948, at the dawn of the high-rise era, compared tenant satisfaction in four projects in New York City. It found that 91 per cent of the tenants in a 400-unit, row-house project were satisfied with their accommodations, but only 55 per cent in a 3,149-unit apartment project were satisfied.[143] Designers did not understand or were unable, within cost limitations, to meet the needs of poor people with large families. Members of the middle class, particularly those without children, may like the easy maintenance and convenient location of elevator buildings afloat in a pool of asphalt or grass and fenced off from the surrounding community. High-rise buildings are not as suitable to poor people with big families. It is trite by now to remark that mothers of small children cannot manage their families from the sixteenth floor of a public-housing tenement. Large families do not adjust as well to elevator living as elderly couples. To take one simple and obvious matter, toddlers trembling on the brink of toilet training cannot reach high-up apartments in time to avoid disaster; this may be one major source of that "stench of urine" in the elevators which is held up to the noses of a nauseated public, sometimes as evidence that the poor are not ready for or do not deserve the government's gift. Moreover, public housing is usually minimum housing. In middle-class housing, there will usually be enough elevators for the tenant population. Not so in public housing. A thirty-minute wait for elevators was not uncommon at one project at the peak period of the day when the children came home from school.

Changes in public housing design were slow to reflect a major fact of public housing: over the years, the "better class" of the poor have left or been pushed out, to be replaced by broken families, dependent families, and welfare families, many of them jobless Negroes locked in the urban ghetto. A treatise on housing management, published in 1937, mildly suggested that housing projects might well accept a scattering of problem tenants—big families, families in ill health, families "who do not quite come up to a designated standard of cleanliness."[144] Such proposals would seem merely ironic today. In some housing projects, high percentages of the families receive

---

[142] Jane Jacobs, *The Death and Life of Great American Cities* (New York: Vintage Books, 1963), p. 15.

[143] *JH*, 5 (1948), 192.

[144] Rosahn and Goldfield, p. 35.

welfare checks as their sole source of income. In 1963, 39 per cent of
the new families moving into PHA housing were "receiving assistance
or benefits,"[145] and in some cities the percentage was much higher,
e.g., 50 per cent of the families in public housing in St. Louis and
62.7 per cent in Detroit.[146] The design of big-city projects has not
been generally tailored to special needs of the dependent poor, even
though this group occupies more and more of a prominent place in
big-city projects. Today, serious attempts are being made to rectify
some of the worst errors of design—to humanize landscapes and to
improve playgrounds.[147] Very recently, special attempts to help large
families have been made. New York has even rented and remodeled
storefronts for big families.[148] But an admittedly impressionistic
overview of the literature suggests that it is somehow easier to envision
and design special apartments and projects for the physically disabled and for old people, with ramps, hand-rails, and other such
devices, than to approach the general problems of the texture of life
inside public housing by the actual tenants who are there. In what
respect are these good homes to live in? In what respect are they not?
Until recently not many people seemed to care about the answer.
City planners and city thinkers, whether orthodox or, like Jane
Jacobs, radical innovators, have spent their mental energy on the
projects as if they were table-top models or aspects of a pedestrian's
vision; life within has been shuttered away.[149]

Site, too, has been a persistent problem for public housing—perhaps the most serious problem of all. Indeed, difficulties of design
have been partly due to difficulties of site. The equivalent-elimina-
tion concept tied public housing to slum clearance. The community

---

[145] HHFA, *17th Annual Report,* p. 281.

[146] Figures supplied by the respective housing authorities of these cities.

[147] Albert Mayer, "Public Housing Design," *JH,* 20 (1963), 133ff; "Public Housing
Design Seminars" (imaginative plaza in public housing project), *JH,* 22 (1965), 23,
86. A particularly imaginative playground has been built in the court of the Jacob
Riis houses in New York (see *New York Times,* May 24, 1966, p. 1, col. 2) at long
last answering Henry Churchill's agonizing question: "Why are all city playgrounds so dreary and bleak, so bald, woebegone and desolate . . . as bare and
functional as the inside of a toilet bowl." *The City Is the People* (New York:
Reynal & Hitchcock, 1945), p. 114n.

[148] *New York Times,* May 5, 1966, p. 49, col. 1.

[149] Because of the "slurs of the social and architectural aesthetes, who condemn
. . . poor exterior designs," the "position of public housing has . . . been weakened." Herbert Gans, "The Failure of Urban Renewal," *Commentary,* 39 (April,
1965), 29, 33.

passion for income and race segregation has tied public housing with firm bonds to the crowded, wounded core of the city.

Early projects were, as we have seen, low-rise; they were also built on open land to a significant extent. Even in the city, vacant land was available to a certain degree, and tax-delinquent properties were fairly abundant. Income segregation was kept in check by the sheer numbers and wide dispersion of people whose incomes were lower than in the 1920's. But with the approach of prosperity, sources of cheap land in the city dried up; people proceeded once more to sort themselves out into income areas in and about the city. From that point on, the very suggestion that a low-income "project," particularly the bulky, high-rise type, might be insinuated into a neighborhood was enough to arouse a storm of protest. The great ghetto gates swung shut.

Perhaps income segregation would have been substantially weaker had it not joined forces with powerful feelings about race. Here again demographic trends conspired against public housing. The postwar migration of poor Negroes into urban centers created a huge, new clientele for public housing but, at the same time, added to the troubles of the program. Some newcomers have not easily adjusted to city life in general and to public housing in particular. Many whites have resented the race, class, and habits of the southern Negroes who moved up North. The wall of white hostility forced Negroes into ghettos. Negro public housing followed them into the ghettos. There it has essentially remained. Site, then, has been powerfully affected by race. The siting of public housing has become, in some cities, one major mode of segregation.

Race discrimination in public housing was at one time fairly open and explicit. Public-housing officials restricted Negroes to Negro housing projects; whites-only projects were also built. This was done in both the North and the South, and sometimes even beyond the apparent dictates of public opinion. In San Diego, where housing segregation had not been the prevailing custom, the federal Public Housing Authority "adopted a segregated pattern for its federally managed projects" during the war.[150] Laws against discrimination in public housing were slow to be passed. The practice was forbidden in New York in 1939 and in Massachusetts in 1948; Connecticut

---

[150] Davis McEntire, *Residence and Race* (Berkeley: Univ. of California Press, 1960), p. 320; see also Robert C. Weaver, "Integration in Public and Private Housing," *Annals,* 304 (1956), 86.

and Wisconsin followed in 1949, and several other states passed legislation in later years.[151]

The "stroke of the pen"—the famous, long-delayed Executive order on "Equal Opportunity in Housing"—did not appear until 1962.[152] Federally supported housing projects could not then use race as a criterion in selection of tenants. Incoming tenants, under PHA policy in 1966, were free to choose the project in which they wished to live.[153] Since the "stroke of the pen," official federal policy strongly rejects "open discrimination." But integration in public housing has not resulted from the Executive order; its actual impact has been small. Integration remains a vain hope in many cities. Projects in southern cities are either white or Negro, rarely both. On December 31, 1965, Tampa, Florida, reported ten housing projects in operation: five all-white, five all-Negro. Savannah, Georgia, had nine projects: three white, six Negro.[154] Outside the South, segregation is probably less deliberate, but there is *de facto* segregation nonetheless. At the end of 1965, Raymond Rosen Apartments in Philadelphia had 1,122 dwelling units; every tenant was Negro.[155] In St. Louis, as of December 31, 1964, 83.3 per cent of the occupants of public housing were Negro; the whites were concentrated in five projects, in one of which they constituted a bare majority.[156] Inevitably, public housing in St. Louis means low-income Negroes, and a neighborhood which accepts public housing must be prepared to accept low-income Negroes. In Chicago in 1964, there were only

[151] Joseph B. Robison, "Housing—The Northern Civil Rights Frontier," *Western Reserve Law Review*, 13 (1961), 101, 110–11; Robert A. Sauer, "Free Choice in Housing," *N. Y. Law Forum*, 10 (1965), 525.

[152] Executive Order No. 11063, Nov. 24, 1962, 27 F. R. 11527, *U.S. Code Cong. Adm. News,* 2 (1962), 4386, §101(a), directed all departments and agencies of the Executive Branch to "take all action necessary and appropriate" to prevent racial discrimination in the renting of residential property financed or supported by the federal government. Pursuant to this Executive Order, PHA issued a regulation on equal opportunity in public housing, 24 Code Fed. Reg. §1500.6. This regulation has now been virtually superseded by regulations issued under Title VI of the Civil Rights Act of 1964.

[153] Jordan D. Luttrell, "The Public Housing Administration and Discrimination in Federally Assisted Low-Rent Housing," *Michigan Law Review*, 64 (1966), 871, 881–85.

[154] HUD, *Low-Rent Project Directory* (Dec. 31, 1965), pp. 53, 67.

[155] *Ibid.*, p. 30.

[156] Figures supplied by St. Louis Housing Authority. Since 1955 Negroes have been in the majority in St. Louis public housing (the racial breakdown in 1955 was 63.4 per cent Negro, 36.6 per cent white). Segregation was total until 1956.

2,472 white families out of the 29,386 families in public housing. They were strangely distributed. All of the 1,638 families in the Stateway project were Negroes; but the 139 families in the Bridgeport project were whites, as were 93 per cent of the families in Chicago's Trumbull project.[157]

Considerations of need and of neighborhood along with the reluctance of whites to live with Negroes, when they have any choice, explain the situation. Cities frequently place projects in neighborhoods where segregation is virtually certain to result. Indeed, many communities have shown that they prefer to have no public housing or no new projects rather than to interfere with existing patterns of income and race. The story has been told in all its tragicomic detail for Chicago in an excellent study by Meyerson and Banfield.[158] Race and income prejudice lie behind many of the referenda in which, with some frequency, cities in some states reject public housing for themselves.[159] An alderman votes "yes" to a Negro housing project next door to his white home-owners at his own political peril. Snobbery, as well as race prejudice, may be the villain. And rationally, why should middle-class Americans want to live in the shadow of huge, grim, overpowering high-rise projects bursting with problem families and with thousands of "culturally deprived children" to debase the currency at the neighborhood school? The only solutions are radical design change, true integration of small projects into the larger community, greater use of vacant and fringe-area land, and class and race mixing within as well as without the projects. These solutions, on a grand scale, are at present impractical, to say the least. The

---

[157] Figures taken from Chicago Housing Authority fact sheets.

[158] Martin Meyerson and Edward C. Banfield, *Politics, Planning and the Public Interest* (Glencoe, Ill.: Free Press, 1955). See also Julia Abrahamson, *A Neighborhood Finds Itself* (New York: Harper, 1959), pp. 254–57, 260–61, on the objections raised to public housing even in Hyde Park-Kenwood, a relatively liberal and more or less interracial Chicago community near the University of Chicago campus. On Baltimore, see "Local Politics—Possible Housing Pitfall," *JH*, 7 (1950), 197.

[159] In Illinois, an act of 1949, Laws Ill. 1949, p. 1027, applicable only to Chicago, forbade the Housing Authority to acquire a site without the approval of the city council (the "governing body of the municipality"). This statute sealed the fate of the Authority's program to develop sites on vacant, outlying land. In November, 1950, California adopted a constitutional amendment that provided that "no low-rent housing project shall . . . be . . . constructed . . . until, a majority of the qualified electors of the city, town or county . . . approve such project by voting in favor thereof." Cal. Const. Art. 34, §1; see *JH*, 7 (1950), 395. See also Nebraska Rev. Stat. §71–1507.

vacant-land solution has long been obvious; it is believed to be political suicide.[160] Mayor Lindsay of New York has proposed building new projects in New York City on vacant land and in outlying areas; at this writing, it remains to be seen if he can carry it off.[161] As things now stand, the price of local acceptance of public housing is continued and even heightened segregation. The public will support decent housing for the Negro and the dependent poor if they will stay in their place, geographically speaking. Otherwise, all deals are off.

Problems of the *identity of the tenants* have already, necessarily, been adverted to. In the big cities, public housing has come to be occupied mostly by the permanent poor and by victims of discrimination; the two categories overlap. Yet law and administration have continued to resist this fact. Money and effort have only reluctantly, belatedly, and recently been spent or contemplated to refurbish the program and to recast public housing in the light of reality. The postwar years were the dark ages of public housing. When the war ended, delight that the killing had stopped was somewhat tempered by fear that the palmy days of full employment were over. The suburban housing program met the needs of the new middle class; it also generated jobs and sparked a great deal of economic activity. Suppliers, laborers, and artisans all benefited. "Housing-starts" have habitually been eagerly counted as a measure of the pulse of the economy. No inducement was to be given to people to stay put in their urban apartments; they were to be encouraged to move lest a decline in housing-starts touch off a new depression. This was probably one strong, largely unspoken reason for rigorous enforcement of maximum rent limits in public housing. People should not sit tight in subsidized housing when the economy needed their housing dollars.

During the war, evictions from public housing were suspended because of the housing shortage. Many tenants earned far above the normal maximum income. In 1947 evictions were resumed, but under the terms of an act sponsored by Senator Joseph McCarthy, local authorities might decide to forego evictions at least up to March 1, 1948, if

> in the opinion of the administering authority [eviction] . . .
> would result in undue hardship for the occupants of [the] hous-

---

[160] "Vacant Sites . . . First," *JH*, 7 (1950), 123.

[161] *New York Times*, May 11, 1966, p. 29, col. 2; May 12, 1966, p. 48, col. 2; June 2, 1966, p. 24, col. 3; June 7, 1966, p. 39, col. 5.

ing accommodations, or unless in the opinion of such authority other housing facilities are available for such occupants.[162]

In *Chicago Housing Authority* v. *Molis* [163] a tenant resisted eviction from a Chicago Housing Authority project. His earnings were considerably above the ceiling of $5,000 which was set by the authority for a family with three or less dependents. The "undisputed evidence" showed that "in the Chicago Metropolitan Area there is no substantial rental housing available, and that purchase housing is available and can be secured with a down payment of $1,000 or $1,500." Molis insisted that the McCarthy Act was "designed to protect 'renters.' " But the court disagreed. The phrase "other housing facilities" in the McCarthy Act "includes housing available for purchase." The federal housing program was for low-income families exclusively. In its decision, the court (consciously or not) reflected the drive to induce or force those tenants of public housing who could afford it to join the middle class in the suburbs. In American thought, the normal tenure is tenure in fee; public housing was designed not to reward or foster indolence, but to furnish quarters in a "slum of hope" for the submerged or potential middle class, pending their rise in the world.[164] In accordance with PHA directives, local directives, and federal law, a crackdown of over-income families took place in 1948 and 1949—in some places attended by considerable pain, in others with relative smoothness.[165] The flight to the suburbs was hastened; new poor replaced the old poor in housing projects.

Renters outside of public housing had been protected in their tenure during the war years; restrictions on evictions were coupled with stringent control of rents. Whatever the merits of rent control, it is supposed to be a program for the benefit of renters. It was gradually dismantled after the war, but survived here and there, most remarkably in New York City. As one consequence, middle-class

---

[162] 61 Stat. 704, 705 (1947).

[163] 335 Ill. App. 491, 82 N.E. 2d 370 (1948).

[164] See "High-Income Tenants Urged to Purchase Homes," p. 47; "Purchase of Homes by Tenants of Middletown Gardens, Muncie, Indiana," p. 47; *JH*, 6 (1949), 45, also on the Muncie project, where the Executive Director of the Authority declares that "we have used every means at our command to impress upon the tenants the importance of securing a home for themselves"; N. H. Dosker, "Public Housing is Training Ground for Home Ownership," *JH*, 7 (1950), 278 (Louisville).

[165] See, e.g., Geraldine Russell, "All 'Excess Income' Families Moved—No Hard Feelings," *JH*, 7 (1950), 27 (Houston).

renters retained a toe hold on Manhattan Island, New York, and especially Manhattan, is predominantly a culture of apartments, not single-family houses. Many New Yorkers want to be close to work, theater, and the excitement of midtown; commuting is difficult and time-consuming. The vast numbers of middle-class renters in the city exert a pressure far more potent than the middle-class renters in cities less concentrated and insular. This distinguishes the case of New York from the underlying situation in *Molis*. Even in New York, protests against rent control by real estate men have been constant and unremitting. The program survives, though riddled with exceptions and loopholes. We may justifiably assume, then, that what is left is the heart of the rent control law, in that it corresponds to the material or social interests that have most intensely resisted repeal. These interests are middle-class interests. The poor are not the major beneficiaries of rent control. Many of them live in public housing, in reconverted brownstones, or in "remodeled," i.e., chopped-up, remnants of large apartments. All of these are exempt from rent control. Many luxury apartments, too, have been decontrolled.[166]

In Manhattan, slightly decaying rent-controlled apartments are often inhabited by middle-aged, middle-class couples, who cling to them, or by lucky young families, who discover them. The money saved in rent can be used to buy theater tickets or private school tuition for the school-age child. Thus rent control, often justified on the grounds of the hardships of high rent, does not primarily benefit the poor, i.e., those whose life is richest in hardships. New York's solicitude for renters can be explained because the city has a bigger and better class of renters than most towns. In public housing, on the other hand, the submerged-middle-class renter had enough power only to delay and monitor the rate of eviction. Most working-class families were probably only too glad for a chance at suburban life. As the middle class moved out, the political influence of the renting class in public housing drained out like water from a tub.

The period of veterans' housing had barely begun to peter out when urban redevelopment was enacted into law in 1949. Public housing became legally and socially tied to the apron strings of urban redevelopment and its successor programs. Up to very recent

---

[166] *New York City Charter and Administrative Code*, V, (New York, 1963), §Y51-3.0(e)(2) i-7.

times, new interest in public housing was sparked chiefly by the appearance of programs of housing for the elderly.[167] These programs are not restricted to low-income old people who live in public housing. Section 202 of the 1959 Federal Housing Act, for example, authorized low-interest loans to nonprofit organizations and governmental bodies for construction of rental housing or cooperatives to be occupied by "senior citizens" whose income was too high for public housing and too low for the private market.[168] But the elderly are able to kindle enthusiasm for public housing, too—a characteristic which invites comparison with the veterans, the defense workers, and the poor of the depression decade. One plausible basis of comparison is that so many of the elderly are members of the submerged middle class; they are members whose sun has set. The elderly, like children, are not "guilty" of any crime; they are merely old and weak and out of work. It is easy to sympathize and empathize with the elderly poor. Housing for the aged also solves a problem for many middle-class people which is perhaps more serious for them than for the poor. The nuclear family of the middle class lacks a clear-cut economic and emotional role for its old folks. Homes for the aged are dreary and institutional. A child who puts his parent in such a home may be deemed guilty of impiety. Moreover, old-age homes are charity. Public housing for the elderly is not, strictly speaking, charity; it provides decent accommodations—one of the necessities of life—at a bargain price.[169] At least it can be so viewed. The movement to use public housing for the elderly poor has, therefore, had a rather wide appeal.[170] Milwaukee was long known to be extremely chary of public housing. But in 1956 a Common Council Resolution proclaimed a "definite and growing need for low rent housing for

---

[167] See Housing Act of 1959, 73 Stat. 665–669 (1959), as amended. The act of 1959 authorized loans to nonprofit corporations for the provision of homes for the elderly. An amendment of 1961, 75 Stat. 162 (1961), added loans to "any consumer cooperative, or to any public body or agency." 12 U.S.C.A. §1701(q). The term "families of low income," 42 U.S.C.A. §1402(2), has been defined to include "a single person in the case of elderly families." Under 42 U.S.C.A. §1410(a) an extra subsidy in the annual contributions contracts is allowed for dwelling units occupied by elderly families.

[168] 12 U.S.C.A. §1701(q). See Sidney Spector, "Housing for Senior Citizens," *N.Y. Law Forum*, 11 (1965), 30, 39.

[169] *A fortiori*, the middle-income programs for the elderly have the virtues of public housing (chiefly the subsidy) without the vices (e.g., the stigma).

[170] See "Housing for the Elderly News," *JH*, 18 (1961), 15; "Public Housing for the Elderly," *JH*, 20 (1963), 77; and *115,000 Senior Citizens* (PHA, 1961).

aged people," complained that "present housing programs do not
adequately reflect the needs of such aged people to secure convenient
and comfortable housing," and importuned Congress to do something about the situation. A Resolution of 1957 requested the local
Housing Authority to survey the community's needs; and in 1958
the Common Council directed work to be done immediately on finding sites for 300 units, even though the survey had not been completed.[171] In city after city, the story is the same; much of their new
construction is for the elderly. In Chicago, out of 5,661 units under
construction as of June 30, 1964, no less than 4,347 were reserved for
the elderly.[172] In Omaha, the Housing Authority began work in 1964
on five buildings with 580 units. This was the first new public housing construction in more than a decade in Omaha. All were "designed especially for the elderly."[173] The first public housing ever
to be built in Vermont was a project of 80 units for the elderly.[174]
In other cities the percentage, though less, is substantial; housing
for the elderly is popular. After all, among the elderly a formidable
number of recruits to public housing can still be found who are respectable white citizens of middle-class background. Forty per cent
of the white families in public housing in 1964 were elderly, as
against 18 per cent of the non-white familes.[175] They may be lonely,
poor, and sick; but they do not break windows or soil the elevators.
And in a politician's view, the old folks are better tenants than
young Negroes with big families. When a public housing authority
proposes to move senior citizens into a neighborhood, the outcry is
apt to be much less strident than otherwise. Then, too, the emphasis
on the elderly is only the latest of many attempts to separate some
class of the worthy poor from the unworthy. It is similar to the
categorical approach to welfare, that is, the development of programs for specific categories of the needy, e.g., fatherless children,
the blind, and the disabled. Public housing, too, is distinctly categorical. It has moved from the submerged middle class, which is admittedly a quite diffuse category, to veterans, and now to the elderly
and the disabled. But probably all of these are merely subcategories

---

[171] Quoted in *Housing Accommodations of Elderly Persons in the City of Milwaukee* (Milwaukee Housing Authority, 1958).

[172] Chicago Housing Authority fact sheets.

[173] Housing Authority of the City of Omaha, Nebraska, *25th Annual Report*
(1964), pp. 2, 3.

[174] *JH,* 21 (1965), 413.

[175] *Families in Low-Rent Projects* (PHA, Sept., 1965), p. 46.

of the submerged or potential middle class. John P. Dean, a regional economist for PHA, urging public housing for the aged in 1946, suggested that policy should develop along the lines of excluding "the house-bound, the bedridden, the senile, those with serious recurring maladies, and those unable to perform daily housekeeping tasks."[176]

An extreme, but revealing instance of the political and social state of public housing, is the case of the Dante Place Housing Project in Buffalo, New York. Dante Place was built as low-income housing. Later, the project turned out to occupy a strategic location in an area considered suitable for upgrading through urban renewal. It was therefore concluded that the location was too choice for the riff-raff of public housing. The city proposed to move out the tenants, remodel the project and convert it into a limited-dividend co-operative for people with substantially higher incomes. The plan was challenged in court by a tenant; but the Supreme Court of Erie County turned down his suit in 1960, remarking that "the conversion . . . is a step forward with the proper planning to a better Buffalo that will benefit everyone in Buffalo, including the plaintiff." Plaintiff would be excused if he found the last phrase ironic.[177]

Problems of Management

Public housing was originally aimed at the submerged and potential middle class which was lower class in income, but middle class in values or aspirations. The original statute was built on this idea, as we have seen, and it has remained a vital force in public housing ever since. For a "middle-class" clientele, it might be tolerable to structure the landlord-tenant relationship in the same way as it is structured in private housing. This would be particularly true if low-income families had reasonable alternatives to public housing so that some kind of market control would temper the power of management. As a matter of fact, outside alternatives are not very attractive; but the more middle-class in culture the tenants are, the more feasible the alternatives. Elderly whites, for example, have a better chance on the open market than a Negro AFDC mother with small children at the same level of income per family member.

---

[176] John P. Dean, "Public Housing for the Aged," *JH*, 3 (1946), 203.

[177] *Chelcy* v. *Buffalo Municipal Housing Authority*, 24 Misc. 2d 598, 206 N.Y. Supp. 2d 158, 170 (1960). For a different view of the meaning of the Dante Place incident, see Jacobs, pp. 393n, 394; and see also "Buffalo: What It Takes to Change Low-Rent to Middle-Income Housing," *JH*, 17 (1960), 73.

Morever, tenants of the submerged middle class are more likely to
be skillful in asserting their rights against management. They would
have different needs for social services and different abilities to protect themselves against excessive paternalism or despotism.

However, protections for tenants have never been built into the
administration of public housing. *Informal* checks on management
power have been treated with great suspicion—if they come from
the tenants, that is. In 1950, the New York City Housing Authority
banned "tenant organizations purporting to represent residents in
all or several projects"; such organizations were "no longer permitted to present grievances and problems to the authority's director, commissioners, or project managers." Only individuals and
unorganized groups had that right. The reason given was administrative convenience.[178] Tenant councils and organizations have
functioned in public housing as social organizations or adjuncts of
management policy. They have not usually been allowed to rock
the boat. Only very recently (1965–66) can one speak seriously of
tenant protest movements and meaningful tenant unions. A big
project is likely to be faceless and bureaucratic; tenants may have
no feeling that there is someone willing and able to hear their tale.
In any event, until quite recently there has been little discussion of
informal controls on management and little interest in the subject
throughout the hi.'ory of public housing.

The *formal* power of management remains virtually unchecked.
Selection, retention, and eviction are matters largely of local discretion. Housing authorities, probably without exception, use a lease
form which allows speedy eviction of undesirable tenants. Tenancy
is on a month to month basis. In Norfolk, Virginia, for example,
the public housing lease provides that it "may be terminated by the
Landlord at the end of any calendar month by giving the Tenant
not less than 30 days advance notice in writing."[179] The language
of New York City's lease is substantially the same. The lease in
Portland, Oregon, runs "for the term of one calendar month . . . re-
newable thereafter from month to month by the payment and acceptance of rent"; either party may terminate by giving "notice in
writing of the intention to terminate at any time not less than
twenty (20) days before the expiration of the term thereof, or in any

[178] *JH*, 7 (1950), 212.
[179] Norfolk Redevelopment and Housing Authority, *Lease Agreement*.

other manner provided for by the laws of the State of Oregon"; no conduct of the landlord "shall constitute a waiver of . . . the twenty-day written notice of termination."[180] Lease clauses such as these lay the legal basis for an argument that housing managers may evict on short notice and without assigning cause. Management, it must be recalled, does not suffer any immediate economic consequences from a vacancy or two. The projects are not run for profit, and slight losses through vacancies may be cured by manipulation of rentals. Moreover, management has plenary rule-making power. The New York City lease contains a promise by the tenant to comply with the landlord's rules and regulations. The printed list of rules and regulations which the tenant must sign hammers home the lack of formal controls over management. The tenant must promise to comply not only with the long list of existing rules, but with "such Rules and Regulations as may hereafter be established by the Landlord." The landlord also may enter the premises at any "reasonable" hour, with or without permission, to investigate any conditions in violation of law or of the "Rules and Regulations of the Landlord."[181]

It might have been otherwise. Statutes, case-law, or administrative rulings might have circumscribed the power of management. But statutory control is minimal. In general, the only important restrictions on management are negative, i.e., those which effectively limit occupancy of public housing to poor people. The Wagner Housing Act provided that only "families of low income" were eligible. Federal law in 1966 also asks local agencies to adopt admission policies which "give full consideration" to their "responsibility for the rehousing of displaced families," servicemen, veterans, and those with particularly urgent housing needs. Federal law requires over-income tenants to be evicted unless "special circumstances" make alternative housing unavailable.[182] State statutes do not add much to the cri-

---

[180] Housing Authority of Portland, Oregon, *Lease*, "Terms and Conditions of Occupancy," paragraph 5. Of more than thirty public housing authority leases sampled by the author in 1965, none failed to contain provisions which in essence create a month-to-month tenancy; and of the reported cases on lease violations in public housing, none to the author's knowledge revealed the existence of any public housing lease which was not written on a month-to-month basis—at least as of mid-1966.

[181] New York City Housing Authority, *Tenant Rules and Regulations*, paragraph 2(z), paragraph 3(b).

[182] 42 U.S.C.A. §1410(g)(2), (3).

teria for selection of tenants.[183] In general, then, the selection of
tenants, the criteria for continued eligibility, and eviction policy,
except in rent-controlled New York where eviction is a difficult matter, have been assigned to the virtually absolute power of local housing management.[184] No public housing statute has guaranteed any
rights to the tenants; a low-income family has no right to get in and
no right to stay. The former is explainable, perhaps, since Congress
has never seen fit to supply enough units for all those who might
want a place in public housing. The latter is a matter of policy and
is questionable.

In a sense, it would be foolish to expect judicial review of management practices to have much impact upon selection and eviction.
First of all, public housing tenants are normally not the suing kind.
Second, the words of the lease and the silence of the statutes place
great legal obstacles in the tenants' paths. The powerlessness of the
tenants was secured by an act of deliberate policy; and moreover it
can be argued that judicial review is a poor way to reform public
housing. Judicial review is bound to be at best sporadic; reform
from within the system or imposed administratively upon the system is more efficient and more likely to be lasting in effect. This is
certainly true; but reform from *any* source has been slow in coming.
And some guerrilla wars against welfare authorities have used court
cases with skill and success.

All this is recent, however. Some cracks in the armor are appear-
ing; and more are likely soon to appear. In the past, court cases have

---

[183] E.g., Wis. Stat. §66.402(1), requiring authorities to rent only "to persons of
low income" and fixing rent-income ratios. In some states there are preferences
for veterans or for persons displaced by the slum clearance program of which the
housing project is a part, or both, e.g., Nev. Rev. Stat. §315.550. Many authorities, of course, add formal criteria of their own, which may include preferences.
In Denver, applicants "must be living in substandard housing at the time of application," but veterans, families of veterans or deceased veterans, persons 62
years of age or older, permanently disabled persons, and applicants "without
housing," are exempt from this requirement. *Denver Housing Authority Information Handbook*. A one-year residency requirement has been waived in San Francisco for preferred groups—including veterans, students, families without housing,
and families displaced by slum clearance projects. San Francisco Housing Authority, "Low Rent Housing—Policy" (Feb. 1964 revision), Part I, Sec. I, page 3.

[184] Additional federal controls might be exerted through regulations; or the
federal government might insist on imposing particular terms in the annual contributions contracts which housing authorities execute with PHA. But in fact
the terms of these contracts had not as of 1966 *materially* altered the distribution
of power between local authority and Washington with respect to tenant selection, eligibility, and eviction.

gone badly for tenants. In *Walton* v. *City of Phoenix*[185] the precise legal question was whether the Phoenix Authority had the right to "terminate defendants' tenancy by giving a ten day notice," in accordance with the lease and the ordinary Arizona statutes on landlord and tenant. Walton insisted that state statutes on evictions had "no application to other than private landlords." This argument was not terribly persuasive. Walton could not point to any other statute which governed the Authority's power to evict, if the Arizona statutes did not. The court felt it was "anomalous" if a "person once obtaining possession" of a slot in public housing "had a continuing and indefinite right of tenure." The Authority, said the court, "may in its sound discretion act as any other landlord in the preservation and maintenance of the property under its control." Like "any private landlord," it might "impose reasonable restrictions on the use of the privilege so granted." Walton's eviction was upheld. The reasoning sounded good to housing authorities. In a number of cities the Housing Authorities have gone to court or been taken there, and the same issue of landlord's rights has been fought out. In most cases through 1965, the decision in *Walton* has been followed. Some of these later cases are unreported; but local management knows they exist; and managers act on that basis.[186]

Despite great formal power over tenants, many managers rarely evict. Some managers do not like to make evictions, if for no other reason than the time, trouble, and money it takes to move in a new tenant, straighten up the apartment, and start afresh.[187] Probably all managers would like to keep formal, court-ordered evictions to a minimum. But in some projects there may be a heavy use of threats

---

[185] 69 Ariz. 26, 208 P. 2d 309 (1949).

[186] *Pittsburgh Housing Authority* v. *Turner*, 201 Pa. Super. 62, 191 Atl. 2d 869 (1963), discussed in *JH*, 20 (1963), 335, is an example of a reported case following the reasoning of *Walton;* see also *Chicago Housing Authority* v. *Ivory* (decided by the Illinois appellate court in 1950), *JH*, 7 (1950), 432, reported in abstract form, 341 Ill. App. 282, 93 N.E. 2d 386 (1950).

A Milwaukee housing manager reported in a personal interview (Aug. 12, 1964), that,

Back in the early history of the Project . . . we had what we called a test case, and it was established at that time that the Housing Authority was in the same position as any private landlord. . . . It held that all that was required was the serving of a thirty-day notice. . . . When we get into court the judge as a rule does not bother about the reasons involved. . . .

See also *JH*, 6 (1949), 150 (unreported cases from Stockton, California, and Buffalo, New York).

[187] Project Manager in Chicago, Illinois, Personal interview, August 4, 1965.

of eviction. A study was made of move-outs from public housing in nine localities between December 1, 1956, and May 31, 1957. One-quarter (25 per cent) of all the move-outs were "by request of management"; somewhat more than a third of these were for in-eligibility, including those for excess income; the rest were requested to leave for "other reasons." These tenants either did not pay their rent or violated rules and regulations.[188]

When questioned, some managers defend the short-term lease and their resultant powers on the grounds of reciprocity; the tenants can leave on short notice, which presumably they could not do if they had security of tenure. This argument is a *non-sequitur*, of course. There is no reason why tenants could not have the right without the liability. If pressed further, managers might defend the short-term lease and their powers over tenure and eviction as a simple and efficient way to reduce annoying external controls, rather than as a license to act arbitrarily, which they deny they ever do. There is no particular reason to believe that Congress and the states meant otherwise than to grant them this power. The general history of public housing gives no support to the view that Congress and the states meant to shower any rights onto tenants. The sole exception was the over-income tenant protected by the McCarthy Act. Once the emergency was over, he too lost his rights.

The decision to evict Walton had been based on the fact that he was "undesirable." There has been some litigation since *Walton* dealing with this type of problem. Up to 1966, most of the cases were unreported; the authority won without much fuss, and there was no appeal. Relatively few troublesome tenants even got into court. They accepted the demands of authority and moved out. Reported cases came chiefly from New York State, which publishes lower court decisions, where rent control has made eviction a justiciable cause, and where there are more public housing tenants than elsewhere. Except for these special circumstances, the law of tenant eviction would have remained even less visible to legal literature than it did.

The reported decisions, too, usually went against the tenant.[189] In *New York City Housing Authority* v. *Russ* (1954),[190] a tenancy was terminated "for non-desirability." The Authority, by resolution,

---

[188] *Mobility and Motivations: Survey of Families Moving From Low-Rent Housing* (Public Housing Administration, 1958), pp. 15–19.

[189] As far as can be ascertained, the tenants lost the unreported cases, too.

[190] 134 N.Y.S. 2d 812 (1954).

had set up a system of procedure for such cases. If the tenant's conduct became "objectionable and his continued occupancy non-
desirable," the manager of the project could make "a finding of
ineligibility." This was done in the *Russ* case, and the finding was
reviewed and approved by a "tenant Review Board." A lower court
decision refused to allow summary eviction proceedings against
Russ. But the appellate term reversed this ruling and upheld the
view of the Housing Authority. Administrative findings of fact were
not to be reviewed by the courts. The Authority, in its petition to
evict Russ, had stated that his conduct was objectionable. These
allegations, said the court, were necessary "merely" to "show the
reasons for the termination of the tenancy and compliance by the
authority with its regulations. It was unnecessary for the landlord
to offer any testimony as to the objectionable behavior of the tenant."
In *New York City Housing Authority* v. *Watson* (1960),[191] the tenant,
Willis Watson, was in jail; the Authority evicted his wife and
children. The court said that the Authority "must establish that it
went through [its] procedures"; the tenant may contest this, but
"he can not contest the finding of undesirability." The eviction was
sustained. In *Smalls* v. *White Plains Housing Authority* (1962),[192]
the basis for eviction was "the misconduct of petitioner's children."
The issue raised by Mrs. Smalls was whether the authority was
obligated to grant her a hearing before deciding to terminate her
tenancy. The court reminded Mrs. Smalls tartly that "the Authority
[of White Plains] is composed of public-spirited citizens serving
without compensation" who make decisions "for the administration
of the project and the welfare of all the tenants." It was "inconceivable that the . . . Authority is required to grant a hearing whenever
it exercises its rights to terminate a month to month tenancy pursuant
to a written lease." This decision probably went beyond the prior
cases since Mrs. Smalls was merely asking for a few procedural rights.
Even these the court was unwilling to concede. Presumably an
authority had to abide by its rules; but nothing required it to make a
rule that would grant hearings as of right to tenants about to be
evicted.

Sander v. *Cruise* (1958)[193] went against the trend. In this case, tenants succeeded in winning their battle; an eviction for "undesirabil-

---

[191] 207 N.Y.S. 2d 920 (1960).
[192] 34 Misc. 2d 949, 230 N.Y. Supp. 2d 106 (1962).
[193] 10 Misc. 2d 533, 173 N.Y. Supp. 2d 871 (1958).

ity" was annulled by the court. The eviction had been based on the fact, or the charge, that the tenants' 25-year-old son was a "confirmed drug addict, three times convicted of narcotics offenses." The tenants insisted, to the court's satisfaction, that the addict son John did not live with his parents and that it was unreasonable to evict them under the circumstances. The New York City Housing Authority made a forceful argument for exclusion of addicts from housing projects. The addict "tends to involve other tenants, particularly teen-age children," in his vice. He attracts "pushers" to a project. He tends to associate with "other addicts and criminals in the project." He "tends to become involved in criminal activities to obtain sufficient money for drugs"; in particular, he may steal plumbing fixtures in the project to finance his drug needs. In short, his presence "tends to make the project unacceptable to normal families." But the court saw no "overt act detrimental to the health, safety or morals of the other tenants in Astoria Houses"; it was not clear that the son's "addiction to narcotics was known to the neighbors or the community." To evict a family simply because their adult son was an addict "exceeds any reasonable requirement" for the peace and good management of the project. "Approval of the Authority's determination would, in effect, sanction the perpetual isolation from the community of all drug addicts. Such a result is repugnant to current concepts of the problems of drug addiction."

These cases graphically illustrated the desire of some authorities for a free hand in management. They also suggest some of the ways in which authorities would like to control their clientele. The court in *Sanders* v. *Cruise* found "repugnant" the idea of "perpetual isolation" of drug addicts from society. But perpetual isolation of addicts from *public housing* was precisely the goal of the Authority; it wanted to ensure for itself a supply of "normal families" and to eliminate the worst sorts of "problem families." To an increasing extent, housing authorities were not getting what they wanted; the flow of problem families into public housing constantly increased in the period after World War II. But it remained a goal of public housing to provide room mostly for normal families with low incomes; and management policies were still geared to that goal. This, too, is a reason for the fact that leases are written so as to deprive tenants of rights and make tenancy a matter of administrative discretion. A rigid scale of preferences, based on some objective standard of need, might curtail the freedom of management to get and to keep the "better" class of the poor.

In defense of management, it must be pointed out that the projects were not and are not equipped as such to handle addicts and other serious delinquents, if indeed society is equipped to handle them at all. Since there is less public housing than there are poor families who want to get in, some basis of selection and retention has to be adopted. Even Senator Wagner in 1937 agreed that "character" would be one basis of choice and that "people of ill-repute" would "of course . . . not be permitted to occupy the premises."[194] Managers choose tenants who can "benefit" from project life by virtue of their normalcy. Roughly, normalcy means adherence to the middle-class way of life or to as close an approximation as possible.

A lot can be and has been said in favor of this general policy. But there are two bothersome points that must be raised. First, the great freedom of management, both formal and informal, enables it to adopt good, bad, and indifferent policies without sufficient debate or review. In 1957, for example, the New York Housing Authority announced a "get-tough" policy to "evict families who cannot be made to control their delinquent children." The Cincinnati Housing Authority in the same year decided to evict unmarried women who gave birth—a policy pursued by many other authorities as well.[195] Most housing authorities refuse to allow their tenants the right to have pets.[196] These policies are all debatable; but they cannot be debated by the tenants. Authorities devise these policies themselves, and they may also proceed to act as judge, jury, and prosecutor in determining who does and who does not violate their rules. Some of these practices and rules may not be unfair or may be fair on paper and unfair in operation. Others may be more benevolent; but there has been no way to separate and control.

Second, the search for a "normal" population has not been successful in large cities. Big-city projects steadily continue a descent to the subnormal. There are many causes. Considerations of site and prevailing winds of opinion emphasize income and race segregation. Affluence sharpens the difference between "adjusted" and "alienated" segments of society.

---

[194] *Cong. Rec.*, 81 (August 3, 1937), 8098.
[195] "Take the Case of 'Undesirables,'" *JH*, 14 (1957), 119. The New York City Housing Authority was accused of excluding unwed mothers, *New York Times*, Dec. 10, 1965, p. 45, col. 2.
[196] See Lawrence M. Friedman, "Public Housing and the Poor: An Overview," *California Law Review*, 54 (1966), 642, 661.

Enlightened management and enlightened cities have long been aware of the problem tenant. One solution is to accept difficult families and try to help them. Many projects subscribe to a rehabilitation theory. They look upon themselves as providing welfare as well as shelter. In Columbus, Ohio, the Lincoln Park Homes has "meeting and craft rooms" in the Administration Building along with a weekly "well-baby clinic." The management "cooperates with South Side Settlement, St. Stephens Community House, and the nearby schools, Lincoln Park Elementary and St. Ladislas." The Columbus Metropolitan Housing Authority operates jointly with the City and State Boards of Education a "Family Living Center," providing adult education classes in "sewing, cooking, and home furnishing with arts and crafts being taught the children of the parents attending classes at the Center."[197] In some cities, branch offices of welfare agencies operate within housing projects. The Missouri Department of Welfare opened a branch office in April, 1962, in the Pruitt-Igoe project in St. Louis; the Department was pleased with results, and a similar office was opened in other projects.[198] Housing authorities, at least the larger ones, have staffs of tenant relations officers, found or support boys' clubs, golden-age clubs and day nurseries, and cooperate with city, state, and federal agencies working with, for, or among the poor. In January, 1965, there were at least 3,300 youth programs, 3,000 recreation programs, and 2,700 adult education programs in public housing.[199] The range of activities is broad—from grandiose pilot projects to the Annual Domino Tournament of the Hunters Point Boys' Club in San Francisco.[200] All these represent an attempt to broaden and deepen the impact of public housing. But at the same time, these worthwhile programs imply a certain disillusionment, a sense that public housing *in itself* is insufficient and has not accomplished rehabilitation by itself. The submerged and potential middle class is no longer in sole possession of public housing. Once inside public housing, problem families were, in the words of Daniel Seligman, "the same bunch of bastards they always

---

[197] Information supplied by Columbus Metropolitan Housing Authority (1965).

[198] "Open-Door to Low Rent Public Housing in Saint Louis," (St. Louis Housing Authority pamphlet, n.d.), p. 18. A similar system is in operation in Chicago.

[199] *Community Facilities and Programs Serving Public Housing* (HHFA, Sept., 1965), p. 3.

[200] Housing Authority of the City and County of San Francisco, *27th Annual Report* (1964–65), p. 12.

were" outside.[201] They needed more than a roof over their heads.

As the problem of problem families seemed to deepen, public housing lost further support. Rather than make public housing more institutional in an attempt to rehabilitate the tenants, some began to
ask that public housing be abandoned altogether. The new left and
the old right both fear and distrust the manipulation of human
beings by persons in authority. To avoid this, the best thing to do
with the high-rise ghettos is to give them up. Housing experts are an
unexpected ally of these critics. Indeed, the *disillusionment* of the experts has become the fourth major problem of the traditional public-
housing program, along with site, design of housing, and identity of
tenants. The cause of public housing has been psychologically abandoned by many of its former supporters. In the last ten years, assessment of public housing has been more and more negative. It has been
argued with great force that public housing does not reduce social
costs of the slums—and does not help the poor. "We have merely in-
stitutionalized our slums." This was said by Harrison Salisbury, of
the *New York Times*, in a book published in 1958. Salisbury had
spent many years in Russia. When he came back to New York, he was
appalled at what he saw. Conditions in New York City's public
housing made a bitter catalogue:

> shoddy shiftlessness, the broken windows, the missing light
> bulbs, the plaster cracking from the walls, the pilfered hardware,
> the cold, drafty corridors, the doors on sagging hinges, the acid
> smell of sweat and cabbage, the ragged children, the plaintive
> women, the playgrounds that are seas of muddy clay, the bruised
> and battered trees, the ragged clumps of grass, the planned ab-
> sence of art, beauty, or taste, the gigantic masses of brick, of con-
> crete, of asphalt, the inhuman genius with which our know-how
> has been perverted to create human cesspools worse than those
> of yesterday.[202]

Housing projects destroyed slum communities and created new
slums of rootless, malintegrated people who turned to delinquency
and crime for some sense of belonging: lives were "twisted out
of joint." Projects were overrun with gangs; "before a single family
has moved into the project the lines of community warfare have

---

[201] Seligman, p. 106.
[202] Harrison E. Salisbury, *The Shook-Up Generation* (New York: Harper, 1958),
p. 75.

been drawn. The stage is set for hatred, feuds, gangs, rumbles, street fighting and killings." The soul of the neighborhood is destroyed in the process of creating public housing. The "deadly plong of the wreckers' ball and the tattoo of new steel work" destroys the "institutions that gave stability." Gone are the "Neapolitan blocks, the street fiestas, the interwoven relationship of stores and neighbors"; instead there is an "absence of churches . . . political deserts . . . lack of political and social organization. . . ."[203]

Salisbury's indictment was serious; public housing, in his view, had destroyed more than it built. He proposed a vast increase in social services. By implication, these services would be far more important than public housing itself. Jane Jacobs, too, would just as soon dispense with public housing as continue the erection of walled-in "ghettos."[204] Both Salisbury and Jacobs are thoughful critics. His assessment was basically from the standpoint of social organization, hers from the standpoint of urban design, though neither adopted an exclusively narrow perspective. The problems of big-city housing projects have also attracted more superficial attacks. Newspaper exposés in various cities have heaped scorn and disgust on public housing. There is a willing audience; bad news about public housing seems to sell newspapers. In April, 1965, Chicago readers of the *Daily News* could soak up details of their "$70 Million Ghetto," a sensational series about the Robert R. Taylor homes, "the world's biggest and most jam-packed public housing development." Taylor—"virtually [an] all-Negro city within a city"—may be Chicago's

> leading civic movement to misery, bungling and a hellish way of life. . . . Its own tenants label it a "death trap," a concentration camp, and even, with sardonic self-derision, "the Congo Hilton." . . . Here live 28,000 people, all of them poor, grappling with violence and vandalism, fear and suspicion, teen-age terror and adult chaos, rage, resentment, official regimenting.[205]

Newspaper articles of this kind are symptoms of the political troubles of public housing. Equally serious, perhaps, are the slings

---

[203] Salisbury, pp. 74, 75, 79, 80.

[204] See Jacobs, pp. 392–401, where Mrs. Jacobs suggests a number of necessary "reforms," which would have the effect of destroying traditional public housing.

[205] M. S. Newman, "Chicago's $70 Million Ghetto," *Chicago Daily News*, April 10, 1965, p. 1, col. 1.

and arrows aimed by professional scholars and housing experts. Disillusionment here runs deep. In 1957, one of the most famous of American housing specialists, Catherine Bauer, wrote a bitter attack on public housing in *Architectural Forum*.[206] The program, in her opinion, had reached a stage of "dreary deadlock," too strong for decent death and burial, too weak to move on to a more progressive stage of life. The next issue of the magazine carried comment by eleven housing experts on how to "break" the "dreary deadlock."[207] The eleven had many and different things to say, but they all accepted the notion that public housing had in some way failed and proceeded from that point on. Indeed, outside the government bureaucracy, that feeling seemed quite general.[208] One specialist, Robert K. Brown, who studied public housing in Pittsburgh, wrote in 1959 that public housing was "not capable of furnishing" a solution "which will begin to approach the dimensions of the problem." Public housing had "apparently failed to achieve even a temporary solution to the housing problems of the low-income group, let alone a lasting solution."[209] Brown suggested that no new public housing be built; he proposed, in its place, making use of some form of rent subsidy for low-income families. The rent subsidy notion had been suggested before, and since the 1950's the idea has steadily gathered strength. A form of rent subsidy was gingerly insinuated into the 1965 Housing Law, though over bitter opposition.[210] We shall consider it later in more detail. Charles Abrams, writing in the *Architectural Forum* symposium, suggested an even more radical approach. He proposed selling existing projects to their occupants and converting them into cooperatives.[211] In 1934 Charles

---

[206] Catherine Bauer, "The Dreary Deadlock of Public Housing," *Architectural Forum*, 106 (May, 1957), 140.

[207] "The Dreary Deadlock of Public Housing–How to Break It," *Architectural Forum*, 106 (June, 1957), 139.

[208] Among the many critiques of public housing, see Wendt, pp. 190–96; Maxim Duplex [a pseudonym], "The New Issue in Public Housing," *JH*, 7 (1950), 202, 238; and James C. Downs, "New Social Goals proposed for public housing for the '60's," *JH*, 19 (1962), 566. The attacks of men like Salisbury and of experts like Catherine Bauer are generally accepted as valid even by (or especially by) liberals with a profound commitment to helping the poor. See, for example, Michael Harrington, *The Other America* (New York: Penguin Books, 1963), pp. 148–157; and Seligman, pp. 105–8.

[209] Robert K. Brown, *Public Housing in Action: The Record of Pittsburgh* (Pittsburgh: Univ. of Pittsburgh Press, 1959), p. 77.

[210] Title I, P. L. 89–117, 79 Stat. 451 (1965); for comment in a House Committee Report, see *U.S. Code Cong. Adm. News* (1965), 2687–90.

[211] Abrams, *Architectural Forum*, 106 (June, 1957), 141, 218.

Ascher, another housing specialist, had written that cooperative ownership was socially and economically impractical for low-cost housing. He felt that "something nearer the landlord-tenant relationship will best serve. . . . Under continued public ownership, the risk is distributed socially as widely as possible."[212] But in the span of one generation, the wheel had turned. Now it was the government-landlord who was an evil, misshapen, soulless bureaucrat; now it was public housing which was "sick unto death," and its administrators who were "bankrupt" and "inflexible," with a "smug and complacent attitude."[213]

Had conventional public housing really failed? Politically, of course, its failure was palpable. Yet on balance, it may have done better than its critics concede. Most of the noisy criticism is directed at the big urban projects; small-town and suburban projects probably do not deserve to be tarred with the same brush. For big-city projects, income segregation and race segregation are inescapable facts, for the time being at least, both for public and private housing. The accomplishments of public housing must be judged against this background. If public housing uproots communities, it does so because it has no choice; urban renewal, federal highway construction and private business expansion also uproot, and more brutally and thoroughly. Public housing creates or maintains urban ghettos; but the ghettos would exist without public housing. A ghetto can be a place of relative safety and security—a community— as well as a symbol of discrimination. There are better ghettos and worse ones. Arguably, if public housing projects did not form huge enclaves, they could not even *try* to build new communities. Big projects have their own schools, well equipped and modern, if nothing else. These projects gather together a whole host of social services; they are safe islands in the teeming slums for social workers and welfare administrators who, probably for the most part in honesty and good faith, try to help those who need them. Is there any reason to believe that social help is any more fumbling and misguided within the enclave than without? If not, then what most needs reform is the administration of welfare programs, not the idea of building houses for the poor.

Public housing is grim and ugly; but so is most of the new architecture of the middle class, the stilted stilt-houses and the ticky-tacky

---

[212] Ascher, pp. 250, 252–53.
[213] *House and Home,* 14 (July, 1958), 61, quoting Warren Jay Vinton, a former assistant PHA Commissioner.

tracts. What effect does "grimness" or "monotony" actually have on the lives of people who live in ugly places?[214] We have really no idea; any more than we know what it means to the soul, if anything, to grow up in the shadow of the Cathedral of Chartres. The controversial differences between the external appearances of public housing and middle-class housing are superficial. Substantial differences are in interior details which middle-class critics are never close enough to see. In the public housing projects of most cities, mothers sleep without fear of fire, and rats do not bite sleeping babies. These are concrete improvements in the life of disadvantaged people. They may conceivably outweigh the disadvantages of high-rise projects and excess bureaucracy—at least as compared to the alternatives available during the high days of public housing. Public housing has not worked magic. It has therefore been deserted intellectually by those who expect magic and by those who care less for the welfare of the inhabitants, about which little is known, than for the assumed social costs of bad urban planning. If public housing needs to be reformed— and it is certain that it does—perhaps one step might be to ask tenants and potential tenants what should be done. They are the ones who suffer personally, if anyone does. Loneliness, loss of community, and fear and suspicion of management are not produced by the way public housing looks. The destruction of neighborhood values, the bureaucracy and anonymity of project life, and the ghetto siting are not inherent in public housing but have been largely forced upon the program by a hostile community.[215] Public housing has committed many crimes, no doubt; but ironically its conviction and sentence stem from crimes it did not commit and conditions over which it has little or no control.

In the *Architectural Forum* symposium, James W. Rouse expressed a common and significant view. Public housing, and indeed, slum clearance in general, was an exercise in futility, he believed. The whole city had to be reformed. Out of the "vast, sprawling blocks of the inner city," there must be created "self-contained neighborhoods which have a soul, a spirit and a healthy pride— neighborhoods which people will vigorously defend against the forces for decay."[216] Rouse meant to tie in public housing with the

---

[214] Some authorities are sure that an ugly environment saps the soul, e.g., Churchill, p. 111. But the case has not been proven.

[215] See Patricia Sexton, *Spanish Harlem, Anatomy of Poverty* (New York: Harper, 1965), pp. 35–46.

[216] James W. Rouse, "Use Public Housing to Make Renewal Work," *Architectural Forum*, 106 (June, 1957), 140.

new panacea, the program which had already succeeded in capturing and subduing what remained of the public-housing movement. Slum clearance was not enough; public housing was not enough. The whole city was the laboratory of society. Slums have to be conquered within the context of the total metropolitan problem.

The program which was to do this has bore two names: urban renewal and urban development. It became the most grandiose and the most expensive of the plans to abolish the slums. Here, too, there set in distinct signs of disillusionment—academic disgust and, what really hurts, budget stagnation. Yet from 1949 to the early 1960's, it was a favorite of reformers and a prime object of federal spending. We proceed now to examine its relationship to the problems of slum housing.

CHAPTER IV

Urban Redevelopment and Renewal: The Ultimate Weapon?

AMERICAN CITIES are ugly and sprawling; city visionaries and architects have dreamt of rebuilding them in the image of the "city beautiful." City planning is not really new—Washington, D.C., was a planned community—but the planning *profession* is young. A movement to build model cities and to rebuild old ones in the light of good design belongs to the end of the nineteenth and beginning of the twentieth centuries.[1] In the early years of city planning, paper schemes far outnumbered actual projects. For planners, the process of renewing America was painfully slow. If only sound planning had a base in firm legislation! If only the green belts, open areas, civic centers, boulevards, plazas, and pleasing architectural masses could be realized with generous government aid! Then wishes would be transformed into reality. The planners gradually gathered influential allies. The dream of more beautiful cities was also a dream of cities more economically sound, cities grappling with the social and economic costs of blight. As a first and partial step, zoning laws were passed. Zoning came to be an accepted, though limited, city-planning technique. Other developments followed. State laws authorizing urban redevelopment began to be enacted somewhat later, e.g., by Pennsylvania in 1945.[2] Although many cities engaged in some form of redevelopment planning, the resources allocated were plainly dwarfed by the size of the job. Federal help was badly

---

[1] See, in general, Christopher Tunnard and Henry Hope Reed, *American Skyline* (Boston: Houghton Mifflin, 1956), pp. 142–53; John Reps, *The Making of Urban America* (Princeton, N.J.: Princeton Univ. Press, 1965), covers the nineteenth century background thoroughly.

[2] Laws Pa. 1945, ch. 385; HHFA, *1st Annual Report* (1947), p. 43. For a discussion of the pre-1949 laws, see William H. Brown, "Urban Redevelopment," *Boston University Law Review*, 29 (1949), 318, 327–34.

needed. World War II delayed serious efforts to involve the federal government. When the war ended, the drive to pass a federal law was resumed. A four-year struggle ended with passage of the urban redevelopment law of 1949.[3]

URBAN REDEVELOPMENT

Famous Title I of the 1949 Act,[4] reduced to essentials, offered federal money to subsidize the buying, assembling, and clearing of land for redevelopment. The federal government could make grants under Title I of up to two-thirds of "net project cost." The process contemplated was roughly this: Local authorities would draw up plans, buy land, clear it, and sell it to a private developer. The developer would pay for this land at its market value. This value would be, naturally, less than what the local authority had paid. Before clearance, the land was typically occupied by commercial structures, tenements, rooming houses, and the like. The authority had to pay what these were worth as income-producing properties; instead of using them as such, of course, it tore them down and bulldozed the land. Demolition, too, was an additional cost. The developer paid "fair value"; but it was "fair value" of raw land. Two-thirds of the difference between what the developer paid and the net cost to the local agency would be borne by the federal government; the local community had to pay the other third. The local contribution did not have to be paid in cash. The law allowed the city to make contributions in kind by donating land, by making "site improvements," by providing "parks, playgrounds, and public buildings and facilities."[5]

---

[3] For a concise account of the legislative history, on which much of the account here is based, see Ashley A. Foard and Hilbert Fefferman, "Federal Urban Renewal Legislation," *Law and Contemporary Problems*, 25 (1960), 635. There are a number of studies of urban redevelopment and renewal. I have found two recent ones particularly useful: Scott Greer, *Urban Renewal and American Cities: the Dilemma of Democratic Intervention* (New York: Bobbs-Merrill, 1965); Charles Abrams, *The City Is the Frontier* (New York: Harper, 1965). A good collection of essays on various aspects of renewal has been edited by James Q. Wilson: *Urban Renewal: The Record and the Controversy* (Cambridge, Mass.: M.I.T., 1966).

[4] 63 Stat. 413, 414 (1949); "The Housing Act of 1949," *Illinois Law Review*, 44 (1949), 685.

[5] Title I, §110(d), 63 Stat. 420 (1949). Where a park or other facility benefited both the project and other areas, the Administrator was to prorate the benefits in computing the amount of the local grant-in-aid.

Opposition to urban redevelopment was much more diffuse than opposition to public housing in the post-war period. There was no uniform business opposition. For example, the National Association of Real Estate Boards (NAREB) had been a consistent enemy of public housing; it was much less sure of the proper position to take toward redevelopment. NAREB in 1945 announced that it "strongly favors a program for urban redevelopment." In 1947, the Association reversed itself; in 1949, it mildly criticized the act as passed; by 1954, NAREB was officially in favor of some aspects of urban renewal.[6] In short, urban redevelopment and renewal never drew down upon themselves from this and other conservative real estate groups the kind of bitter opposition which the AMA offered to Medicare. Indeed, few groups seriously attacked the redevelopment provisions of the proposed law in the whole four years of struggle. Some conservative rural congressmen balked at spending their constituents' money to clear up big-city slums. Congressman Meyer of Kansas, for example, asked why "the lowly taxpayers of southeastern Kansas . . . have to contribute to the rebuilding of slums in New Jersey."[7] But the biggest stumbling block to passage was the fact that urban redevelopment was yoked to the unpopular public housing program in one omnibus bill. It was this, rather than any particular intense opposition, that delayed urban redevelopment until 1949.

Urban redevelopment was in fact appealing to many diverse groups; and the act was so framed as to allay some potential doubts. Under the act, the "governing body of the locality" in which a project was to be situated had to approve any redevelopment plan, so that local control or at least local veto was assured. The plan was supposed to "conform" to "a general plan for the development of the locality as a whole." This pleased the planners. The developer, of course, had to agree to devote the land "to the uses specified in the redevelopment plan for the project area." Business interests were pleased that private enterprise had at last been given a chance to show what it could do. Government helped out by assembling land through its powers of eminent domain and by demolishing substandard structures, the product of years of error and decay. But redevelopment was a far cry from the "socialism" of public housing. For the decent, ordinary citizen, the program promised relief from the city's worst blight, its eyesores, its festering slums; for the down-

---

[6] Foard and Fefferman, pp. 635, 642n.
[7] Quoted in *ibid.*, p. 652n.

town merchant, the program promised a chance to revitalize his declining business district which was suffering from suburban competition and the automotive habit.

The urban poor were frequently mentioned in the discussions of the bill. Low-income housing was never far from the center of debate. Contracts with local public agencies for federal aid were to require that the agency have a "feasible method for temporary relocation of families displaced from the project area," and that a supply be made available of equivalent "decent, safe, and sanitary dwellings" at reasonable rents and reasonably accessible to places of employment. The program administrator had to "give consideration" to whether "appropriate local public bodies" had "undertaken positive programs" both to encourage housing cost reductions through building code reform and to prevent "the spread or recurrence, in such community, of slums and blighted areas through the adoption, improvement, and modernization of local codes and regulations relating to land use and adequate standards of health, sanitation, and safety for dwelling accommodations."[8] This provision, the ancestor of the "workable program" requirement,[9] implied, though it did not yet require, stringent use of local housing codes to jack up housing standards in renewal areas, if not elsewhere in the city. Furthermore, urban redevelopment was bound to residential constructon. The 1949 Act limited urban redevelopment projects to areas which, before redevelopment, were "predominantly residential" *or* which were "developed or redeveloped for predominantly residential uses."[10] Thus, by the 1949 law, federal money could be spent for a project only if the area to be redeveloped *had been* a slum or, if it had not been a slum but, for example, a blighted commercial area, the developer planned to convert it into a residential area after the land had been cleared.

But note that it was possible to tear down a slum and put up a totally nonresidential project! Urban redevelopment was not a program to build houses, not a program for sheltering the urban poor, but a program to remake the cities in a physical sense. At the

---

[8] Title I, §101, 63 Stat. 414 (1949). Redevelopment plans had to conform "to a general plan for the development of the locality as a whole." §105(a)(iii), 63 Stat. 417 (1949).

[9] Charles S. Rhyne, "The Workable Program—A Challenge for Community Improvement," *Law and Contemporary Problems*, 25 (1960), 685. F. David Clark, "Basis for Measuring 'Workable Program' Success," *JH*, 19 (1962), 524, 525.

[10] Title I, §110(c), 63 Stat. 420 (1949).

base of the program lay a rigid social-cost approach toward slums and blight. "Blight" was a broader concept than "slum." It was a concept that included dreary, unprofitable, commercial strips, rotting midtown warehouses, and obsolete factories. The social costs of blight were conceived in many different ways. Some people saw them largely as economic costs, e.g., as loss of tax dollars through business decline or as general economic stagnation. In the eyes of city planners, they were the "costs" of bad planning and city decay—vague malconsequences hard to enumerate. Downtown business interests were concerned less with housing than with their own monetary problems as the core of the city eroded economically. Professional planners were less interested in housing than in parking, open spaces, new buildings, civic centers, and other projects that seemed essential to the grand design of the ideal city. The historic social costs of bad housing were only secondary considerations. Those legislators who, like Senator Taft, were deeply concerned with housing reform, did succeed in writing into the law a connection between housing and redevelopment; but this was done in an arbitrary and superficial way through the "predominantly residential" clause.

Nor did the clause in any way require the construction of low-cost housing. The focus of the act was not upon the urban poor, but upon the urban slum; high-cost housing, it was thought, eliminated blight and slum conditions just as efficiently as low-cost housing, and perhaps a good deal more so. Not that anybody deliberately set out to disguise as a low-cost housing program one which was secretly intended to build apartments for the rich; but the act was a planners' and businessmen's act, with nods to the housing worriers. Those who had the "big picture" in mind contemplated urban and regional planning; they wanted to revitalize and reform metropolitan areas and thus counterbalance what seemed to them to be the senseless, planless sprawl of the cities, their decay at the center, and the foolish and uneconomical land uses of blighted zones. Others had a somewhat smaller picture in mind; they saw the end of particular slums in particular areas. But they saw this in purely physical terms: tear down the bad and replace with the good.

Neither group, perhaps, anticipated what in fact took place. Urban redevelopment and its successors became flexible devices, statutory charters under which cities could tap federal coffers for all sorts of hopefully useful purposes. Urban redevelopment could be used to finance big coliseums, for example. Nothing in the act suggested coliseums as one of the purposes of redevelopment; but New York City was willing to interpret the act broadly, and Robert Moses built a coliseum. Washington did not stand in the way.[11] The Columbus Circle project used redevelopment funds. The proper jurisdictional findings were made by local authorities; the area was duly declared to be "substandard." An action was brought in court to stop the project. But the New York Court of Appeals deferred to other agencies: "when [authorized] . . . bodies have made their finding, not corruptly nor irrationally [n]or baselessly, there is nothing for the courts to do about it."[12] The facts of the case showed that the phrase "predominantly residential" was a weak reed indeed. Thirty-nine per cent of the Columbus Circle area was "occupied by nonresidential structures." Yet the neighborhood was residential enough for the agencies and courts. Nothing restrained the authorities from drawing maps in such a way as to include enough houses to meet the statutory requirement. In the coliseum case, opponents of the plan insisted that the lines were gerrymandered. Whether true or not for that case, it is undeniable that lines could be drawn, under the urban redevelopment law, in such a way as to achieve quite diverse ends—not merely housing or slum clearance ends.

---

[11] Congress objected at one point. See *New York Times,* April 10, 1954, p. 1, col. 4. And HHFA disliked unilateral changes in plans made by Moses, *New York Times,* April 20, 1954, p. 1, col. 2. But these were late, technical objections.

[12] *Kaskel* v. *Impellitteri,* 306 N.Y. 73, 115 N.E. 2d 659 (1953). Abrams, pp. 116–23, is a brilliant critique. The attitude underlying *Kaskel* is typical of judicial review (or lack of it) in this field. In *Despatchers' Cafe* v. *Somerville Housing Authority,* 332 Mass. 259, 124 N.E. 2d 528 (1955), plaintiffs complained that the Authority wanted to change a residential area into an industrial park. The court refused to go into the question of administrative motivation. See also *In re Bunker Hill Urban Redevelopment,* 37 Cal. Rptr. 74, 389 P. 2d 538, 574 (1964); and *Housing and Redevelopment Authority of Minneapolis* v. *Minneapolis Metropolitan Co.,* 259 Minn. 1, 104 N.W. 2d 864 (1960).

In *64th St. Residences* v. *City of New York,* 4 N.Y. 2d 268, 150 N.E. 2d 396 (1958), the project was New York's Lincoln Center. The attack in the case, however, was against the acquisition of land by Fordham University. See also *Kimberline* v. *Planning Board of The City of Camden,* 73 N.J. Super. 80, 178 A. 2d 678 (1962) (expansion of Rutgers University); and *Kintzele* v. *City of St. Louis,* 347 S.W. 2d 695 (Mo., 1961) (expansion of St. Louis University; first amendment argument). On the question of what constitutes blight and what constitutes deciding what constitutes blight, see *Wilson* v. *Long Branch,* 27 N.J. 360, 142 A. 2d 836, 854–56 (1958); and *City of Chicago* v. *Zwick,* 27 Ill. 2d 128, 188 N.E. 2d 489 (1963). But see *Bristol Redevelopment and Housing Authority* v. *Denton,* 198 Va. 171, 93 S.E. 2d 288 (1956).

The significant fact about the coliseum case is not that a coliseum was built, and the significant questions are not whether it should have been built and whether it was needed. The significant fact is that all levels of government either positively favored the coliseum or acquiesced in its construction, though the area cleared was not a slum and, indeed, contained relatively few substandard homes. All levels of government by implication assumed or agreed that the best use of this batch of redevelopment money was for a New York coliseum. The program also could be and was used for industrial parks, "civic centers," and other nonhousing purposes. An article in the *New York Times* in late 1963, for example, told of a redevelopment plan for New York's Battery Park which, according to Ada Louise Huxtable, intended "to use the machinery of urban renewal to put together a 12.8-acre site for the [New York] Stock Exchange."[13] Manchester, New Hampshire, got rid of "vest pocket slums" in its downtown area and replaced them with a "much-needed 219-space public parking lot."[14] New York, Chicago, St. Louis, and many other cities have used the program to expand college campuses. By and large, citizen protests coming from displaced tenants and businessmen have been futile; by and large, reviewing agencies have gone along with plans and determinations made by others on the local level. Who, then, shaped the plans under Title I and later legislation? In Newark, where redevelopment and renewal have been notably "successful"—meaning that much has been spent and much has been built—the Housing Authority, under skillful and aggressive leadership, has been prime mover.[15] In other cities, large institutions have dominated or strongly influenced planning and conception of the program. The University of Chicago played this role in the Hyde Park area in Chicago.[16] In still other

---

[13] "Upheaval at Battery," *New York Times*, Oct. 10, 1963, p. 53, col. 5. According to this article "the city justifies applying the urban-renewal process to benefit a private commercial group by pointing out the enormous and pivotal role that the Stock Exchange plays in New York affairs—that is, the public economic good."

[14] "New England's First Completed Renewal Project," *JH*, 14 (1957), 345.

[15] The Newark experience has been described in Harold Kaplan, *Urban Renewal Politics: Slum Clearance in Newark* (New York: Columbia Univ. Press, 1963).

[16] Julia Abrahamson, *A Neighborhood Finds Itself* (New York: Harper, 1959); Peter A. Rossi and Robert A. Dentler, *The Politics of Urban Renewal* (New York: Free Press, 1961).

places, local business groups or downtown merchants have led the way.[17] But in all these instances, the interests served were hardly housing interests. Unlike public housing, urban redevelopment and renewal have been malleable enough to be deflected from a housing course, even if we assume that housing was intended to be the core concern of Title I. But that assumption would be misleading. Housing goals were never a major prop of the program. Indeed, rich flexibility of goals and means has been the strength of Title I. The law provided a vast pot of federal money which local communities may use for a wide range of projects which appeal to them. This is not to minimize the degree of federal control. But federal control has *not* been applied so as to force urban redevelopment to adhere strictly to a housing role or, indeed, to any single formula or goal.

Certainly, it would be vain to expect HUD, or its predecessor, the Housing and Home Finance Agency (HHFA) to stress housing aspects of redevelopment and renewal when Congress itself did not. The legislative history of the program demonstrates legislative impatience with any attempt to bind renewal to housing. Even the minor restraints of the "predominantly residential" clause have been too tight for Congress. The 1954 Housing Act provided that up to 10 per cent of the total amount of capital grants could go to areas which were not "predominantly residential," if they contained "a substantial number of slum, blighted, deteriorated or deteriorating dwellings or other living accommodations, the elimination of which would tend to promote the public health, safety, and welfare" and if these areas were not "appropriate" for residential redevelopment.[18] In 1956, the residential requirement was waived for urban areas "in need of redevelopment or rehabilitation as a result of flood, fire, hurricane, earthquake, storm or other catastrophe."[19] In 1959, the 10 per cent limitation was raised to 20 per cent, and the requirement was excused for "urban renewal areas involving colleges and universities."[20] Still later, hospitals were given the same benefits as colleges and universities,[21] and the 20 per cent limit was increased to 30 per cent.[22] These changes rendered the residential requirement

[17] *New York Times*, July 12, 1965, p. 1. col. 1 (upstate New York).
[18] 68 Stat. at 627 (1954); Foard and Fefferman, pp. 657ff.
[19] 70 Stat. 1101, 1102 (1956).
[20] 73 Stat. 675, 677 (1959).
[21] 75 Stat. 169 (1961); 42 U.S.C.A. §1463.
[22] 75 Stat. 168 (1961).

virtually toothless. Foard and Fefferman, writing in 1960 from posts in the General Counsel's office of the HHFA, at a time when the limitation was only 20 per cent, noted a land-use analysis of 53 municipalities which found that about 73 per cent of the land in developed areas was used for residential purposes. They felt that

> the twenty per cent exception, along with special purpose exceptions, should often be adequate to permit nonresidential urban renewal projects to be undertaken in about the same proportion to predominantly residential projects as nonresidential land use in the locality bears to residential land use.

They saw nothing improper in this trend. They said:

> there seems to be widespread agreement that the federal interest in urban redevelopment does not depend strictly on housing betterment as such . . . [but] on improving the living environment of the urban population,

including "commercial and industrial development" and "public facilities and transportation."[23]

Urban redevelopment showed a predilection for two major kinds of projects. One of these we might call construction-minded, the other clearance-minded. The Columbus Circle area was cleared to build the coliseum that Robert Moses wanted; the urge to clear this particular area did not precede or even influence the plan for a coliseum. This is construction-minded redevelopment; land clearance is valued chiefly as a step to further a specific plan, project, or building. In other cases, the emphasis is on clearance *per se*; i.e., getting rid of obnoxious areas. What is constructed is, in a sense, less important than what is torn down. As an archetype of this kind of project, we may take a venture in Nashville, Tennessee.

> Tennessee's distinctive State capitol at Nashville once was surrounded by some really sorry slums. These now have been leveled, eliminating an eyesore that was increasingly difficult to explain to visitors.[24]

---

[23] Foard and Fefferman, p. 671.

[24] "Slums and Blight, A Disease of Urban Life," address by Urban Renewal Commissioner James W. Follin, delivered on May 3, 1955, and printed as *Urban Renewal Bulletin No. 2* (HHFA). See O. L. Hubbard, " 'Operation Eyesore' Stops Urban Decay," *American City*, 77 (May, 1963), 165 (Dearborn, Michigan).

Similarly, the urge to redevelop parts of St. Louis was stimulated by the fact that

> people going and coming to work . . . are offended by the state of decay they witness. . . . Unfortunately, too, every visitor . . . by train is given a poor impression of St. Louis [by] . . . dismal districts.[25]

The remedy is to eliminate these "dismal districts" as quickly as possible. In fact, many projects do "seem to be chosen for show."[26] In any case—whether a project is chosen for show, for commercial reasons, or to eliminate an eyesore—the welfare of the residents in that particular area is not a central concern of the program.

Both clearance-minded and construction-minded projects are appealing to groups other than residents of the areas affected. Some experts in urban design like bold, radical solutions to the congested ugliness of the city core. They like big clearance and big building. Daniel Burnham, one of the patron saints of these experts, wanted American cities to "make no little plans"; his dreams were big and brassy. Unfortunately, little people sometimes need little plans. The bold solutions of redevelopment have not offered much to the urban underdog. Rather, they have appealed to the pocketbook interests of some city businessmen. Downtown merchants may see direct monetary benefit from a project to replace dirty slums and low-income customers with expensive apartments occupied by people with spending money. The merchants also like federal help for parking ramps and civic centers that bring the customers downtown. Other businessmen sense an onrush of indirect benefits resulting from an enhanced city image. Big redevelopment spreads the idea that the city is a vital, growing place, not a stagnant or decaying community. The reputation of a city is a matter of some importance. There are many adherents to the cult of the shiny, the big, and especially, the new. Clean-lined, "functional," new buildings which embody the latest technological and pseudo-esthetic developments are a valuable goal in themselves. So long as the cult of the new remains strong, businessmen are right in thinking that a dynamic image is an

---

[25] Quoted in George B. Nesbitt, "Relocating Negroes from Urban Slum Clearance Sites," *Land Economics*, 25 (1949), 275.

[26] Greer, p. 91.

important economic asset for their city. It matters less *what* is built than the fact of new buildings. Moreover, bold plans of redevelopment are important to the self-interest and prestige of city leaders and the officials of the local redevelopment authority. The city's enhanced image reflects glory on the mayor and council; a high volume of building, many projects, and acres of clearance add to the empire and the reputation of the authority.

The cult of the new is an important mainstay of clearance-minded redevelopment. Blighted areas seem to be displeasing to the middle class; wide support can be enlisted for projects which destroy them. New construction, whatever its esthetic merits and its contribution, or lack of it, to urban needs and form, can be justified as "better than what was there before." Some cities, in their passion to rid themselves of eyesores, have cleared without stable plans for new construction. The slums are gone, but the fields of rubble stay. Years go by, and the bombed-out look remains. One such area in St. Louis was called Hiroshima Flats by the natives; another in Detroit was "ragweed acres."[27] In Buffalo, 13 years after approval of plans to clear a tract of 160 slum acres, the bulk of the area, called the Ellicott district, was "an overgrown lot with a few junked cars, piles of garbage and rat nests. Trees that were saplings when the land was cleared have grown tall."[28]

Construction-minded redevelopment, especially of the coliseum type, is arguably a perversion of the redevelopment concept. Charles Abrams, for one, has so termed it, stressing particularly its abandonment of the public-housing concept: "Public housing . . . had done its reverence in justifying urban renewal and could now go."[29] Clearance-minded redevelopment at least seems true to the ideal of clearing the slums; but it rests implicitly on a one-sided theory of social costs. Society's losses from the slums are caused presumably by eyesores, by economic "stagnation," and by something called "blight" which has a pathological tendency to spread. The remedy is to clear the slums, that is, the buildings. But where do the people go? They are in theory relocated in better housing. But what is the

---

[27] Roger Montgomery, "Improving the Design Process in Urban Renewal," in Wilson, *Urban Renewal,* pp. 454, 459.

[28] *New York Times,* July 29, 1965, p. 58, col. 1.

[29] Abrams, p. 82.

source of this housing?[30] Relocation has been criticized from the outset. The government insists that "most people displaced by urban renewal find decent housing," and it points to studies which so indicate.[31] But some nagging doubts remain. The quality of the government's studies has been questioned by other housing experts.[32] Some families better themselves, to be sure; but others go from substandard house to substandard house, one step ahead of the bulldozer. Some families move to better houses, but at higher rents that may work a hardship. Some small businesses are crushed to death. The very threat of renewal casts a pall upon a neighborhood. Relocation problems have not generally been allowed to impede urban "progress"; the urge to tear down is stronger than the desire to relocate the poor. Recently, relocation has been strengthened and humanized; new programs of aid to the dispossessed have been devised. A 1964 amendment to Title I authorized not only "reasonable and necessary moving expenses," but also a "relocation adjustment payment" of not more than $500 to help a displaced family find a "decent, safe and sanitary dwelling." This payment was to be computed as the difference between 20 per cent of the annual income of the displaced family and the average 12-month rental for a decent place to live.[33] In effect this may amount to a one-year rent subsidy. Yet, though these programs are better than what preceded them, Charles Abrams calls them "neither enough nor good enough."[34]

---

[30] Martin Anderson, the sharpest and most intemperate of the critics of renewal, has put the question this way:

> If standard housing is available at rents they can afford in convenient locations, why haven't they moved long ago? Perhaps they were not aware of it. If this is the case wouldn't it be far simpler and much cheaper to advise people of these attractive bargains without going to all the trouble of tearing their homes down?

Martin Anderson, *The Federal Bulldozer* (Cambridge, Mass.: M.I.T., 1964), p. 56. Occasionally, a sufficient supply of housing of this kind does exist; and relocation is a "success." See James C. T. Mao, "Relocation and Housing Welfare: A Case Study," *Land Economics*, 41 (Nov., 1965), 365 (Stockton, California).

[31] *New York Times,* Mar. 19, 1965, p. 9, col. 3; "Census Bureau Relocation Report," *JH,* 21 (1965), 210; but see "Inequities Seen in Slum Renewal," *New York Times,* Apr. 27, 1965, p. 44, col. 3, describing a report by the Advisory Commission on Intergovernmental Relations and quite critical of renewal and relocation.

[32] See Alvin L. Schorr, *Slums and Social Insecurity* (London: Thomas Nelson, 1964), pp. 46–50; Abrams, pp. 132–54; and Chester W. Hartman, "Omissions in Evaluating Relocation Effectiveness Cited," *JH,* 23 (1966), 88. A further discussion of evidence and experience appears in Astrid Monson, *et al.,* "Relocation Program," *JH,* 23 (1966), 135–62.

[33] 78 Stat. 788 (1964); 42 U.S.C.A. §1465(c)(1) and (2).

[34] Abrams, p. 153.

The root of the problem lies in the nonwelfare orientation of redevelopment and renewal. Cities, for example, are passionately eager to tear down skid row. But skid row is a social, not an architectural phenomenon.[35] The skid-row bums do not vanish from the earth when their bars and their flophouses vanish. Moreover, renewal tends to judge neighborhoods by looks and to judge looks by the esthetics and the biases of planners and the middle class. Stable, low-income neighborhoods can be destroyed on the basis of criteria which do not fit. Herbert Gans has defended the West End in Boston as a sound place to live for Italian workmen; yet this neighborhood fell before the seige-guns of redevelopment.[36] In a 1960 pamphlet, the government warned of the dangers in a neighborhood of "incompatible land uses," "serious, widespread overcrowding of buildings on the land which robs the area of light, air, and sunshine," and "streets . . . which are unsafe, congested and poorly located."[37] Yet these are characteristic traits of Beacon Hill, Oldtown, Georgetown, and Greenwich Village—districts which are safe from destruction because they are quaint, fashionable, and expensive. Urban redevelopment has been used to tear down areas which, whatever their impact on their residents, offend the eye of some outside beholders and are, like the Nashville slums, "difficult to explain to visitors." It has also been used as an excuse to get back-door federal help for a major building plan like the coliseum. Finding blight merely means defining a neighborhood that cannot effectively fight back, but which is either an eyesore or is well-located for some particular construction that important interests wish to build. The neighborhood must also be one that can be squeezed into some statutory formula. This last is not a critical problem. It can generally be done.

In any event redevelopment and, after it, renewal destroyed thousands of homes and displaced thousands of people. The program itself did not build new homes for the poor. Only a tiny amount of public and low-cost housing was erected on urban renewal sites be-

---

[35] Some cities show an enlightened attitude; see *JH*, 20 (1963), 319 (Detroit proposal for dormitory style public housing for homeless men from skid row).

[36] Herbert J. Gans, *The Urban Villagers* (Glencoe, Ill.: Free Press, 1962), especially pp. 308–26.

[37] These are listed in "Selecting Areas for Conservation," *Urban Renewal Service Technical Guide No. 3* (1960), p. 10, as conditions which, if widespread, cannot be remedied by conservation—that is, they mean the neighborhood is fit only for the bulldozer.

fore 1960.[38] Much more emphasis was placed on luxury and middle-income housing.[39] Arguably this helps the poor, since the good houses and apartments abandoned by the rich will filter down and upgrade the housing for the poor. The arithmetic of this idea is questionable. Even if the idea were sound, it means that the poor are asked to bear the personal costs of disruption and dislocation,[40] while government subsidy enables the middle class and the rich to live in a convenient part of town more cheaply than otherwise. The situation would be grimly ironic, except that a like distribution of burdens and benefits is not uncommon in the history of welfare laws. Social security, for example, is supported by a regressive tax; benefits are scaled not to need but to contribution. To be sure, it suits fairly well some of the middle-class interests that supported it and which benefit by it. Moreover, it avoids the stigma and paternalism of public assistance; but at a cost of failing to meet the needs of those who need the money most. Laws for the benefit of labor tend to preserve jobs for relatively well-paid members of craft unions; they shut out the army of underemployed and unemployed men. Urban redevelopment may be an extreme but not an isolated case. Welfare legislation is not immune to the laws of human nature and of politics. Laws that affect social and economic interests are passed by those who can muster a majority—measured in enthusiasm as well as in upraised hands. And enthusiasm, as a rule, often follows the pocketbook. It is no surprise, then, that urban redevelopment does not aid the urban poor. They were not consulted on its adoption. They have always been represented by proxies who, when the chips are down, abandon with varying degrees of reluctance the claims of the poor in the interests of compromise or some assumed greater good.

---

[38] Anderson, pp. 104, 105; Herman D. Hillman, "Public Housing Sites," *JH*, 19 (1962), 79.

[39] Recently urban renewal has given more of a role to low-income housing. There has been experimentation with various pilot and demonstration programs; and the actual number of low-income projects being built in renewal areas is increasing. In 1964, 55 such developments, containing 7,799 dwelling units, were approved by HHFA. (In 1957, there was only 1 low-income development approved, with 372 dwelling units.) HHFA, *18th Annual Report* (1964), p. 248.

[40] See Marc Fried, "Grieving for a Lost Home: Psychological Costs of Relocation," in Wilson, *Urban Renewal*, p. 359.

URBAN RENEWAL

The Housing Act of 1954[41] was a major overhaul of federal urban policies. Previously, President Eisenhower had appointed a committee to recommend a "new and revitalized . . . program . . . of housing and sound community development."[42] Title I operations under the 1949 Act had not been satisfactory. The redevelopment program had proved difficult to mobilize. Money commitments were far less than authorized. The Renewal Commissioner told Congress in 1954 that "there is plenty of grant money left, and plenty of loan money."[43] The President's Committee reported that $214,000,000 out of the $500,000,000 authorized by Congress for grants to the cities was still "available."[44] Yet the underlying idea of Title I retained solid support. People were still dazzled by the dream of rebuilding the cities. Urban problems were increasingly visible and seemed increasingly complex. The new law, based in part on the Committee's recommendations, was designed to translate the dream into reality. By increasing efficiency and flexibility, the new law aimed to broaden the program and make the federal dollar go farther.

Redevelopment was in essence a bulldozing technique. It tended to throw the baby out with the bathwater; valuable, usable buildings were destroyed along with the slums. In addition, only major capital could undertake to buy an entire cleared area and erect a new "city." Big business had not adequately responded to the bait of redevelopment. Moreover, many areas of the city were on the downgrade but had not yet touched bottom. Spot changes might be enough to arrest their decay. Techniques less radical than the great bulldozer might be effective.

For urban redevelopment the new act substituted a broader concept: urban renewal. Federal support would now be available to help finance a wide variety of projects, not merely bulldozing. Thus, for example, the Administrator could advance funds for urban

---

[41] 68 Stat. 590, 622 (1954).

[42] The President's Advisory Committee on Government Housing Policies and Programs, *Report* (Dec., 1953), p. 1.

[43] Quoted in Abrams, p. 86.

[44] President's Advisory Committee, *Report* (1953), p. 110. Moreover, $110,000,000 of the $286,000,000 "used up" by then simply represented what would "perhaps" be required by "projects now in the planning stages."

renewal projects including "plans for carrying out a program of voluntary rehabilitation of buildings or other improvements" in accordance with an urban renewal plan.[45] Conservation, rehabilitation, and code enforcement were all tools of the new program. An official of HHFA expressed hope that "the old gerrymandering of boundaries will not be confronting us so constantly"; the new act might foster "real neighborhood planning and replanning."[46] The bonds between urban renewal and general urban planning were drawn tighter. No city could qualify for urban renewal funds without a "workable program" to "utilize appropriate private and public resources to eliminate, and prevent the development or spread of, slums and urban blight, to encourage needed urban rehabilitation, [and] to provide for the redevelopment of blighted, deteriorated, or slum areas."[47] The Workable Program promptly acquired capital letters and became a positive set of requirements imposed by Washington on all cities that wished to share in the federal money. Generally, a municipality had to adopt or show itself ready to adopt acceptable building, fire, plumbing, electrical, and housing codes before HHFA would certify its Workable Program. The Program also contemplated a "comprehensive community plan . . . [which] includes plans for land use, thoroughfares, community facilities, and public improvements, as well as zoning and subdivision regulations."[48] The Workable Program concept has gotten tighter over the years. Housing codes, for example, were first authorized and encouraged, then required by HHFA, and finally in 1964 made mandatory by statute.[49]

---

[45] 68 Stat. 624 (1954), on the new programs, see H. N. Osgood and A. H. Zwerner, "Rehabilitation and Conservation," *Law and Contemporary Problems*, 25 (1960), 705.

[46] Richard L. Steiner, "Urban Renewal—Federal Programs," in *Planning 1954* (Chicago: American Society of Planning Officials, 1954), p. 60.

[47] 68 Stat. 623, 624 (1954); 42 U.S.C.A. §1451(c).

[48] Rhyne, pp. 685, 690–91, 692.

[49] ". . . commencing three years after September 2, 1964, no workable program shall be certified . . . unless (A) the locality has had in effect, for at least six months prior to such certification . . . a minimum standards housing code, related but not limited to health, sanitation, and occupancy requirements, which is deemed adequate by the Administrator, and (B) the Administrator is satisfied that the locality is carrying out an effective program of enforcement to achieve compliance with such housing code." 78 Stat. 785 (1964); 42 U.S.C.A. §1451(c).

See HHFA, *15th Annual Report* (1961), pp. 26–27, for a description of the increased administrative importance within HHFA of the Workable Program requirement; and Robert C. Weaver, *The Urban Complex* (Garden City, N.Y.: Doubleday, 1966), pp. 97–105.

After 1954, the urban renewal program continued to develop along lines demanded by its inner logic. Emphasis on overall planning has constantly increased. The Housing Act of 1956 created the concept of the General Neighborhood Renewal Plan (GNRP) which was defined as a "preliminary plan" which outlines the "urban renewal activities proposed for the area involved [and] provides a framework for the preparation of urban renewal plans."[50] A GNRP allows local agencies to make plans of broader scope than previously, e.g., plans for projects which "may have to be carried out in stages, over a period of not more than 10 years, rather than as a single project."[51] In 1959, legislation authorized planning grants for statewide agencies, to help out the planning work of smaller communities, and similar grants to "official State, metropolitan, and regional planning agencies" for planning to cover "entire urban areas."[52] The 1959 Act also introduced grants for the "preparation or completion of community renewal programs" which could include identifying "slum areas or blighted, deteriorated, or deteriorating areas," measuring the blight, determining "the financial, relocation, and other resources needed and available to renew such areas," finding potential project areas, and "scheduling or programing of urban renewal activities."[53] The 1964 Act authorized federal support of code-enforcement projects and a new program of rehabilitation loans.[54] The simple view of 1949—that government's role and subsidy could be limited to assembling and clearing tracts of land—has been obscured if not buried under layers of complexity.

Urban Renewal and Local Communities

The Workable Program requirements seem to be symptoms of tight federal control; moreover, HHFA (now HUD) puts out an Urban Renewal Manual, in three volumes, full of rules, regulations, stipulations, and requirements. Despite all this, the localism of renewal is striking, persistent, and unabated. Nothing in any of the renewal acts took away the veto power of local governing bodies. At many

---

[50] 70 Stat. 1099 (1956).

[51] HHFA, *10th Annual Report* (1956), p. 246.

[52] 73 Stat. 672 (1959).

[53] 73 Stat. 672 (1959); 42 U.S.C.A. §1453(d); see HHFA, 15th *Annual Report* (1961), p. 294; Howard Hallman, "The Community Renewal Program (The CRP)," *JH*, 19 (1962), 70.

[54] 78 Stat. 785, 790–91 (1964); Melvin Stein, "The Housing Act of 1964: Urban Renewal," *New York Law Forum,* 11 (1965), 1, 3–5, 11–12.

specific points this is made explicit. So, for example, contracts for
surveys and plans under the 1954 Act called for approval by the
"governing body of the locality involved."[55] Local control is, indeed,
of three sorts. First of all, the local public agency, i.e., the renewal
body proper, proposes even if some other body disposes; and without proposals there are no disposals. Second, the local "governing
body" plays a major role, both legally and factually. Few, if any,
projects are built which arouse the detestation of a city council.
Third, citizen participation is built into the law. The Act of 1954
included in its definition of an "urban renewal project" a project
which carried out "plans for a program of voluntary repair and
rehabilitation of buildings."[56] This implied some kind of formal or
informal public association, perhaps modeled after those of the Baltimore plan. In conservation projects, neighborhood associations
played a critical role. One of the requirements of a Workable Program, without which urban renewal plans could not be certified,
was "citizen participation."[57] Federal acts encourage, cajole, bribe,
and sometimes compel local action once it is initiated; yet action
taken in response to federal urging is nonetheless local in concept
and execution. And projects almost invariably originate locally.
Washington does not drum them up.

The three types of local control result in extremely subtle and
complicated political adjustments and maladjustments in the cities.
The tremendous increase in federal emphasis on planning has been
balanced, if not frustrated, by the legal and factual need to appease
local politicians and their neighborhoods. In many local communities, subcommittees have sprung up, which mold their own plans or
unmold the plans of others. There are rehabilitation and renewal
projects in which the prime mover is a tight little neighborhood
association and other projects in which such a neighborhood association is the prime immovable.[58]

Local participation is highly praised in Washington and elsewhere. Urban renewal on the neighborhood level looks like grass-
roots democracy at work. Indeed, urban renewal does reflect

---

[55] See 68 Stat. 624–25 (1954); §304(d), and §307, Housing Act of 1954.

[56] 42 U.S.C.A. §1460(c)(5).

[57] See the excellent study, Comment, "Citizen Participation in Urban Renewal,"
Columbia Law Review, 66 (1966), 485.

[58] Rossi and Dentler, *The Politics of Urban Renewal*, richly document the role
of organizations in the struggles for and against renewal of the University of
Chicago neighborhood.

grass-roots sentiment, but of a somewhat special and very complicated type. Money and effort are spent ratifying the plans of local
institutions, such as colleges, churches, and hospitals, of local merchants, and of local politicians. Washington's control over urban
renewal, in essence, merely generalizes the desires of local communities and turns them into vaguely worded rules. And in some respects
there is no federal control at all. Criticism that a renewal plan for
Salem, Massachusetts, was insensitive to historic and esthetic values
brought these reported comments from Dorn McGrath, the head of
project planning and engineering for URA:

> Federal review of local urban renewal plans does not judge
> quality or suitability; it is concerned with legal compliance.
> There . . . are no design criteria . . . [U]rban renewal is not
> much more than the power of eminent domain. It acquires and
> clears the land. It plans and builds nothing. That is local respon-
> sibility.[59]

The renewal program has been in part the enthronement of middle-class, suburban values, in part a subsidization of commercial
aims and goals, in either case sugar-coated with a veneer of "city
planning." Local-run renewal can be defended as a form of coopta-
tion,[60] a means of safeguarding the program by absorbing local interests into the program, securing their consent, minimizing potential
opposition, but paying a high price in that the program must commit itself to policies and plans favored by the coopted groups. Or
it can be compared, for example, with occupational licensing in
which, ostensibly for the best of motives, trade groups create puppet
governmental agencies; through these agencies they govern their
membership and forward group interests as they perceive them; typically, they legitimize their private government in the name of the
public good, posing as the regulated while in fact behaving as the
regulators.[61] This is not to say that HUD is the prisoner or the
puppet of, for example, redevelopment and renewal bodies func-
tioning in Omaha or Atlanta. The interaction among the federal

---

[59] Ada Louise Huxtable, "Urban Renewal Plan Threatens Historic Sites in
Salem, Mass.," *New York Times*, Oct. 13, 1965, p. 31, col. 2, p. 51, col. 3.
[60] The classic study is Philip Selznick, *TVA and the Grass Roots: A Study in
the Sociology of Formal Organization* (New York: Harper, 1966), especially pp.
13, 217.
[61] See Lawrence M. Friedman, "Freedom of Contract and Occupational Licensing 1890–1910: A Legal and Social Study," *California Law Review*, 53 (1965),
487, 494–510.

government, local agencies and neighborhood associations is complicated; waves of power and submission move from one to the other.
But no yoke can be imposed on local communities, in the long run,
which they do not choose for themselves.

Renewal plans are, and continue to be, highly controversial in
specific instances; renewal in the abstract is much less so. Some
communities have turned down renewal; others will do so in the
future. This political situation is perfectly natural, since the program is essentially a sweepstakes prize of federal money which can
be used as powerful leverage by one group against another; one of
the few defenses of the defeated is to use the counterleverage of the
polls. Urban renewal takes sides; it uproots and evicts some for the
benefit of others; no wonder then that it creates much controversy.
And yet some profess to be baffled by the controversy and find it
incredible that so many people fight progress.

Since renewal controversies are so highly local, they cannot be
easily generalized. Probably no one political or social factor can
explain why renewal "succeeds" in Newark, "fails" in St. Louis, and
is defeated at the polls in South Milwaukee. We would even find it
hard to agree on a definition of success and failure. But the program
lends itself to a diversity of experience. It invites the clash of local
interests. In some communities particular interests are stronger than
others. But one might guess that everywhere the worst losers would
be those with least economic or political leverage—the poor. And
indeed, the poor do seem to be the losers, even in a program that
sometimes claims to be for their benefit. They lose their homes, their
small businesses, their community organization. What they gain, if
anything, are hand-me-down houses and a few of the jobs generated
by the federal spending on construction and demolition.

Urban Renewal and the Poor

Local control is arguably "democratic" in the sense of seeking
constant advice and consent from the people affected by government
programs. Yet local control lends strength to the forces which want
to preserve income segregation. A neighborhood can mobilize itself
to clean out pockets of blight; a community may conserve neighborhoods in danger of succumbing to this urban disease. Conservation
can be used to foster race segregation and income segregation. Undoubtedly many communities have helped themselves to federal

money and power for precisely this purpose. Even under the Act of 1949, some communities used redevelopment for "Negro removal."[62] Redevelopment was particularly suitable for small suburban communities with, for example, only a single Negro section near the railroad tracks. If this one site were redeveloped, the suburb could rid itself of its eyesore, upgrade its image, and enhance its property values. At the same time the suburb could solve its race problem by exporting nonwhites to the urban core where they belonged. Urban renewal was, therefore, an additional reason why it was valuable for a neighborhood or community entity to constitute a legal entity as well. A city or incorporated village has effective means to control the race and income of its residents through zoning ordinances, architectural control, and other land-use techniques, if not through blunter methods. Renewal added one more to the arsenal of techniques. It made it possible to clear blight that happened to correspond to the poor part of town or, better yet, the Negro section. Moreover, the federal government would pay much of the cost.[63] Large cities are too sprawling and heterogeneous to be able to clear out all undesirable people and places through land-use controls or through redevelopment. This indeed was one reason why annexation has been unattractive to suburban towns since the turn of the century. Urban renewal helped make up for the weakness of city neighborhoods compared to suburban towns and villages. Neighborhoods might form structures that were the functional equivalents of suburban governments. Techniques of income and race segregation that had been available only to suburbs became available to quasi-suburbs in the city. An amendment to the Illinois Neighborhood Redevelopment Corporation Law in 1953 authorized formation of companies to "conserve" neighborhoods which were "deteriorating" as well as to eliminate "slums." With the consent to its plan of the owners of 60 per cent or more of the land in its area, a Neighborhood Redevelopment Corporation could have that mighty symbol of sovereignty, the power of eminent domain. The law was forged by the leaders of the Hyde Park-Kenwood community, who were

---

[62] The phrase is widely used; see *New York Times*, July 26, 1965, p. 11, col. 1 (Danbury, Conn.). See also, in regard to Hyde Park-Kenwood, Elinor Richey, "Splitsville, U.S.A.," *Reporter*, 28, No. 11 (May 23, 1963), 35. But see the defense by Weaver, *The Urban Complex*, pp. 132–37.

[63] Abrams, p. 145.

engaged in a struggle to roll back the slums on Chicago's south side.[64] Although the slums that surrounded the neighborhood were Negro, the leaders of Hyde Park-Kenwood were probably less concerned with race than with culture and class. Other quasi-suburbs have probably not been so particular.

Recently, there has been much discussion of how to democratize urban renewal and how to maximize a benign kind of citizen control. In truth, citizen control means many different things, depending upon the nature of the project and its effect on particular citizens. It is futile to ask people if they want their houses torn down; a solid, perhaps violent, "No" is the inevitable answer. "In clearance areas," said one local official, "you don't organize [participation]; you prepare people for moving."[65] James Q. Wilson has suggested that "the higher the level of indigenous organization in a lower-class neighborhood, the poorer the prospects for renewal in that area."[66] Lower-class organizations fight urban renewal because it hurts them; middle-class organizations mold urban renewal to their tastes which include, all too often, income segregation and race seggregation. Citizen participation of the middle-class type may have many valuable consequences; but it carries a price in disruption of lives of the poor. The jury system, too, is a valuable check on potential tyranny, yet the jury can be a weapon of tyranny when, as in the deep South, public opinion is itself antidemocratic. Washington has, by and large, been willing to pay the price of this kind of citizen participation. More accurately, it has been willing to let the poor pay it. Just as segregation in public housing was winked at or even fostered by PHA for many years, so the dysfunctions of urban renewal were long accepted by administrators as necessary if not downright desirable. Since the rise of the Negro protest movement, government has become more sensitive to the problem.

---

[64] Laws Ill. 1953, p. 1138, §2, Ill. Stats. Ann. 67½ §292(1)(a); Rossi and Dentler, pp. 85–86; see Comment, " 'Conservation'—A New Area for Urban Redevelopment," *University of Chicago Law Review*, 21 (1954), 489.

See Cal. Health & Safety Code §33701 (redevelopment plans to "provide for participation" of owners of property in redevelopment areas); and "Conservation and Rehabilitation of Housing: An Idea Approaches Adolescence," *Michigan Law Review*, 63 (1965), 892, 893–94.

[65] Edmund M. Burke, "Citizen Participation in Renewal," *JH*, 23 (1966), 18, 20.

[66] James Q. Wilson, "The Citizen in the Renewal Process," *JH*, 20 (1963), 622, 625. For a critique of some of Wilson's views, see Comment, "Citizen Participation in Urban Renewal," *Columbia Law Review*, 66 (1966), 485, 598.

Despite the fact that urban renewal was not directly beneficial to the urban poor, supporters of the program customarily placed heavy rhetorical emphasis on the evils of the slums and what slums did to the people who lived in them. James W. Follin, Commissioner of URA in 1955, made an argument typical for its time. In a speech (later printed) called "Slums and Blight . . . a disease of urban life,"[67] the Commissioner excoriated blight as a "kind of cancer. . . . Unless checked, it tears at the very foundations of urban life." The wise businessman constantly "renews and improves his facilities" to avoid falling behind "in the competition for markets"; so the wise city must undertake renewal "for its very survival." So far, this was tough-minded economic talk. Next, Follin introduced Gussie, an imaginary little girl, to act as the "symbol of the deadly effect of slums on human lives." Gussie is pictured as a big-eyed, forlorn-looking child; she holds a limp doll in her arm and stands in a heap of garbage. Gussie lives in the slums where she witnesses the "old, ugly story" of "killing diseases, vicious crime and juvenile delinquency, charred bodies in tinderboxes, infants assailed by rats and vermin," and, in short, "shattered American lives." In a later picture, Gussie is shown smiling at a big broom labeled "Code Enforcement"; the broom is cleaning up some of the garbage. There follows a glowing description of urban redevelopment and renewal. In the last picture Gussie, forlorn no longer, grins broadly at the world. "Her community has achieved its goal of urban renewal and she looks forward to a better way of life." Her city has benefited, too; it takes in more tax money, and "commerce and industry have expanded." But a certain gap in the logic remains unplugged; during the discussion of the mechanics and structure of renewal, no mention is made of the precise impact of renewal on Gussie. How did she earn her grin? Was it because her home was replaced by luxury apartments, a civic center, a park, or a college campus? If cheap and decent housing was built for her, Commissioner Follin oddly failed to make mention of it.

Failure to make a connection between Gussie and the actual process of renewal awakens the suspicion that Gussie is merely a propaganda tool. The same *non sequitur* crops up over and over again in discussions of renewal, rehabilitation, and conservation. How are poor Negroes and poor urban whites helped by neighbor-

---

[67] *Urban Renewal Bulletin No. 2* (1955).

hoods which upgrade themselves? They upgrade themselves by getting rid of Negroes and poor whites. Great praise has been poured
on such one-time slums as Oldtown in Chicago,[68] now a mecca of
quaint shops, elegant town-houses, and popular coffee-houses. It is
no longer a place of destitution and economic despair. But where
are the people who once lived there? It is not at all clear that they
have bettered themselves along with the neighborhood. The opposite result is quite possible. In recent years, the relationship of
urban renewal to the poor has been discussed in more realistic
terms. Yet the sufferings of the poor are still used as an argument
for altering neighborhoods in the physical sense. William R. Slayton,
Commissioner of URA, said in 1963 that "renewal is a necessary and
desirable means of eliminating blight, aiding those people afflicted
by it."[69] We applaud an improved neighborhood, like a repentant
sinner who has abandoned his evil companions. Is it peoples' lives
we are concerned with or their buildings?

Political compromises are bound to occur as urban renewal
dreams become realities; naturally, these compromises tend to be
at the expense of the urban poor. The urban poor live mostly in
the biggest cities. The worst slums are located where they live. But
to sell renewal politically, it had to provide something for everyone; consequently, there is renewal for places like Madison, Wisconsin, Santa Barbara, California, and Lincoln, Nebraska, as well
as for Chicago and New York. According to URA statistics, "late
1964 tallies show that some 70 per cent of the 800 cities carrying out
1600 federally-assisted urban renewal projects had populations of
less than 50,000."[70] Politically, renewal must help suburbs as well
as central cities. Yet this policy strengthens the hand of suburbs who
want "Negro removal" or who plan to maintain patterns of income
segregation. Money goes to protect the economic position of the
older suburbs by revitalizing their downtown areas. Some of these
are converted to shopping centers. They can, therefore, compete
better with the downtowns of the central city, which are also using
renewal money to revitalize themselves. The government robs Peter
to pay Paul and then robs Paul to pay Peter again. These inner con-

[68] "Chicago Slum Street Changes into a Mecca for Shopping and Fun," *Wall Street Journal*, Feb., 1965, p. 1, col. 4.

[69] William R. Slayton, "The Operation and Achievements of the Urban Renewal Program," in Wilson, *Urban Renewal*, pp. 189, 229.

[70] "Small City Renewal Job," *JH*, 22 (1965), 251.

traditions of urban renewal have become more apparent with the passage of time; controversy over the program has become quite strident. A polemic and scholarly literature of opposition to urban renewal has begun to develop.[71] In addition, renewal has suffered serious setbacks in many communities where it has been forced to the vote. Curious and shifting coalitions of far right, far left, and every gradation in between have opposed particular renewal proposals.[72] Home-owners have revolted against the bulldozer. Their opposition is one root of the policy shift toward emphasis on neighborhood conservation. Conservation enlists the aid, not the opposition, of small home-owners with working-class backgrounds, though sometimes the Negro serves as overt or covert bogeyman.

Nonetheless, urban renewal is here to stay. Federal aid to the cities will grow increasingly voracious of federal funds. The new cabinet post of Housing and Urban Development is a straw in the wind. Urban renewal is one of the jewels in the crown of this newest department. Urban renewal, after all, despite its political troubles, has many ways to disarm opposition. It makes enchanting promises to solve urban problems and holds out glittering visions of the City Beautiful; it gives voice to slogans of humanitarianism and covers itself with the banners of the war on poverty; moreover, in any given case, urban renewal can appeal to strong economic or political

---

[71] Most egregiously, Martin Anderson in *The Federal Bulldozer,* a bitter attack on the economics and welfare results of urban renewal. The book was greeted with horror and dismay by professionals; e.g., "Urban Renewal Issues," *JH,* 22 (1965), 92; " 'Federal Bulldozer's' Fallacies," *JH,* 22 (1965), 199. A more balanced review is Scott Greer's "Far from the Heavenly City," *The Nation,* Jan. 25, 1965, p. 87. Anderson can be dismissed as a troglodyte; but some of his charges are annoyingly hard to refute. He has gained some strange bedfellows, e.g., Herbert Gans in *The Urban Villagers* and later writings, and Charles Abrams in *The City Is the Frontier.* This last book, gentle and judicious in tone, and written by a housing expert of enormous prestige, will not be easily ignored. Another recent, very thoughtful, and beautifully executed critique is Warren Lehman, "Thinking Small about Urban Renewal," *Washington University Law Quarterly* (1965), 396. It is interesting, too, to look back at Henry Churchill's predictions in *The City Is the People* (New York: Reynal & Hitchcock, 1945), pp. 170–74.

[72] See, for example, "Phoenix Repeals Housing Code, Renewal," *JH,* 18 (1961), 287; "Referenda in Five Cities," *JH,* 19 (1962), 31; "Urban Renewal Bond Issues Bite the Dust in Two Missouri Referenda Votes," *JH,* 19 (1962), 73; Donald H. Bouma, "What's Behind 'Yes' and 'No' Votes When Housing and Renewal Are Issues on Local Ballots?" *JH,* 20 (1963), 628; "Newburgh Divided on Urban Renewal Plan," *New York Times,* May 7, 1965, p. 43, col. 1; "Urban Renewal Gains Upstate; Residents' Fears Yield to Need," *New York Times,* July 12, 1965, p. 1, col. 2, p. 14, col. 1.

interests. Not least of all is its bureaucratic power, not only in Washington, but in the hundreds of local agencies created in states, cities, and villages—agencies which will fight for their life with great passion. The program, then, may be wounded or altered; it may be transmuted or absorbed into a Model Cities program; it may change names; but it will not die. Its critics can only hope that new plans and proposals to humanize renewal will shift the emphasis in renewal in a welfare direction. Some aspects of renewal, e.g., housing-code enforcement and stimulation of the economy, may genuinely help the urban poor. But the urban renewal program, as it exists, was not designed as a plan to solve the housing problems of the poor, nor has it acted as such. Without radical change, it never will.

CHAPTER V

The Current Scene and Future Prospects

THIS STUDY has assumed that housing the poor is a matter of government concern. Some people feel that it is best to leave housing alone; the rich will build for themselves, and their houses will filter down to the poor. Some feel it is hopeless to tamper with the market. Others argue that it is senseless to single out housing. The poor need jobs and money; give them these, and they will take care of their housing themselves. These are serious points of view. This study avoids confronting them. It assumes that its readers feel a duty of government toward the poor. It also assumes that, at least for now, government will treat slum housing specially, as a problem separable from other problems of the poor; it assumes that programs specifically concerned with slum housing will be debated, evaluated, and tried. This chapter and the epilogue should be read with these assumptions in mind.

Bright promise has been followed by disenchantment several times in the history of housing. Tenement-house laws, model tenements, and public-housing programs all failed to live up to the dreams of reformers. Disillusionment with urban renewal is also running deep. The program has absorbed large amounts of money and energy; it has no serious prospect of housing the poor safely and honorably. Indeed, as we have seen, housing the poor is hardly part of its program at all. The search continues for new arms and new ideas.

Efforts are being made to intensify certain old programs, such as code enforcement. These efforts do not attack the problem at its roots. Code enforcement, for example, cannot in itself provide enough good housing for the poor. It cannot cure overcrowding in one area without creating overcrowding in another. Of course, it may be worthwhile to improve and intensify code enforcement and to reform the housing bureaucracy, even if the whole of the housing problem cannot be solved this way. There is no reason not to solve little problems merely because big ones are intractable. It is good to cure minor and sporadic injustices and to strengthen limited but useful programs. If New York City, for example, sets up a centralized, prompt, and efficient office, with a single telephone number, to handle tenants' housing complaints, one can only applaud. A phone number will never clear the slums of Harlem or integrate the poor into American society; but it might help particular people in particular ways. A war on red tape may make it possible to give tenants better service; it may keep them from freezing in winter and roasting in summer. In the long run, however, the housing problem cannot be solved by a crackdown or, for that matter, by codes or by rent strikes or receivership laws.

Existing laws, including the housing codes, are ineffective. This is due in part to defects inherent in the state of mind which led to their enactment. Programs to punish and destroy the evil slum landlord have helped to create or at least perpetuate the evil slum landlord. Intensification projects and administrative reforms run the risk of making slum housing more expensive than ever before, both financially and emotionally. A program of hatred and coercion may make some landlords give heat, make repairs, and get rid of their rats. But the crackdown approach is indirect and perhaps self-defeating. It does not provide new investment in the slums; it discourages it. Something new must be tried.

No one can complain that new tactics are not being considered. In the last few years, new programs, strategies, plans, and devices have sprouted like dandelions. Some of them are pregnant with great hope. The so-called rent subsidy or supplement is one of these. The rent subsidy is really two plans. One is a plan to pay low-income families a subsidy "equal to the difference between the amount that the applicant is able to pay and the amount of the actual rent to be charged."[1] Public-housing rents are subsidized, but the subsidy is available only to people who live in the government's houses.

---

[1] Robert K. Brown, *Public Housing in Action* (Pittsburgh: Univ. of Pittsburgh Press, 1959), p. 88. The idea is not entirely novel. See a discussion of a rent "certificate" plan—substantially a rent subsidy—in *JH*, 1 (1944), 10; The President's Advisory Committee on Government Housing Policies and Programs, *Report* (1953), pp. 261–64; Carol Aronovici, "Housing the Poor: Mirage or Reality," *Law and Contemporary Problems*, 1 (1933), 148, 156.

Under the rent-subsidy plan proper, the subsidized poor could live in middle-income housing, if they wished. The government would pay part of their rent. Ultimately, the increased demand for decent housing at reasonable cost would stimulate private enterprise to build enough new houses, and the slums would wither away. This program has extremely avid supporters in high places. The New York Housing Authority announced in May, 1966, that it intended "to buy 2,000 to 3,000 apartments in publicly financed middle-income cooperatives and rent them as public housing at normal rates."[2] In a number of cities, experiments in this kind of subsidy were carried out as demonstration projects.[3] The Johnson Administration was convinced the effort was worth a further try. The 1965 Housing Act contained a modest program authorizing public-housing authorities to lease space in private buildings.[4] Functionally, this is similar to the first form of rent subsidy; the authority, however, signs the lease rather than the tenant.

The success of this form of rent subsidy is not easily judged in advance. The program has gotten off to a rather slow start. To make a serious impact, the program would have to be pursued on a grand scale; if this were done, the short-run effects might be a general rise in rents, since there would be no immediate increase in supply but a great increase in demand for housing of a certain quality. An even more serious obstacle is the attitude of the middle class. What the program, in essence, plans to do—and what *must* be done—is to strike at the heart of race and income segregation. But the middle class and working class are not apt to be happy at the prospect of low-income neighbors. In New York State, the voters killed, by referendum, a proposal called LIFE (Low Income Financing Experiment) which planned to produce 5,000 low-rent subsidized apartments in middle-income projects.[5] More recently, pilot projects of a similar nature in New York City have evoked bitter reactions from middle-class tenants.[6] The mixing of full-pay and subsidized tenants is most palatable if the subsidized tenants differ from their neighbors in income only, that is, if they belong to the submerged or potential middle class, both

---

[2] *New York Times*, May 5, 1955, p. 1, col. 5, p. 36, col. 4.

[3] Commonwealth of Massachusetts, *Final Report of the Special Commission on Low-Income Housing* (Boston: April, 1965), pp. 84–89.

[4] Title I of P. L. 89–117, §103, 79 Stat. 451 (1965).

[5] State of New York, *Report of the Joint Legislative Committee on Housing and Urban Development* (1963), p. 37.

[6] See the account in *New York Times*, Mar. 1, 1965, p. 1, col. 4, p. 24, col. 4.

Negro and white. The problem poor are not made socially acceptable by subsidy. Those who do not fit in respectable society will continue not to fit, at least for a while; and respectable society will continue to resent their proximity. Successful experiments have been those which carefully selected their tenants. An Ann Arbor project which mingled subsidized and unsubsidized old people in one building was of this type. Although their present incomes were low, tenants "represented" the "lower half of the middle class"; they were "clergymen, nurses, librarians, school superintendents, teachers, small businessmen, store clerks, and factory foremen." The population was "fairly homogeneous." There were "few status differentials."[7] A program in Washington, D.C., leased 50 houses from private owners and inserted low-income tenants in them. But the tenants were carefully selected to blend in with their surroundings: "Evidence of good housekeeping potential was essential for families selected."[8] The law carefully protects local option; the federal leasing program does not "apply to any locality unless the governing body of the locality has by resolution approved the application of such provisions to such locality."[9] Consequently, it will be hard to use leasing in the white suburbs which strangle major cities.

Another kind of rent subsidy was also made part of the 1965 Housing Act.[10] It was an attempt to goad private enterprise into building more housing for the poor. The plan thus can be compared to the model-tenement movement, but with this difference: the builder charges fair market rental, and the government picks up the difference between the rent and one fourth of the tenant's income. The program as enacted has many interesting features. For example, individuals and profit-making corporations are not authorized to build qualifying housing under the act; only nonprofit corporations, limited-dividend companies, and the like may receive the subsidy. There are important justifications for such a provision; but classic prejudices against the ordinary slum landlord are part of the reason for this provision. By now, of course, such prejudices

[7] Wilma Donahue, "Rent Supplement Experiment," *JH*, 22 (1965), 477.

[8] Edward Aronov and Hamilton Smith, "Large Families, Low Incomes, Leasing," *JH*, 22 (1965), 482, 483. See also, on the New York state program, James W. Gaynor, "Subsidized, Unsubsidized Tenants," *JH*, 22 (1965), 493; *New York Times*, Mar. 1, 1965, p. 1, col. 4; on a leasing program in New York City, *New York Times*, Jan. 31, 1966, p. 1, col. 6, p. 17, col. 3.

[9] P. L. 89–117, §103, 79 Stat. 451 (1965).

[10] Title I, P. L. 89–117, §101, 79 Stat. 451 (1965).

may be warranted in many cities. One point of the act is to entice into housing a respectable class of owners and operators. Respectability, however, is equated with limited profits or no profits at all. Moreover, the act shows distinct traces of a search for the submerged and potential middle class. The Administration, in fact, had originally proposed a bill which would extend the subsidy to the lower ranks of the honorable middle class. Here Congress demurred. Under the act as passed, no one can qualify as a tenant unless his income is "below the maximum amount which can be established in the area . . . for occupancy in public housing dwellings." But Congress kept the Administration's "categorical" approach to the selection of tenants. The rent subsidy is limited to families who have been "displaced by governmental action," to the elderly who are "sixty-two years of age or older," to the physically handicapped, and to those occupying substandard housing or housing in a "disaster area" which "has been extensively damaged or destroyed as the result of such disaster."

Success of a program like the rent subsidy cannot be measured by whether a pilot program works. Success is volume; and the most damning thing that can be said of the rent subsidy is that Congress has been desperately shy of voting any funds. The rent subsidy barely attained a toe-hold in the 1965 Housing Act. "Renticare" passed the House of Representatives by six votes, and the Senate by seven;[11] but Congress refused to grant money other than for planning the program and drawing up regulations.[12] That a scaled-down program could barely clear Congress in a session of unparalleled Democratic strength was ominous. In 1966, it took extraordinary efforts by President Johnson to coax out of Congress the paltriest sum for the program. The ins and outs of this legislative struggle would weary all but the most dedicated reader. The meaning of the struggle is clear, however. The rent subsidy goes against the Congressional grain. This is a symptom of deep distrust of the program among the Congressmen's constituents. The source of this distrust may well be the fear of low-income neighbors. The rent supplement, in other words, faces the same pitfalls as the leasing program: it will have trouble getting enough money, and it will have trouble placing anybody but members of the submerged and potential middle class. Within these severe limitations, no doubt the subsidy can do some

---

[11] *New York Times*, July 16, 1965, p. 1, col. 4.
[12] *New York Times*, Oct. 22, 1965, p. 26, col. 1.

good. But in the short run, the rent subsidy is unlikely to provide a major solution to the housing problems of the very poor.

Another great hope has been to use some form of rehabilitation to conquer the slums. Can government, private foundations, or subsidized free enterprise provide good housing for the poor by buying and repairing existing houses?[13] This is not the same idea as neighborhood conservation under the urban renewal laws. The idea is to fix up houses, not quarantine neighborhoods, and thus to serve the poor, not shut them out. Better housekeeping and improved community facilities will upgrade the neighborhood for those who already *live* there, not for a "better" class; people are not to be displaced merely because they are poor. It is an exciting idea in many ways: public housing without its defects of design, code enforcement without punishment and segregation, renewal without snobbery and relocation. Particularly attractive is the idea of avoiding the misery of dislocation which large-scale building inevitably brings. In some pilot programs, tenants have remained in their apartments while buildings were upgraded.[14] Rehabilitation has in recent years captured the imagination of government and of private foundations.[15] Since foundation buildings are usually expected to break even or a little better, foundation participation has many overtones of the model-tenement movement.

Rehabilitation can obviously succeed in each particular instance. No "pilot programs" are necessary to demonstrate that pouring enough money and services into a building and its tenants will improve the building and the tenants. Who will provide the money? Code enforcement programs seek to make private landlords bear the cost. This is only feasible if the amounts required are such that the buildings will still be profitable after the money is spent. It may also be feasible in small sections of big cities and in big sections of very

---

[13] See 75 Stat. 168 (1961).

[14] *New York Times*, June 27, 1963, p. 53, col. 2. Some programs have acquired houses, fixed them up, and resold them. See "Rehab Program Uses Architects," *JH*, 19 (1962), 64.

[15] *New York Times*, May 4, 1964, p. 31, col. 1 (work of Conservation, Rehabilitation and Renewal Foundation, financed by Laurence Rockefeller); *New York Times*, April 14, 1965, p. 43, col. 1 (work of foundations and City of New York). The *Times* reported on July 14, 1965, p. 58, col. 1, that a "syndicate of real estate investors, who prefer to remain anonymous, plan to purchase and rehabilitate as many as forty run-down residential buildings," aided by city loans. Another "pilot project" was announced on July 28, 1965. *New York Times*, July 28, 1965, p. 54, col. 1.

small cities. But in the heart of the slums, rehabilitation has to be nonprofit or low-profit. Private rehabilitation there is not possible without massive subsidy. Low-income householders, under the 1965 Housing and Urban Redevelopment Act, can qualify for outright grants of up to $1,500 to repair their buildings.[16] This is a good idea and a humane one; but it probably applies more to shanty-towns than to the tenement districts of big cities. The potential class of beneficiaries is probably too small for any major impact. Yet the use of a massive subsidy would turn rehabilitation into a form of public housing. Philanthropic foundations probably do not have enough money to do the job unaided. Moreover, foundations tend to be fickle. They may have their fling and turn elsewhere for promising "pilot studies."

Rehabilitation by government is another story. Philadelphia's Housing Authority has initiated a "used house" program of buying "old houses in decent communities," rehabilitating them, then furnishing them to poor families. In this way the "stigma of massive projects is . . . avoided."[17] In 1965, the Philadelphia City Council created a nonprofit city corporation to buy and rehabilitate substandard housing for sale or rental to low-income families.[18] Some cities are combining experiments in rehabilitation with attempts to humanize public housing, to soften the blow of urban renewal, and to increase social and racial integration, or to do all of these things. In planning the West Side Urban Renewal Area in New York City, announcement was made of provisions for "vest-pocket" public housing, for middle-income housing with slots reserved for low-income tenants who may remain in their homes even though their income rises, for extensive rehabilitation of existing houses, and for a carefully staged and phased program of construction to minimize the tortures of relocation.[19]

[16] 79 Stat. 457–8 (1965). *New York Times,* Dec. 24, 1965, p. 19, col. 8; *Chicago Sun-Times,* Mar. 23, 1966, p. 84, col. 1.

[17] Philip Herrera, "Philadelphia: How Far Can Renewal Go?" *Architectural Forum,* 121 (Aug.–Sept., 1964), 190. See also David Hunter, *The Slums* (New York: Free Press, 1964), pp. 237–38.

[18] "Philadelphia Seeks Low Income Housing Via City Corporation," *JH,* 22 (1965), 203.

[19] Described by Delma Dennehy, "Progress in Strategy: New York Turns to 'Invisible Renewal' to Save Its West Side," *Architectural Forum,* 123 (July–Aug., 1965), 73. In New York City, a 20-story building can be "vest pocket," e.g., the houses, fixed them up, and resold them. See "Rehab Program Uses Architects," col. 4.

The line between extensive, government-backed rehabilitation and public housing is slim. It makes little functional difference whether government itself rehabilitates houses and rents them out or pays other people to do it. Virtually all of the suggested new approaches to the housing problem are either variations of public housing or functionally equivalent to it. This is true of the rent supplement plans, for example. Why should this be so? It is so because by definition a massive subsidy means massive public participation; and the term public housing may be applied to any slum housing program in which the public contribution is dominant. Those who attack "public housing" have an image in mind: big ghetto structures that are bureaucratically run. But this image may be changing. The smaller towns have never had public housing of this type; and many big cities are now trying, against great political odds, to get away from it. The Lindsay administration in New York plans to build public housing on vacant land that is scattered about the city—including some housing in middle-class neighborhoods.[20] Whether he can succeed is not clear at the time of this writing. The opposition is strong and loud; but so is the support from liberals and minority-group blocs.

Moreover, the very fact of an outpouring of plans, proposals, demonstration projects, pilot projects, bills, laws, rules, schemes, devices, and propositions is an important *new* fact. Some proposed techniques will turn out to be better than others. None of the techniques in themselves are likely to be true solutions to the housing problem. The cumulation of them all is no solution either, but is a symptom of a *will* to succeed, which is tremendously important, and perhaps also of an inclination to devote the necessary resources, which is the *sine qua non* of success. The housing problem is not going to be solved by gimmicks, but by spending enough money on very simple things. The curse of American housing movements has been inadequate cash. Even anti-slumlord campaigns, which we have criticized here, can be analyzed as symptoms of public miserliness. It is an infinitely cheaper response to a concrete problem to pass a law and blame somebody else. If rats are a slum problem, it is cheaper to make rats a crime and landlords criminals than to take positive

---

[20] *New York Times,* May 11, 1966, p. 29, col. 2; May 12, 1966, p. 48, col. 2; June 2, 1966, p. 24, col. 3; June 8, 1966, p. 39, col. 5.

public action against rats. Moreover, if the rats are not eliminated, the "criminals" can be blamed and the public absolved. Public housing, in the broad sense, is the only program which might perhaps *actually* provide a significant supply of decent homes for people below the poverty level. Other programs, such as code enforcement, are not inherently incapable of making a major contribution. But they are less likely to do this because they are so strongly imbued with notions of fault and attempt to place the moral and financial burden on private shoulders.

The *scale* of housing reform is a critical factor, too, in that it indicates a shift in the alignment of political forces in regard to housing. One major point made in this study is that the problem of slum housing can be in part reduced to a problem of political leverage. The dependent poor and the Negroes have never had much social and economic power. Laws have sometimes been passed *for* them, to be sure, but usually much compromised and weakened in passage or in administration. In the age of the war against poverty, government claims to be willing to spend time, energy, and money to eliminate poverty. Logically, much of this time, energy, and money ought to go toward solving the problem of the slums. The cynic will remind us, however, of many past wars against poverty. The history of housing reform is a history of such wars. They have usually ended in stalemate. This war may be no different. Misdirection and indirection are frequent in the history of so-called welfare laws.

Despite all the setbacks of the past, there are reasons for guarded optimism in the 1960's. The first of these is the militancy of the poor, particularly of the Negro poor. The militancy arose and remains strongest in the civil rights movement; but it has spilled over into other areas. The rent strikes are an example. Militancy, of course, may be and often is maddening, misguided, and ultimately self-defeating. The poor may use new-gained power only to create a whole new set of problems. The poor may turn out to foolishly misconceive their long-term self-interest and perhaps even their short-term self-interest. Yet through militant action the poor gain a chance to state forcefully their views and their wishes. And militancy may succeed by persuading the white, middle-class majority that its own self-interest requires concessions in order to avoid continued riots and confusions—a cruel but necessary calculus. In any given case, success depends upon the precise demands that are made, upon the skill of the leadership, upon the social and economic costs that the whites are asked to incur, and upon how these costs compare with the costs of resistance.

In addition, reform forces committed to the war against poverty were never stronger. Reformers have made many errors in the past; but they have played an indispensable role. Reform is difficult, and perhaps impossible, on welfare grounds alone; yet reform is unthinkable without reformers. There are plenty of them today, and they are supported by powerful interests within government and in foundations, universities, and church organizations. The academic community, the philanthropic community, the enlightened bureaucratic community—each seems more powerful today than in the past. Churches, too, have awakened to preach the social gospel again. The official war against poverty, for all its blunders and hypocrisies, is a hopeful symptom. The new Department of Housing and Urban Development symbolizes increased governmental sensitivity to housing problems. The head of the department, Robert C. Weaver, is a man of rich experience in government and great knowledge in housing affairs. President Johnson's Model Cities plan may yet develop into a significant program. More material resources can be allocated on housing the poor; and unless we are totally deluded, more social understanding is available through research and study than has ever been true before.

Thus three armies—government, the reform community, and the poor themselves—are now engaged in mobilizing resources toward a solution of the problem. What these armies will accomplish remains to be seen; whether they will fight with or against each other likewise will only be revealed by the passage of time. In Syracuse, New York, in 1965, the Office of Economic Opportunity financed a Community Action Training Center, with important leadership supplied by faculty members of Syracuse University. The Center in turn mobilized tenants in public housing; and the tenants tried to wage *organized* battle against the one-sided lease, "high" rents, "pigpen" lawns, "unfair" electric bills, and other tenant grievances.[21] The Authority, which was also a government agency, reacted with rage; government finds it hard to support attacks by its left hand on its

---

[21] "The Tenants 'Report'—Public Housing Syracuse 'Style'—This Is the Way It Is" (1965), a mimeographed hand-out of the tenants' organization. Materials on the Syracuse movement were supplied to me by Professor Warren C. Haggstrom of Syracuse University. See *New York Times*, Aug. 11, 1965, p. 19, col. 3.

right. In San Francisco, in 1966, angry public housing tenants turned to a legal action group—financed by OEO—for help. In October, 1965, 60 tenants "sat in" at the office of the chairman of the New York Housing Authority.[22] In 1966, tenants and tenant groups brought numerous lawsuits against housing authorities, protesting against unfair rules and unfair governance. Some of these lawsuits have been victorious; more will be. Housing authorities and HUD are getting the messages and making some changes on their own. Political, economic, social, and administrative obstacles are enormous. But once started, protests may continue until grievances are met. We are entering a period of militancy and social action. Social forces at work will naturally be reflected in new law and in diversions of old law. But the precise directions taken remain to be seen.

---

[22] *New York Times,* Oct. 13, 1965, p. 36, col. 1.

Some Thoughts
on Welfare Legislation

THIS STUDY concerned itself with law aimed at one special, though important, social problem: housing the poor. We have emphasized the forces that shaped and affected the passage of housing laws. We have not stressed administration and enforcement. This is not because we deny the importance of administration and enforcement but because our major subject was enactment: the authoritative promulgation of formal law by a body empowered to do so.[1]

Housing law is commonly classified as "welfare legislation." The social security law, public assistance laws, public housing laws, and economic opportunity laws are also called "welfare" or "social" laws. Are these laws different in their origins or in the process of adoption from laws which, for example, regulate the dairy industry, impose taxes on cigarettes, or codify the grounds for divorce? It is tempting to say "Yes." But in practice it is hard to draw a meaningful line between welfare and nonwelfare laws. Housing laws "for" the poor have always had a suspicious tendency to be "for" other people too. The building-trade unions were enthusiastically in favor of the Wagner Housing Act of 1937. They expected the law to make jobs for their members. The act as passed specifically provided for the protection of "labor standards" and the payment of

---

[1] Legislatures, city councils, rule-making agencies, executives with the right of decree, and military commanders enact law; and so do common-law judges, to a degree. Difficult questions can be raised about what is and what is not "legitimate" enactment, and what functions are served by different kinds of enactment power held by different enacting bodies. These questions do not concern us directly here. The study has been concerned only with legislative power in the conventional sense—with statutes passed by the federal Congress, by the states, and, to a lesser extent, ordinances enacted by city councils. In the creation of housing law, judges have played only a minor role; and administrative rule-making has not been a major emphasis of this study.

prevailing wages.[2] A humanitarian aim, of course, may be an element in legislation—at times a very powerful one. But mixed motives are the rule, not the exception.

Quite diverse "interests" supply the fuel for the making of law. Each of them has played a role in housing history. There are, first of all, direct pocketbook interests. Downtown merchants support urban renewal because it will help their stores. Other direct interests are institutional: bureaucratic interests of those who gain or conserve power, position, satisfaction, or salary from a particular configuration of government or law. Interests of this kind lay behind New Deal bickering and battling over whose department would run public housing. Bureaucratic interests accounted for the fall of the Wisconsin Tenement House Law of 1907, which had impaired the power of Milwaukee local officials. PHA officers were said to oppose the rent-supplement program because administration was not to be centered in their agency. Still another kind of interest is that which people feel in the advancement or welfare of their own race, national group, occupational group, or even in their club. The interest here is not so much material, in the short run, as emotional. A status-group interest was hypothesized as a force behind the movement to subsidize limited-dividend housing laws. Businessmen wanted to add to their group prestige. They wanted to show that free enterprise (the system under which they themselves had achieved status and success) was capable of solving major social problems.

Other kinds of interest we can call reform interests, defining reformers as proponents of programs whose motives are moral and humanitarian, who are not seeking to advance their economic, institutional, or group interests through law. Not all "reform" is likely to be thought of as welfare reform, by any means. Some reformers work for improvement of the rule against perpetuities, for adoption of the metric system, or for codification of the law of checks. Reform interests may arise from a passion for rational order and planning, as well as from considerations of social justice. Professionals are particularly prone to value clarity and order in those fields of endeavor which they define as within their jurisdiction. So a lawyer's interest in court reform or codification is not necessarily an interest in justice as an ideal; it may be an interest in esthetic or professional order or an interest in seeing that actual life comes as

---

[2] 50 Stat. 896 (1937); now 42 U.S.C.A. §1416.

close as can be to obeying those textbook rules he has learned in the course of his training. Moreover, our society values efficient operation quite highly. Laws aimed at improving an imperfectly operating system are likely to win widespread approval. Reform interests, too, appear at every point in the housing story. Lawrence Veiller was a reformer. The planners who back urban renewal represent the professional element in reform; they are those who seek to bring reality into harmony with professional ideals. Many reformers, of course, have nonreform motives as well, just as nonreform interests may often be tempered by principle.

The history of housing legislation hints broadly that the reform element cannot stand by itself in the dynamics of social-action programs. Pure reform interests are rarely, if ever, sufficient to pass a major piece of legislation. There exists no such category as social welfare laws, if by this we mean laws which differ from other laws in that they arise solely out of a sense of injustice crying out to be rectified. The same interest-group struggles lie behind "welfare" and "economic" legislation.

For most people most of the time, direct material interests are more powerful than indirect material interests or remote material interests; the former are more powerful, too, than ideological or reform interests. Experience tells us that a bill to abolish liquor stores will be opposed by people who own liquor stores. If a proposal is made to build an eight-lane highway through Manhattan, storekeepers who would lose their shops will oppose the plan, even though the highway in the long run is "good for business." In a copper mine, a worker who is ideologically opposed to war will probably support the stockpiling of copper "for defense reasons," if it means that his job is saved. This view of human nature need not give rise to despair. Social justice may be better, more easily, and more permanently served, if its political and legal framework is imbedded in a hard foundation of material interests.[3]

---

[3] Reform motives obviously do play a powerful role in the passage of major pieces of legislation. Perhaps a distinction should be drawn between the general *motive* for a legislative program and its specific *design*. In the case of Social Security, for example, the program obviously gained great strength from an urge to reduce or eliminate the terrible sense of economic insecurity that gnawed at the American people during the depression; one basic pillar of support was reformist and ideological. But many details of the law have baser and more basic origins. For example, labor was eager to keep wages stable and high; the act would enable older workers to retire. Indeed, older workers would forfeit pay-

People's perceptions of their interests are important factors in determining their behavior. This is one reason why the reformer often plays a critical role in enactment. The reformer's job is to convince people where their interests lie. In the history of housing legislation, many reformers have taken up and expounded arguments of social cost to persuade people that housing reform will serve their interests. A man who lives in a comfortable house near a mass of wooden tenements is easily persuaded that his own house is in danger of fire unless something is done about the slums.[4] In addition, reformers, through propaganda and persuasion, may enlist neutrals in their cause by convincing them that they have a little to gain and nothing to lose from reform. Nonetheless, reform is unlikely if the major economic and social interests oppose it. In most cases, we discover that reform or welfare laws passed are not pure reform, but serve as compromises between competing interests. When public utilities are licensed, for example, the companies lose their immunity from governmental interference; they gain a more-or-less guaranteed return on investments and a certain amount of freedom from competition. The reformers influence the calculus of interests, to be sure, just as an adroit arbitrator influences the results of bargaining. The outer limits of compromise are set by economic and social interests as the actors perceive them.

Many theoretical refinements have been worked out by social scientists who have concerned themselves with interest groups and enactment.[5] The *intensity* of reform and nonreform commitments is

---

ments if they held full-time jobs and earned more than a given amount. Conversely, one may argue that no complex, major law can be passed (absent actual corruption and the complication of log-rolling), which serves only narrow special interests and which cannot be rationally subsumed under some more general goal that a reformer could conceivably support. In theory, it is just as easy for a reformer unconnected with the auto business to believe that what is good for General Motors is good for the country as it is for him to believe that the wages of the poor ought to be raised. For various reasons, most "reformers" are usually on one side of a particular issue, rather than neatly divided among the sides. How strongly and on which side of a particular issue the reformers line up is an important fact in determining how that issue will be resolved. However, it is not possible to decide where the reform interest lies in the abstract, apart from the social, economic, and intellectual context in which an issue comes up for decision.

[4] The danger may be in fact remote; and he may lose more than he gains if, as it turns out, building restrictions cripple his land-use rights. We do not need to assume that people can and do make accurate long- and short-run economic and social calculations.

[5] E.g., James M. Buchanan and Gordon Tullock, *The Calculus of Consent* (Ann Arbor: Univ. of Michigan Press, 1962).

an important complicating factor in enactment. A numerical minority that feels strong on an issue may buy off enough of the majority to kill a proposal, perhaps by promising to trade off votes on some other issue, or through making strategic concessions to win a small majority. *Friction* or *inertia* plays an important role in determining the success or failure of legislation. The intensity of interest on the part of proponents has to be enough to overcome the slight but definite interest of the uninterested in avoiding the cost and trouble of action. Concretely, proposals supported by a tiny group, as to which all others are indifferent, is likely to be ignored unless part of a log-rolling process.

Conversely, if no one strongly objects and if government officials or professional groups insist upon some amendment to a program or a codification of law or even some change in the legal order on the grounds of professional esthetics or craftsmanship, in the interests of efficiency, of good order, or of public relations, or to eliminate minor "defects," the change has a high likelihood of success.

Legislation and legal processes themselves play a role in determining the future course of law. Law can and does influence values, and the course of legal development may educate the public on the possibility or feasibility of social action through particular forms of law. A proposed bill suggests a role for government in building houses or in renewing cities. The bill sets off a debate. Groups and individuals are made aware of potential impacts on themselves. The debate itself changes people's ideas of their interests. It also changes their ideological cast, their notions of social justice and injustice; latent concepts and policy considerations emerge from indifference. They may change in the process. Most Americans probably thought of the Negro ghetto, if at all, as an eyesore to be forgotten and avoided; urban renewal evoked the possibility of getting rid of the eyesore. Now the question of Negro life in the ghetto is debated, discussed, and harangued over. The debate is not always edifying, to be sure, but it goes on. Court decisions, legislative discussions, and the pronouncements of executive officials have played an important part in providing material for debate and even in advancing some of the concepts to be debated. Indeed, legal and nonlegal processes of value-formation influence each other and feed each other's growth. The tenement house law of Wisconsin (1907) provides another example of the value-forming use of law. It was a reformer's law; most of the legislature was notably indifferent. Once the law was in effect, it hurt the status-interests of Milwaukee officials, and it seemed to hurt pocketbook interests of builders and their workers as well. The law was then challenged successfully in court. But the debate over the impact of the law sharpened perceptions of interest. A wider public became aware of the problem and its possible solutions. Some segments of the public learned that aspects of the law seemed to threaten their interests in important ways. After the "educational" experience of the act and its downfall, a new act was passed, and all sides conceded that one was "needed." But this time the act was drafted by professionals and reflected with more accuracy the interests of various groups who demanded to be heard. Education by government action is sometimes even more direct. Official investigations, reports, and studies helped mobilize public opinion in favor of tenement house laws. Lawrence Veiller adroitly used these devices to arouse public opinion in New York; he also made heavy use of social-cost arguments to convince the uncommitted. Without a background of muckraking and debate, the tenement house laws could not have been passed, though the political weakness of the landlords must also be considered.

The history of an enacted program has complexities of its own. The Wisconsin Tenement House Law of 1907 has been cited as an example of the use of law as a factor in value-formation. The fall of this law also illustrates how legislation in action tends to change attitudes and alignments. Before passage, the effect of an act is theory; after passage, it is brute reality. In operation, laws may impinge unexpectedly on the interests of a formerly apathetic group and rouse them to new or greater opposition. Consequently "crippling amendments" are likely to be introduced in the early years of regulatory laws. These amendments are in part the continuation of the struggle over enactment, but are in part also the result of new alignments occasioned by the act in operation. Lawrence Vieller's career in New York is pictured as full of hurried flights to Albany to save his tenement house law from this or that "crippling amendment." In Wisconsin, landlords who thought the act "didn't apply to them," builders who had not before realized the inconveniences of the permit system, unions which justly or unjustly now blamed the law for loss of jobs, and local officials who found their positions threatened by a new bureaucracy—all became aroused against the Tenement House Law after passage. The same phenomenon is observable under urban renewal. Groups once apathetic or favorable suddenly demand an end to a project when they realize homes will be bulldozed or that an interracial project will be built in the neighborhood. Acts passed with the aid of reformers' zeal by appeal to rather diffuse values may be particularly vulnerable to dramatic changes in the focusing of opinion and hence in the alignment of perceived interests. This will be true when many members of the original coalition had been persuaded to vote "Yes" by arguments of social cost and when the act in operation invokes more powerful arguments of direct material interest.[6] If, as a result, the original act is compromised, the reformers themselves are apt to leave the scene in disillusionment and fasten their zeal on another mode of reform. Such withdrawal further weakens the original program. This has happened to public housing as well as to the tenement house laws.

Federalism plays a large role in shaping housing law; but the role is difficult to assess. The major slum-control laws are heavily dependent on federal funds. Even code enforcement may become more and more an adjunct of urban renewal. At the same time, no major program—urban renewal, public housing, or code enforcement—is run directly from Washington. There is some overlordship, some regulation, but local administration is the rule. Typically, existing local governments are bypassed in favor of autonomous, "nonpolitical" bodies, i.e., the local authorities. In this manner, administration can be local and yet give free play to the operation of experts, professionals, and civil servants, somewhat independently of municipal politicians. Not that administration is immune from

---

[6] Paradoxically, opposition interests may have a better chance to amend a program *after* the battle against passage has been lost. Beforehand, these forces may be tempted to try to keep *any* law from being passed. They thus forfeit a role in drafting the bill. Afterwards, if they concede that the program will be permanent, they may present their amendments and proposals not as saboteurs but as potential members of a new coalition. The AMA took a do-or-die attitude toward Medicare. By so doing, they lost some of their power to modify the law *before* passage. At this writing (June, 1966), the automobile companies have thrown in the towel on federal safety regulation and are desperately asking for a role in making and running the program. If the big companies agree to a law, its passage will be certain. Concessions may thus seem worthwhile. The phenomenon discussed here helps in part to explain, for example, why regulation so often appears to be "captured" by the regulated. One reason is that the reformers lose interest in a program once it is law; but another is that the interested parties—those that are regulated—give up the fight and ask for a place at the table. They will usually get it, since the alternative is endless and pointless struggle. The history of federal regulatory agencies provides a rich mine of examples.

local politics; the problems of public-housing site selection in Chicago are graphic, perhaps extreme, illustrations to the contrary.

The complex, mixed, federal-state-local nature of housing law presents reformers and pressure-groups with problems and opportunities. A group that wishes to divert or destroy a particular urban renewal project, for example, has a hard time exerting its power where it would count. The governing statute is federal and relatively impervious to local pressures. Washington cannot easily veto a project once it has been approved. Local governing bodies may lack direct control over projects run by autonomous authorities. If they have control, they may be unresponsive to protests because of the sharp clash of interests that renewal occasions. The many referenda on public housing and urban renewal represent the exasperation of those dissatisfied with the operation of the programs, but who find no other clear channel to effectuate changes in policy or administration. Since referenda, however, are posed in black-and-white terms, the result is a certain brittleness in public housing and urban renewal plans. They are voted for on a "Yes" or "No" basis; they tend to crack or stand firm, rather than bend. Another device of the disappointed is the test case in court. This too leaves little room for compromise.

SOCIAL CLASS AND SOCIAL WELFARE

Laws *for* the poor, we have suggested, are unlikely to be generated unless (a) the poor are a majority and have fair and adequate political representatives, or (b) on balance, proposed legislation serves the interests of some class larger and broader than the poor. The history of American housing law suggests that the second condition has been much more important in the genesis of housing policy than the first. The early tenement house laws were buttressed by social cost arguments. Public-housing laws first appeared in a few states in the 1920's as laws to stimulate the establishment of "homesteads" among sturdy yeomen of the lower middle class. The federal housing program of the 1930's made jobs for workers and contracts for manufacturers with idle plants; in addition, the depression added millions of new, if unwilling, recruits to the lower orders of society. When increased prosperity removed the conditions for passage of the original program, political support for public housing melted like butter in the sun. The shift in emphasis to veterans' housing and then to housing for the elderly finds at least a plausible, partial explanation in considerations of the social and economic interests of groups other than the dependent urban poor. The urban renewal program uses the plight of the poor for propaganda purposes; but the size and character of urban renewal is determined by other interests—e.g., downtown merchants, university presidents, city officials—united only by a common desire to use federal money for their own ends. Model tenement house programs turn out to be lower-middle-class programs. Even in the midst of the "war against poverty," the Johnson Administration introduced a supposedly radical, new, rent-supplement bill—designed for the lower middle class. (Congress removed this feature.)

There should be no cause for surprise in these facts. The United States is a middle-class nation and will remain so. However one defines poverty, the poor are a minority of the nation. The middle class is so numerous that the "general good" is apt to be identified with middle-class interests. Mobility into the middle class has always been high enough to make this equation tolerable to the potential middle class. The concept of class, indeed, is repugnant to Americans both on ideological and pragmatic grounds. The idea that America is classless is at least halfway plausible by virtue of the sheer weight of numbers of those with some stake in the economy. The interests of the urban dependent poor are minority interests.

Moreover, the middle class is white, and the lower class is disproportionately Negro. What bargain, realistically, can the poor, urban Negro strike? He can hardly achieve goals which conflict with the strong material interests of major economic forces in this society and especially with the vital interests of his reluctant white neighbors of the lower middle class. These neighbors deeply cherish the value of their homes and the stability of their neighborhoods. Whether or not the presence of poor people or Negroes around the corner impairs or ought to impair these values,[7] clearly people *think* that they do. Moreover, largely for ignoble reasons, millions of whites are uncomfortable or worse in the presence of Negroes. They are also uncomfortable in the neighborhood presence of "inferiors" in culture or cash. Income and race segregation have been powerful

---

[7] See, on this question, Luigi Laurenti, *Property Values and Race* (Berkeley: Univ. of California Press, 1960).

villains in housing history. Public housing has suffered terribly from their effects. Majority interests have denied public housing its best sites and boxed it into urban ghettos, effecting unfortunate results for the poor and for the public housing program. Those safely outside the ghetto walls have, in the past, been willing to tolerate the existence of a ghetto. Urban renewal capitalizes on the harm and disgust that the ghetto evokes; but it is not a response derived from or conducive to social justice.

Are the slums then incurable, short of revolutionary change? The answer is not necessarily "No." Social change has not been impossible in this country; quite to the contrary, social change has been rapid and unceasing. Indeed, one chronic source of the current problem of the slums lies in the constant upgrading of the working class to the point where the really poor are a national minority. One reason the poor lack politcal leverage is because so much political and economic power is in the hands of the masses who are *not* poor and, indeed, are rather hostile to the poor. The working class has achieved striking gains at the bargaining table, in the market, and in the legislative forum. In the late nineteenth and early twentieth centuries, the working classes used industrial unrest as a tool of bargaining—they raised the price of social order. A strike is a cost to business just as it is to labor. Over the course of years, various groups and interests have asserted claims to legislative attention, claims that sharply conflicted with each other. In time, elaborate compromises have been worked out in the form of programs emanating from farm bills, labor bills, bills for and against business, bills appealing to or unattractive to doctors, lawyers, barbers, bakers, and countless other groups. Each articulate interest has staked a claim and, quite frequently, succeeded in winning a share of legal protection or subsidy. The legal system is largely built up of a constant, shifting succession of compromises between demands of interest groups, taking the form of legislative programs. In this series of compromises, the lowest class, i.e., the very poor, has been conspicuously underrepresented. The poor have had neither the power nor the numbers to assert their claims with success. Consequently much "welfare" legislation is really for unionized workers, for the submerged middle class, for the half-poor or the pseudo-poor, or is so riddled with measures aimed at quarantining the larger society from by-products of poverty that the *true* interests of the poor, whatever they are, are entirely left out of calculation.

As we have mentioned, the way is open to the poor to achieve some goals by raising the price of good behavior. The poor have the power to harass, to annoy, to riot, and to picket. They may make plenary use of their power to disrupt, of their vote, of their small but definite economic power, and of the impact of domestic problems on foreign affairs. Not least of all, they may appeal to the conscience and invoke classic American values. An uneasy conscience is unpleasant and therefore a burden to its owner; he may be willing to take some action to put an end to the pangs of the heart. Some people—those only slightly opposed to a given reform—can sometimes be called upon to change their minds in the name of conscience.

Many reformers are at work today to enlist the neutrals on the side of the poor. Some nonreform interests are tending in the same direction, e.g., status-group interests and even the desire of political leaders, such as the President, to make a name in history by solving major social problems. Ranged on the opposite side are groups with interests in the status quo. It is by no means clear that the tactics of the poor, on or off the streets, are proper and effective ones. A riot may provoke appeasement if the majority is convinced that the price of civil order has been effectively raised and that the minority must be bought off with reforms. It provokes suppression if the majority feels the price is too high, that is, that the only reforms which would end unrest impinge too dearly or directly on the interests of the majority. Or, by enraging the good neutral citizens, a riot may destroy the necessary reform coalition and encourage formation of a coalition of suppression. Genuine reform through legislation is politically possible; the housing problems of the poor can be solved even though the poor are a minority; but a solution will not *necessarily* come around. Are there ways in which sound policy can curb unrest and satisfy both sides?

REWARDS AND PUNISHMENTS

Legislation seeks to influence human behavior. The statute books are full of overt and covert appeals to the population to do or not do various acts, to refrain from robbery, to buy more milk and less liquor, to put accurate labels on drugs, not to shoot pheasants out of season, to pay tax before April 15th. Legislation issues commands that are backed up by positive and negative sanctions. *Punishment,* the negative sanction, raises the costs of certain actions to the actor or decreases satisfactions; *subsidy* lowers costs of action to the actor or increases satisfactions.[8]

Some housing laws stress punishment, others subsidy. The heart of the distinction between positive and negative approaches to the housing problem is the distinction between punishment and subsidy. One approach attempts to influence behavior through increasing costs, chiefly to landlords. The other expends public funds in direct or indirect subsidy. One of our main theses is that the housing problem has not been and will not be completely solved by negative legislation, that is, by using punishment rather than subsidy. Merely to impose costs on the suppliers of slum housing will not abolish the slums. It is probably true that enforcement of restrictive laws has had a wholesome effect in many cities and has succeeded, perhaps at some human cost, in upgrading the physical standards of many slum areas. This impact is not easy to measure. For the past century, legislation has persistently concerned itself with increasing the costs of the landlord. This process may well have had quite harmful results. The added costs have not been high enough to drive the landlord out of business; but they have been high enough to stimulate the least scrupulous class of landlords, to encourage the "milking" of property, and to inflate the rents of the poor. Successive waves of indignation have done nothing more than exaggerate the process. The New York rent-strike law is only one of the latest steps in this process. The slum landlord has high costs. He has uncertainty costs; he is likely to be operating in violation of the law, and therefore he runs the risk of crackdown. He has high costs of upkeep and compliance, particularly if his tenants are irresponsible. He has the psychic costs of operating a hated business on the fringes of the law. The result is the process we have described as the "filtering-down" of landlords.

---

[8] By punishment is meant any raising of cost; a tax, for example, on beer but not on cheese, punishes users of beer compared to those who use cheese. Honor, prestige, authorizations to act, dispensations from existing laws, absence of forms or formalities—all of these are subsidies in the sense used here. Some statutory programs offer *service,* a subsidy in kind—free booklets, vocational guidance, national parks. Many statutes embody combinations of punishment and subsidy in one complex enactment dealing with one subject. Such statutes attempt to channel (or *regulate*) behavior by raising some costs and lowering others, inducing or favoring one kind of behavior over another. The distinction between punishment and subsidy is not in terms of the statutes themselves, but in terms of their effects on potential subjects. A statute may act as a subsidy to A and a punishment to B at the same time.

For the city, however, punitive laws are a cheap solution to *its* problem. The rent-strike law, for example, mollified the strikers while costing government virtually nothing. Other things being equal, a government will look for the cheaper solution to a social problem, i.e., the solution that demands the least money, taxes, staff— and public disapproval. Expensive solutions will be avoided if there is an alternative. Punitive laws are an alternative which has appeared all too often in housing history—laws unreasonably increasing costs to landlords or, in other words, laws attempting to shift the burden of the slum-housing problem upon the shoulders of private citizens. Since the landlord is a businessman and since the system does not contemplate that he be anything but a businessman, he must in turn shift all or a part of the cost to his consumers.

The use of punishment rather than subsidy is all the easier for government in that it seems like an appropriate reaction to consumer rage. The slum landlord looks like, and may well be, a despicable creature, interested in quick returns, contemptuous of human suffering, socially undesirable in every apparent way. Thus, all agree that punishment is appropriate: we must "take the profit out of the slums." But making the job expensive does not necessarily take out the profit; it simply means that to earn any profit, including psychic profit, in a dangerous, unpopular business, the mark-up will have to be great, the returns on *some* buildings quick and high. Punitive laws, in the short run, may satisfy the leaders of the poor, who see "results" stemming from their efforts; the city has struck a position of rectitude and has responded to pressures at little cost to itself. But the problem has not really been solved. The iron logic of profit and loss has not been altered. Neither the character nor the habits nor the prices of the slumlords will be permanently improved in the process.

Punitive laws may also be difficult to enforce except sporadically. A law which requires landlords to maintain their buildings at a level where profit is impossible without illegal overcrowding imposes a punishment upon landlords, and the rational landlord must decide either to disobey, to run the risk of incurring sanctions, or to abandon the building. If he abandons the building, it will eventually end up either in the hands of the city or in the hands of an "unscrupulous" landlord. All buildings of the class in question will eventually be city-owned or "in violation." Since violations under an oversevere law must occur on a wholesale basis, the city will find it exceedingly difficult to enforce the law without an enormous staff of inspectors. Inspectors already at work will be offered bribes because the surviving landlords are precisely those who would offer bribes and because landlords will prefer the certainty of regular payoffs to the uncertainties of random enforcement. Some landlords—perhaps the more honorable!— will prefer paying fines to bribing inspectors, provided there is little danger of great stigma or prison. Lax judges, who may merely be judges who see the landlord's point of view, make the payment of fines no more onerous or recurrent than parking tickets. But these judges in turn are under pressure to crack down on the landlords.

The alternative is obvious and simple. For more permanent solutions to the housing problem, government must use subsidies rather than punishments wherever possible. This is the lesson of housing history. The country must decide whether its goal is to house the poor or to harass a miserable and unimportant class of people in the name of a false morality and false economy. If a stock of housing for the poor is to be provided by public action at all, it cannot be provided cheaply. The costs cannot be shifted to landlords, as things now stand. Nor can a massive housing effort be stimulated by small subsidies. Subsidies must be big enough to do their job. Tax abatement or permissive legislation simply did not offer enough to attract great amounts of capital into "model" housing. Modern tax reforms and building-code reforms would help, but not enough. The rent-subsidy program is too small and too flimsy to work miracles. The leased-housing program has many admirers; but it too is small and experimental. Pilot programs merely prove what can be done with the money no one is yet willing to spend.

Public housing programs, on the contrary, are heavily subsidized. But the level of construction has never been high enough to fill the need. Moreover, buildings have been cheap and unsuitable, creating problems as well as solving them. Public housing means in theory a government commitment to build decent houses for the poor. The American program has tended to degenerate into a program to build high-rise ghettoes for Negroes in big cities or, alternately, to abandon the lowest class altogether. Big-city Negroes, it is clear, will not tolerate such public housing much longer. No one can blame them for this attitude. On the other hand, middle-class, urban society

is not ready to receive the poor as neighbors. We have discussed—
and approved of—ways of humanizing public housing. The problem
is to make these ways acceptable to the country at large.

The urban majorities, particularly the working-class whites, look
upon Negro and lower-class neighbors as a cost and, in short, as a
punishment. They have not been willing to assume this burden;
and they have had the power and the votes to make their wishes
come true. They have brought public housing to its knees. They
have limited the program in size and scale and driven it into the
ghettos. The Negro protest movement and the war against poverty
have increased the price of white intolerance; but it is dangerous
to wait until the price becomes so astronomical that it either *has*
to be met or society will crumble.

The traditional attack on prejudice has used two weapons: preachment and punishment. Both are powerful modes of influencing behavior, to be sure. Even exhortations to brotherhood have an impact; they make people ashamed. But the shame is quite small
compared to the inconvenience and economic perils, whether real
or imagined, of social change in the neighborhood. Plenty of coun-
terarguments and rationalizations can cover up a bigot's shame.
Fair housing laws which punish intolerance are hard to pass and
even harder to enforce if repugnant to large segments of the population. Fair housing laws are, from the city's standpoint, a cheap
solution to a difficult problem. Usually, these laws have no "teeth"
or make no use of them; they make big propaganda and small gains.

The boldest way to solve the housing problem is also the simplest:
vastly to increase the subsidy and radically to diminish the punitive
element in housing legislation. Rather than heap costs on slum
landlords, we ought to swallow our distaste and look for ways to
make it profitable to own houses in the slums, to make it as profitable as selling bread to the poor or showing them movies, which are
activities carried on by respectable people. A dangerous kind of
"morality" infuses our housing laws. Current legislation authorizes
outright grants to poor people to fix up their homes in the slums.[9]
We are afraid to subsidize those whom we define as immoral.[10]

---

[9] P. L. 89–117, 79 Stat. 451 (1965) §106(a).

[10] Edgar M. Ewing, "Baltimore's Housing Clinic," *JH*, 19 (1962), 321, describes
a program for "teaching" rather than "fining housing code violators." The violators he refers to are all tenants—they are "newcomers to the city" and "culturally deprived." When a class of violators is defined in favorable terms, it becomes possible to deal constructively rather than punitively with them.

But subsidy is a powerful engine for creating morality. The new rent subsidy is a timid step toward encouraging construction of housing for the poor. Perhaps it could be improved, emboldened, and expanded.

What of the problem of the ghetto? Rather than heap scorn (and punishment, if we could) on little men in frame houses who tremble or rage at Negro neighbors, at Negro housing projects, and at Negro children in their schools, we might find out the price of their prejudice and buy it off. How much is prejudice worth to a man? Imagine the effect of flat money payments on a mixed neighborhood: some whites would not stay for any price; others might stay and even like it for $100, or $1,000, or more. Some might be reconciled if their schools were improved, if more policemen patrolled the streets, if the lighting was fixed and the pavement straightened. Some might remain if they were awarded a medal. These are not intended as concrete proposals, but only as illustrations, bizarre as they may sound, of a direction which might be taken by laws which sought to subsidize good rather than penalize evil. Such an approach would have enormous practical and political problems. But theory suggests that punishment is often costly and futile; raising the subsidy may do a better job in areas where its merits are as yet unsuspected. Mixed income neighborhoods would be stable if they were highly desirable neighborhoods. The proposals in New York for scattering public housing about the city arouse great wrath in Queens. The people in Queens feel, rightly or wrongly, that they are losing something rare and precious. What do we offer in return? Society is a subtle, complicated web of interactions, fueled by the interplay of punishments and rewards. Social problems are not solved by fiat, but by manipulation of the carrot and the stick. The punitive approach has led to deeper and deeper failure in the hard-core slums. Whatever usefulness it once had has long since been expended. The Sphinx has not been moved by threats, bluster, or coercion. Perhaps we might yet bribe him from his seat.

Index

Interests: effects on housing legislation, 14, 186–188; types of, 185–186; relative strength of, 186; intensity, 187–188

Jacobs, Jane, 122: on housing design, 121; criticizes public housing, 142
Jersey City, New Jersey, housing, 40
Johnson, Pres. Lyndon B.: and rent supplement, 177
Judges: laxity with regard to housing offenses, 46–47
Judicial review: of welfare legislation, 7–9; of evictions from public housing, 134

Kazan, Abraham, 88
Klein, Woody: study of New York tenement, 43
Knickerbocker Village, 71, 89

Landlords: of the nineteenth century, 33; as scapegoats of the housing movement, 39–44; and enforcement of tenement house laws, 45, 55; failure to professionalize, 85; prejudice against as affecting rent supplement, 176–177; effects of punitive attitude toward, 195
Leased-housing program, under Housing Act of 1965, 175–176
Lehman, Warren, on housing codes, 54
Limited-dividend housing companies, 88–90: under California law, 8; during World War I, 95; and status-group interests, 185
Lindsay, Mayor John V.: and public housing site location, 126
Lodging houses, 45
Lowell Homesteads, Massachusetts, 98

McCarthy, Sen. Joseph, sponsors law delaying public housing evictions, 216–217
McCarthy Act, and public housing evictions, 126–127, 136
McGrath, Dorn, 165
Manchester, New Hampshire, use of urban renewal, 153
Massachusetts: tenement house law of 1868, 26; building of "homesteads," 97–99; veterans' housing, 117; anti-discrimination law, 123
Massachusetts Homestead Commission, 97–98

Medicare, 190n
Metropolitan Life Insurance Company, 86
Middletown Gardens, 119–120
Milwaukee: housing ordinance of 1905, 26; lodging houses, 45; contents of housing code, 53–54; demolition program, 70; attitude toward housing for the elderly, 129–130
Missouri, anti-loitering law, 57
Missouri Department of Welfare, 140
Model Housing Law: certificates of compliance with housing laws, 62
Model tenements: movement to build, 75–87; effect of neighborhoods on success, 83–85
Model Cities program, 172–182
Moerdler, Charles, 47n
Moses, Robert: and New York coliseum, 152, 155
"Mulberry Bend," destruction of, 27–28

Nashville, Tennessee, 155, 159
National Association of Real Estate Boards (NAREB): opposes public housing, 105; attitude toward urban redevelopment and renewal, 149
National Housing Association, 38
National Industrial Recovery Act (NIRA), 101
National Lumber Dealers' Association, opposes public housing, 105
National Nonpartisan League, in North Dakota, 97
"Negro removal," 167, 170
Negroes: in New Deal resettlement program, 115; in public housing, 123–126; militancy and housing reform, 181; and welfare legislation, 192–193
"Neighborhood effects," 8
Nevada: preference for veterans in public housing, 117
Newark, New Jersey, urban renewal, 153
New Deal: and housing, 15, 101–106
New Jersey, tenement house law, 36; housing conditions, 30
New York (City): fire zones, 25; slum conditions, nineteenth century, 28; cholera epidemics, 29; creation of Metropolitan Board of Health, 29; character of tenements, 32, 86;

DATE DUE
